THE SMALL
BUSINESS BIBLE

The Random House Small Business Library

The Small Business Bible

Special Software Edition

Paul Resnik

RANDOM HOUSE
ELECTRONIC PUBLISHING

New York

CONTENTS

CHECKLISTS

CHAPTER
1

MAKING AND BREAKING THE SMALL BUSINESS

This book identifies and discusses the underlying, basic requirements for success in small business. It will show you how to understand and apply them to your venture.

It is frequently observed that those who fail to learn from the past are condemned to repeat it. And so it is with small business venturers. This book contains the fundamental, decisive lessons in building a small business derived from the experience of your countless predecessors, both winners and losers.

When small business owner-managers understand the basic factors that make or break the firm, their managerial mind-set helps them overcome the inevitable difficulties encountered in all business ventures. When owner-managers concentrate on these basic make-or-break requirements of running a small business, sales and profits will invariably follow—and a lot of fun, as well.

The Promise and the Perils

Establishing your own business is the American dream. Nearly a million new businesses are launched each year.

The rewards of owning your own business are wonderfully alluring. Many founders make their fortunes. There are also the emotional satisfactions of creating your own firm and controlling your own life—feelings of independence, achievement, and personal pride. For many entrepreneurs, running their own firm means an end to the frustrations of working in a large organization—bureaucratic rigidity, politics, and boring routine.

Unhappily, an estimated 80 percent of new ventures fold within the first five years, and many don't even make it through their first year.

Good Management Responsible for Small Business Success

Success and failure in small business, however, is not a statistical crapshoot. Good management is the factor that determines survival and success. Bad management is the factor that determines failure—not the economy, the competition, the fickleness of customers, or bad luck.

Dun and Bradstreet, the guardian of business statistics, has reported that bad management is responsible for over 90 percent of business failures. About half of these failures are attributed to "incompetence" and the other half to "inadequate" prior experience. But that is like saying that someone is not a good tennis player because he doesn't play tennis well. It just begs the question: What particular qualities of "competence" and "experience" should be sought by the aspiring business venturer?

Good management—the capacity to understand, direct, and control the business—is based on an owner-manager's critical attention to the few decisive factors of survival and success that make or break the business.

Effective Management Can Be Learned

The underlying premise of this book is that those make-or-break factors of effective management can be learned—and learned *before* the business falls prey to the basic recurring mistakes that ensnare the 80 percent of small business failures. If these factors are learned and applied early in the game, new owner-managers can concentrate their efforts on making the firm and avoiding the mistakes that I, my colleagues, friends, and countless others have made. Many of those mistakes, in isolation or together, were so serious that they cost their owner-managers their businesses. *Most business failures are neither inevitable nor necessary.*

Management Intelligence

Good management is more than the aggregate of the daily activities of the owner-manager. It also comprises the attitudes, perceptions, thoughts, and knowledge—the management intelligence—that motivate and govern crucial management activities. What you perceive, think, know, and emphasize determine what you do and how you do it.

Good management is purposeful, guided activity. The following vital issues, for example, are all determined by what you think and know.

1. What you believe is important to the success of your business
2. How aware and concerned you are with the special pitfalls that predictably confront nearly all small businesses
3. How you conceive your role and specific responsibilities as owner-manager
4. How much of your business landscape you perceive and the extent to which you grasp or create opportunities for developing and improving the business
5. Which aspects of your business you regard as uncontrollable and which you are willing to manage
6. Where and how you decide to allocate the firm's limited resources

The Ten Make-or-Break Conditions of Survival and Success

Management intelligence is based, in turn, on a real awareness and understanding of the critical make-or-break requirements for managing your business. There are ten of them.

1. *Be objective.* Self-delusion has no place in building a business. An honest, dispassionate assessment of the strengths and weaknesses of the company and your business and management skills is essential (see Chapter 2).

2. *Keep it simple and focused.* In small business, simple is effective. Concentrate your efforts and resources where the impact and profits are greatest (see Chapter 3 [Keep in mind, however, that the entire book is about the priority requirements that generate the best results in small business.]).

3. *Provide excellent and distinctive goods and services that*

meet the wants and needs of select groups of customers (see Chapter 4).

4. *Determine how to reach and sell your customers.* Marketing plans make the job easier (see Chapter 5).

5. *Build, manage, and motivate a winning team to do what you can't do alone* (see Chapter 6).

6. *Keep the accounting records and controls that you must use to understand and manage the business.* Hire a first-rate operations-oriented certified public accountant (CPA) (see Chapter 7).

7. *Never run out of cash.* Cash is king in the small business world (see Chapter 8).

8. *Avoid the recurring pitfalls of rapid growth.* Manage your firm's expansion (see Chapter 9).

9. *Understand and your business inside out.* This is the foundation for controlling the firm and improving the profits (see Chapter 10).

10. *Plan ahead.* Formulate critical and challenging, but achievable, goals and convert them into productive activities (see Chapter 11).

These basic requirements will take on full meaning in the extensive chapter-by-chapter discussions.

Simple, But Not Easy

The make-or-break conditions of small business success are not textbook theories or the easy maxims of the "can-do" tipster. There is no guaranteed formula for small business success. What there is, however—the experience and lessons of your predecessors—is far more valuable. It comprises an approach to effective management that helps you decide what is important and where to apply your time, monies, and resources most productively.

This book is as much a "what-to and why" book as a

"how-to" book. The emphasis is on doing a handful of basic, critical things well, rather than doing everything with indiscriminate energy. The effective manager is a master of restraint.

The basics are "simple"—simple in the sense that they are economical and effective. But, as Clausewitz wrote in his classic treatise, *On War,* "Everything is very simple in war, but the simplest thing is difficult." The failure to *do* the "simple" or "obvious" accounts for most business collapses.

You must commit yourself to applying these few decisive lessons *now* and not later "when there is time." There may be no guarantee for small business success, but there is a demonstrable shortcut to failure, namely, the neglect of the basic, make-or-break factors that separate the winners from the losers.

The Basics Apply to All Small Businesses

These basics apply to all small businesses, be they sophisticated high-tech concerns or no-tech Mom-and-Pop shops. They apply equally to manufacturing, retail, and personal service firms. They apply, in large part, to nonprofit organizations as well.

And every one of these make-or-break factors should be critical considerations *before* the firm has commenced operations. Effective management can, and must, begin before you open shop. If your venture gets off to a shaky start, you will play a miserable game of catch-up for several years, provided the firm lasts that long. Turnarounds are infinitely more difficult than sound start-ups.

Effective Management Is a Must in Small Business

This is not a book about general management. It is about managing *small* businesses.

Small Businesses Are Not Little Big Businesses

There are many ways to define a "small" business (see the Glossary at the end of Chapter 7). But small firms in general have distinctive traits that require special management understanding and skills.

What especially characterizes the small firm (other than a requirement that the owner-manager must manage and stay in overall control of all aspects of the business) is that the resources of the small firm are very limited. For example, most small businesses are cash-thin for at least the first few years of operations and are highly vulnerable to any sudden changes both within the firm and in the overall business environment. Many a small firm, for want of cash, goes under at a time when it is actually making profits.

The margin for error in small business is slim. There is no cushion to support a protracted learning period or to protect against major miscalculations, sudden "surprises," and unproductive indulgences. Most successful business founders, therefore, abhor "risky" business deals. They leave blind risks to the gamblers. They accept very calculated risks, seeking situations in which they feel they can control as many variables as possible and influence the outcome through personal attention and effort. Small business venturers cannot afford to be high rollers.

The small firm cannot "buy" success. It cannot spend its way out of self-inflicted problems, nor can it buy extensive markets or the very best and most experienced employees.

A small business must be especially concerned with internal efficiencies. Unlike the big business, there is no room for idle and wasteful costs that dissipate the scarce cash and assets of the firm.

The Pivotal Role of the Owner-Manager

Because the small firm's resources are so limited and the firm itself so vulnerable, the critical need is effective management that puts the business's scarce resources to work where they do the most good.

Only the owner-manager can determine the overriding purpose, values, and identity of the business. Only the owner-manager can set the business's priorities and objectives and decide how the firm's assets should be allocated to have the greatest impact.

Small business management is the art of the essential. It is making the most out of the least.

The owner-manager alone can fashion the products and services best calculated to satisfy customers in the targeted market segment. And it is the owner-manager who must build a capable, inspired employee team and ascertain where each employee's contribution makes most sense. Similarly, it is the owner-manager who must also attend to the daily operations and, as a *player*-manager, make key contributions in areas where he or she is gifted or experienced, be it the marketing and selling, product development and quality control, or financial management. Finally, no one but the owner-manager can monitor all the activities of the business and decide what changes or improvements have to be put into place.

Ralph Waldo Emerson observed that "an institution is the lengthened shadow of one man." *In a small business, that person is you, the owner-manager.* Unlike the CEO of a large corporation, you are personally responsible for every aspect of the company and its products. No matter how flexible and informal the company's structure, everything ultimately flows top-down. You must not only be the manager in title, but actively *manage* the firm.

Entrepreneurs, Administrators, and Managers

Certainly, you need considerable entrepreneurial skills to launch and inspirit the firm. Entrepreneurs make things happen and get things done. They take new or innovative ideas and convert them into live commercial operations.

But not all entrepreneurs have the knowledge or disposition to manage an ongoing concern and make the *right* things happen and get the *right* things done. Entrepreneurs are preeminently starters, and they are often inattentive to, or bored by, managerial responsibility. That is why so many are replaced by venture capital firms that invest in their companies. In fact, that is why so many of them fail in business. As the founder of a Massachusetts chemical distributorship explains, "Building a company is the easy part. Managing is the tough part. I'm an entrepreneur and a deal-maker, not a manager." Managers are also finishers.

Certainly, you need a modicum of administrative skills to assure that those critical "right" things are done well. But the essential skills of the administrator are different from those of the manager. The administrator attends to custodial duties and minds the store. He is more concerned with efficiency than effectiveness and with stability and survival, rather than development and improvement.

Effectiveness is the hallmark of a good small business manager. The test of this is the capacity to understand and control the firm and direct it beyond the inevitable recurring perils of the small business world toward sustained and profitable growth.

What that means in practical working terms will be spelled out in the following chapters. Let's proceed to examine those make-or-break factors of your business success, one by one.

CHAPTER

2

NO ROOM FOR ILLUSIONS: SMALL BUSINESS REALITIES AND SELF-DECEPTION

Honesty, objectivity, and emotional and intellectual guts are the marks of a successful business founder.

The realities of the small business world are uncompromising, no matter how you choose to interpret them. Among those realities are these.

1. Owner-managers bring to the business both relative strengths *and* relative shortcomings.

2. Many entrepreneurs have subtle, built-in tendencies toward self-destruction after the business is established.

3. There is a very human proclivity for self-deception. In business, this obscures awareness of problems related to both management of the business and the needs of the business itself.

Rigorous and honest assessment of the health of your business and of your role and contributions as owner-manager is one of the make-or-break determinants of a small business's success or failure. This chapter will discuss some of the key obstacles to that rigor and honesty; then it will give practical antidotes to help you face the realities and needs of your firm head on.

All Owner-Managers Have Relative Weaknesses

If the small business is the lengthened shadow of its founder, it reflects not only that person's strengths and enthusiasms but also limitations.

There are no "ideal" owner-managers. There are no Renaissance people at the helms of small businesses. Each owner-manager brings to that individual business unique drives, abilities, work experience, interests, and attitudes. It is not astonishing that each owner-manager also comes with limitations—shortcomings of personality and temperament, of aptitudes and antipathies, of experience and skills. It is as simple as this: Owner-managers with recognizable strengths have recognizable limitations. They, and you, are only human.

Know Your Weaknesses

But here's the rub: Those limitations will be played out to the detriment of your business unless you are open to corrective measures. The key is not just to recognize objectively your relative strengths in the business, but to acknowledge your relative limitations and deficiencies.

A business writer, Michael Maccoby, has written, "Good leaders today are not people who are 'perfect.' They all have faults. The difference between them and old-style managers is that they acknowledge and struggle with their faults, rather than ignoring and becoming defensive about them." Only then can you compensate for, nullify, or correct your own managerial limitations and cope with the problems and needs of your firm before they sabotage your future prospects.

It is not easy. There are no bosses and corporate directors or shareholders telling you there are untended needs in the business and that neglect will be costly. There are no well-staffed departments attending more or less independently to all the varied aspects of the business. As a small business owner-manager, you are perched gloriously and dangerously on your own.

Self-Deception

We all tend to direct our attention to what is comfortable and pleasing, deflecting our attention from what makes us uncomfortable and anxious. That can take the form of "wishful thinking," "forgetting" the facts, or sheer denial. It often involves distortion of reality, whether by selective inattention or rationalization of unsettling circumstances.

A capacity for self-deception is normal. But in some people, it is overdeveloped and exercised frequently, reflecting a gargantuan need to tamper with reality and to avoid coming to grips at all with whatever is disturbing or painful.

But the facts and requirements of small business operations will not be bent, denied or explained away simply because the owner-manager imposes personal emotional perceptions on the realities of the business world. Anyone who thinks, "No Way!" when confronted with evidence of lagging sales, a pattern of customer complaints, booming competition, rising costs, or possible embezzlement will learn far too late how little margin there is for illusion in the small business world. It can't be said too often that objectivity and realism are basic requirements in small business.

Inner Limitations

The founder of a small business may be particularly prone to defensiveness and self-deception. For all the obvious strengths and virtues of the entrepreneurial personality, it may contain the seeds of destruction of its own good works.

Typically founders are dauntless, optimistic, even missionary. Their tendency is to focus on opportunity, not risk. They are inclined more to action and less to reflection and introspection. And there can be tendencies to self-defeating egotism. Consider some manifestations.

1. *Unwitting Self-Congratulations.* Owner-managers normally devote long hours to the business and often think, "I'm working my butt off, giving it my best, things must be more or less right if I can't see any problems." But we see what we want to see, and business problems may sabotage a self-image as an achiever. Blinding, defensive pride sets in.

2. *Disdain for Areas of Limited Business Experience.* Most owner-managers are limited in their general business experience. They often do not acknowledge just how limited that experience is and what there is to learn. Cash flow and balance sheet analyses, for example, or demands for marketing and delegation may be not only mysteries but also regarded as wasteful interferences with "real" work. "I just don't believe in balance sheets," an owner-manager told his accountant shortly before he finally perceived a hemorrhaging of cash. The man

had no experience reading and using an accountant's financial statements. He had also rejected suggestions in the start-up phase for a minimum contingency cash fund. "One accountant will tell you one thing, another the opposite," he rationalized. He had all the comfortable confidence of pure ignorance—and it almost cost him his business.

3. *Rejection of Assistance.* Often, the very individualism that motivated the establishment of the firm is also expressed in a stubborn insistence on going it alone. The venturer finds it difficult to seek or receive guidance and assistance. It is as if such help would encroach on personal independence or sense of achievement.

4. *Resistance to Delegating the Work.* Many business founders are strongly impelled to control every last small detail of the business. While one consequence may be strong personal "leadership," another is reduced capacity to focus on the essential needs of the business. In particular, it means resistance to delegating any real authority to the staff. That can be fatal, especially to growing companies or those with owner-managers who lack decisive talents or experience. Some owner-managers have little tolerance for subordinates who think for themselves. Such owners not only fail to listen actively to others but also harbor a visceral distrust of their ideas. It is as if the views of the staff were perceived not as possible ways to improve the business but as outside controls or infringements on the entrepreneur's valued freedom.

5. *Aversion to Basic Management Tools and the Management Process.* The owner-manager may show a dangerous aversion to basic management processes, such as:

a. Evaluating the business analytically and creatively;
b. Designing basic business controls;
c. Planning for selling the goods;
d. Building a team;
e. Watching the cash needs;
f. Developing specific action plans to meet priority objectives.

But those seemingly "nonactive" mental processes are, in fact, among the essential tools for helping you do the things that really matter in order to enhance your firm's profit potential.

6. *Boredom That Sets in after the Concern Is Established and on Its Way.* For many entrepreneurs, the excitement and sense of achievement come from creating the business. Afterward, they begin to neglect the more ordinary but essential tasks for developing the business beyond the survival stage to growth and prosperity.

Functional Limitations

Probably 90 percent of business founders are adequately gifted in a number of business capacities. If you capitalize on those strengths and acknowledge and compensate for the relative gaps, there should be no insurmountable personal obstacles to business success. But we tend to do what we know, like, and are comfortable with, and it is likely that strengths will be exercised at the expense of other vital needs of the business.

Debbie Fields, founder of Mrs. Field's Cookies, a national chain of fresh cookie stores, gives a succinct illustration of what it means to know your functional strengths and weaknesses. "I knew what I was really good at. I make great cookies; that I really do well. And I'm really good at dealing with people....But there are some things I am just not a whiz kid at. I am not great with numbers...I do rely on [my husband] with numbers because he's so good with them....And so I thought, well, understanding my limitations, I need superstars. I have surrounded myself with superstars. And they know it."

If for any reason you neglect, or are limited in, some basic areas of your business, you will subvert the very strengths that you contribute to it.

Assessment of your business capabilities and dispositions should be seen as an occasion for increasing your company's odds for survival and success. It is not an occasion for diminished self-esteem.

You can use the work sheet in Checklist 1 to assess your own relative strengths and weaknesses in the basic functional areas of the business. Rate yourself 1 (poor) to 5 (excellent) in each category (the worksheet provides a space for notes and comments above each rating). Then, looking at the aggregate ratings, determine honestly in which areas you are likely to make strong contributions to the firm and in which ones some corrective measures are necessary.

Most business founders have solid prior experience or interests in either the product or the marketing and selling areas of the business. But it is rare that they have both.

Engineers and inventors, for example, are notorious one-dimensional business entrants, and, for that reason, most venture capital managers shy away from them. "Investors don't put money in ideas," explains one venture capital manager. "They invest in businesses." Ideas have to be managed to fruition, and products don't just sell themselves. For the inventor or engineer, "financial success may be of secondary importance to artistic success," points out an observer. "The fact that *their* product is on the market is, for them, sufficient success."

The innovative or technologically gifted product designer is frequently not the person to install rigorous business controls systems or to promote a marketing and sales campaign. The engineering mind may, in fact, be insensitive to marketing and other commercial implications when making key technical decisions for the product.

Similarly, if marketing or sales is your forte, it will be your most valuable functional contribution to the business, as long as you understand that other areas vital to the survival and success of the business require equal attention and action. Otherwise, all your marketing or sales efforts will be dissipated. A poor product, inflated costs, or a weak staff will almost surely, in part or combination, undo inspired sales efforts.

Further self-assessment is needed in the marketing and selling area. An eye-to-eye sales whiz may not be a sufficiently adept conceptualist to develop a coherent marketing plan.

CHECKLIST 1 Self-Assessment Work Sheet of Business Capacities

	The Product	Marketing and Selling	Finances	Staff	Daily Operations/ Administration
1. *Interest and proneness to active involvement.* Ask: (1) which do I like; (2) where have I gravitated in the past; (3) which have I avoided, where are the blocks?	___	___	___	___	___
Rating	___	___	___	___	___
2. *Experience and knowledge.* No one is an across-the-board dynamo; the issue is substance and depth.	___	___	___	___	___
Rating	___	___	___	___	___

3. *Abilities, aptitudes, and skills.* Ask: (1) what comes easily; (2) where are the natural "knacks"; (3) where do I feel doltish?

   Rating _____ _____ _____

4. *Aggregate impressions.* Is the likelihood of significant contributions to the firm strong, questionable, or poor? _____ _____

Allan Kennedy, an experienced consultant and coauthor of *Corporate Cultures,* says of the high-tech companies along Massachusetts' Route 128, "These companies are full of entre-preneurs. You couldn't spend a day there without hearing, 'Let's go call on a customer.' They're very real-world oriented. Most of them don't think strategically, but they're terrific at action." That approach may work out well, provided it is the *right* action. Are they concentrating on the *right* markets, the *right* customers, for example?

Conversely, the owner-manager who excels as a marketing strategist may lack entirely the negotiating and sales skills of a natural salesperson. And a super salesperson may fail com-pletely if forced to shift gears and organize a strong sales staff as sales manager.

A key area frequently neglected in small business relates to daily administration of operations and internal controls. Often the owner-manager will harbor a nearly invincible distaste or block towards the accounting and controls function. It is quite natural that the business founder's attention and strengths lie elsewhere. Administrative detail and routine are not at all the attractions that led to launching the business in the first place. But administrative chaos and a consequential loss of control of the firm will very likely topple the venture unless this gaping hole is effectively plugged.

As entrepreneur Derek F. du Toit recalls, "My problem was that, like many entrepreneurs, I was not an adept administra-tor. Good administrators strive for detailed policy execution and orderly business operations. They are happiest when circumstances are controlled and actions are predictable. The person who starts a business has a much different mind-set...where the accent is on getting the job done as quickly as possible....The entrepreneur prefers planning new projects to learning from experience how to run the business effectively." Says du Toit of himself, "I don't have the mind-set of even an average controller." To plug in the gaps in his abilities, he hired well. (See "Confessions of a So-So Controller," *Harvard Busi-ness Review,* July/August, 1985.)

A woman who went into bankruptcy because she could not efficiently process and deliver orders for her $10 million-a-year catalog business says, "We weren't prepared on Day One and weren't prepared the day before bankruptcy. We were in an almost continuous state of crisis management. My talents lie in the area of merchandising, working with vendors—the creative, marketing end of the catalogue. As far as plant operations go—order fulfillment, data processing—I don't feel comfortable at all. I'll leave those to the people who know what they're doing [assuming she can raise new money for a similar venture]."

Selfless Objectivity

A study by Southern Methodist University's Caruth Institute of Owner-Managed Business found that one of the traits of the *successful* entrepreneur is being *very realistic*. Yet, according to one accountant and small business consultant, "It is simply amazing that ego considerations are so frequently dominant and profit considerations are so subordinate, and the owner doesn't even know it."

"Mind-forged manacles" can cripple the business.

Problems, mistakes, and difficulties are the norm in small business. But, as the old adage goes, "an error doesn't become a mistake until you refuse to correct it."

The prerequisite for confronting and dealing with problems and mistakes is acknowledging them. A problem must be identified before it is solved. Similarly, the prerequisite for seizing opportunity and improving the business is acknowledging that every business is capable of improved performance. No managerial effort is complete and no owner-manager infallible. You should try to distinguish with infinite care between what "is" and what "can be."

The objective well-being of the business must always retain supremacy over your other ego needs. In the words of one observer, "Most people have built-in screens which filter out the boos and amplify the applause. Not so for successful entrepreneurs. They know when they are in trouble and have the ego strength to admit they are wrong."

Checklist 2 lists guidelines to help you honestly confront your mistakes and the firm's shortcomings.

CHECKLIST 2 Guidelines for Selfless Objectivity

---

1. Detach your ego from evaluation of performance; that is a mark of a true "professional."
2. Be wary of self-satisfaction; it weakens the capacity to see things freshly.
3. Pay attention to evidence of unachieved performance: Look, for example, not only at the half-full glass but also at the empty half which cries for attention.
4. Understand that while mistakes are inevitable, smart owner-managers correct and learn from them.
5. Remember that constructive discontent is the prerequisite for improving profits.
6. Be aware that what you don't know is just as important as what you do know.
7. Ask hard questions of yourself and others: That is the best way to gain new knowledge and insight.
8. Be strong enough to listen openly and carefully to the ideas of others.
9. Be willing to follow nagging gut feelings no matter where they lead.

Confronting the Limitations

All owner-managers, then, have relative shortcomings as well as strengths. Experience, knowledge, or interest may be limited in some key aspects of the business—a danger compounded by a universal tendency to focus on what is comforting and satisfying. We will now discuss some specific ways you can compensate for any limitations.

Strengthening Your Own Knowledge and Performance

Often we are weak in a particular business area simply because we haven't been exposed to it. Its work and methods may seem forbiddingly mysterious and difficult. Accounting and internal controls are a typical example. Checklist 3 sets out ways you can get on top of an area you don't fully understand, using accounting and internal controls as an illustration.

CHECKLIST 3 Strengthening Your Effectiveness in a Key Function
(Example: Accounting and Internal Controls)

1. *Spend more, not less, time on it.* Pour yourself into the accounting books and the flow of paper work.
2. *Ask lots of questions,* including all the "dumb" ones, of the accountant or bookkeeper. Keep asking until you know as much about their work for you as they do.
3. *Challenge assumptions.* Ask, "Why this way, not that? Is there another way?"
4. *Work with, not apart from, the specialists (in this case, the accountant or knowledgeable outsiders).* Find out what issues are at stake that you don't know about. Determine if there are useful ways of doing things that could be applied to your business.
5. *Take a brief introductory night-school course* in bookkeeping/accounting.
6. *Read a book* on management accounting, or parts of a text on, say, inventory control, or on any other specific area in which you need more knowledge to really get a grip on operations in your firm.

Look for Warning Signs

Pay a healthy respect to early warning clues that something is wrong or neglected.

Here's what one "turnaround" management consultant says: "The bottom-line problem is always top management. The typical client is an entrepreneur who has been in the same business for many years. His strength is in sales or production, seldom finance. By the time we get his call, he's already in deep trouble. We never get an early call. Many managers just can't believe that anyone knows any more about their business than they do. And in a lot of ways, they're right. All we sell is common sense, but there are a lot of managers who just will not take advice until it's almost too late."

Consider these warning signals, for example:

1. Nagging, won't-go-away gut feelings that frequently suggest procrastination or neglect of a problem area;

2. A pattern of confusion or chaos, such as:
   a. Double payment of bills
   b. Recurring customer complaints
   c. Appeals by the staff for guidance;

3. Evidence in the financial reports of unhealthy trends that should be controlled;

4. Subtle suggestions by staff or an outside professional that you seem to be resisting or neglecting some strongly recommended improvements.

Building a Team

Taking on a partner is one way to compensate for your limitations. It may succeed, but it usually doesn't. Checklist 4 lists some reasons why not.

It is much more practical to hire first-rate employees who are strong in key areas where you are relatively weak. If, for example, you understand the importance of tightly run administrative processes but loathe those activities, you can employ a mature bookkeeper with strong office management experience. Likewise, if you are decidedly product oriented, you should look for someone experienced and talented in the marketing or sales functions. If, for whatever reason, you are ducking product development and quality, you will have to assure that this base is covered well. And so on.

CHECKLIST 4 Partnership Problems

---

1. The partner is chosen on the basis of friendship, not contribution to the business.
2. The partners have conflicting goals for the firm.
3. Either or both partners fail to acknowledge limitations and fail to seek compensatory help from each other.
4. Conflicts of personality and ego damage the business.
5. One partner contributes much more than the other, yet they receive equal compensation.
6. Decision making and functional responsibilities are blurred.
7. One of the partners turns out to be dishonest, irresponsible, or lacking in the rudiments of fair play.

Seek Help from Outsiders

For reasons we have mentioned, owner-managers are in jeopardy of insulating themselves from sufficient awareness of their own or the firm's limitations and problems. Independent, experienced outsiders are a wonderful source of help.

Outsiders are objective. They are not "part of the problem." They ask uncomfortable questions and raise new issues. They let you know what you don't know and point to hazardous areas of neglect. They provide valuable sounding boards. Following are some of the more useful outside sources.

1. *The Board of Directors.* The traditional small business Board of Directors is just a formal response to state corporate law requirements, and members are typically friends or officers of the company. An owner is often reluctant to expose weaknesses to outsiders if they comprise a majority on the Board since the outsiders could strip the company's owner of management powers. So, the Board is typically given only nominal authority and functions only to ratify decisions of the owner-manager.

Some owner-managers, though, tout the benefits of placing experienced outside members on the Board. Those members can provide supplementary business know-how where it is vitally needed. They can identify hidden problems and provide crucial, fresh perspectives on the company's needs.

2. *Advisory Boards.* In effect, an advisory board is an informal board of directors. Members have no statutory or any other formal authority, and their effectiveness depends on two factors: how well they are chosen and the owner-manager's willingness to open up the company to them and to respect their observations and recommendations.

Typically, an advisory board will have a useful mix of experience. A four-member board, for example, would ideally include another owner-manager in an allied field, one general business person, and two additional members versed in particular areas of importance to the business, such as technical concerns, marketing, or sales.

In effect, the advisory board would review and approve all major business operations and decisions and make specific recommendations on its own initiative. At the least, its members might simply ask hard questions never considered by the owner-manager.

Advisory board meetings are generally held two to four times a year. They are most effective when the owner-manager provides the board in advance with substantial background materials and extensive oral briefings and allows the board members to wander around the office or plant, talk freely with employees, and examine the books.

Many owner-managers seem surprised at the caliber of talent they attract. A very small or new business may need to attract members with small stock inducements, but $250 to $750 a meeting per member is the common fee for a more established firm. It is enough, in one observer's words, "to establish an obligation of diligence, but low enough to ensure autonomy."

3. *Business Round Tables.* Owner-manager round tables are typically composed of 10 or so owner-managers in the same general business field. They usually meet every month or two to discuss mutual concerns and problems. One large

organization that sponsors such round tables is the American Women's Economic Development Corporation (AWED), whose national office is at 60 East 42d Street, New York, NY 10017. A similar organization is the Smaller Business Association of New England.

One member speaks of his monthly gathering as "an antidote to the isolation of the owner's office....The quality of advice may not be as important as hearing someone in the same position respond to the same issues." Another member notes, "As soon as your staff meets resistance from you, they back off. You can only get this kind of input from an outsider."

In six southeastern states, owner-managers of television sales and service dealers have informally organized the Southeastern Critique Group. Typically, members meet for three days every six months to conduct a "hard-nosed, no-holds-barred" review of an individual business. The entire operation is probed and investigated, from the appearance, pay, and productivity of its employees to reviews of advertising effectiveness, inventory control, financing, and the operations and future plans of the parts departments. The reviews are said to be both "scary and sometimes embarrassing" and "a potential eye-opener of valuable advice."

4. *Informal Contacts with Other Owner-Managers*. The more business owners you can cultivate, the better your possibilities for valuable third-party assistance. If they have been in business a few years, they have already learned some hard lessons and can share common experience and information, as well as advise you on common concerns.

5. *Professionals*. You can convert contacts with your accountant, lawyer, banker, and insurance broker into sources of practical business assistance. Each has a lot of small business knowledge you could actively tap. Because the accountant's contributions in particular are so important, a good portion of Chapter 7 is devoted to this role.

6. *Consultants*. Small business consultants can help you, too. The trick is to recognize the specific areas where you need

help. It is not always easy to find the right consultant who will make specific recommendations tailored to your particular business and its particular needs. Many small business owner-managers have been helped by the Service Corps of Retired Executives (SCORE), which provides a wide variety of assistance in both the pre-start-up and operating stages. A Small Business Administration office can put you in contact with a branch if it's not listed in your local telephone directory.

7. *Friends and Customers.* Chapter 4 suggests the usefulness of seeking feedback from the buyers of your goods and services. Solicit comments, and listen carefully to them. Increasingly, small businesses are using consumer "focus groups," which are organized to elicit customer responses to a variety of questions relating to a company's goods and services.

Any way that you can sharpen your awareness of business realities should be embraced. Personal illusions and ego are huge obstacles to effective management—to understanding, directing, and controlling a small business.

CHAPTER
3

SUTTON'S LAW: SIMPLE IS EFFECTIVE

Several decades back, the country was captivated by the ingenious bank-robbing exploits of Willie Sutton. Once, following a conviction, a reporter asked, "Willie, why are you always robbing banks?" Sutton eyed him as if he were some low fool who had missed the most obvious point in the whole world. "That's where the money is," he replied.

In his own fashion, Willie knew where the payoff was, and he didn't waste his time and energies on sideshows.

So let's call this *Sutton's Law: Go Where the Money Is*. Or, rephrased: *Simple Is Effective*.

Effectiveness in small business means concentrating scarce time, money, and other resources where they will be most productive and the payoff will be greatest. To squander the business's limited assets, including your own funds, your vision and energy, your talents and time, on secondary or unproductive objectives and activities is to dissipate the company's profits and potential for success.

Small business management, I have already noted, is the art of the essential. It is making the most out of a little.

Purposeful and *economical* activity—focused on *leanness, productivity, contribution,* and *impact*—is the key to *effective* small business *management*. What these words should mean to you, as the owner-manager, is the subject of this chapter.

Owner-managers whose operating maxim is "ready, fire, aim" use cannons to shoot squirrels and popguns for the elephants. They create the wonderful illusion of lots of action and drive, when the management reality is a failure of direction and control. Their firms are like corks bobbing in the middle of the ocean.

A West Coast venture capitalist reviewed the business plan of a fledgling company that was planning on producing three different product lines. "You guys are crazy as hell," he said. "What you should do is focus on one thing and make that happen. Now go decide which one that should be."

A successful Silicon Valley entrepreneur recalls, "We had to grow up, focus on what our business was about, and then concentrate on the two or three things that had to be done over the next 12 months. My view is that you should start out with a set of principles or beliefs, and from those you begin to develop business strategies that are consistent. I needed to stick with some fundamental principles."

Another venture capitalist delights in limiting the funds provided by his firm to small businesses because it "focuses them into a very narrow channel. We don't want them moving off whatever they've decided to do."

You can bet that a successful small firm is tight and narrow in focus and that, like a superb athlete, it tolerates no waste and shows an economy of forceful energy.

Purpose, Priorities, and Objectives

In the words of baseball's philosopher, Yogi Berra, "If you don't know where you're going, you probably won't get there." This is an essential aspect of Sutton's Law. Keep your eye on the payoff.

A Clear and Dominating Business Purpose

C. Northcote Parkinson, of Parkinson's Law fame, wrote that "a principal cause of disaster is confusion of purpose. In the foundation and development of a successful enterprise there must be a single-minded pursuit—we will do well, in general, to stick to the point."

Somewhere else it is written, "I cannot give you a formula for success, but I can give you the formula for failure: Try to please everybody." Big businesses sometimes try this, but they rarely succeed, even with all their money, talent, and other resources. Thomas J. Peters and Robert H. Waterman, Jr., in their best seller, *In Search of Excellence,* point out that most successful large firms are driven by a clear sense of mission and purpose.

The small business desperately requires a clear identity and a dominant organizing concept in order to separate the vital managerial concerns from the desirable, the important ones from the trivial, and the muscle from the fat. It must parlay its vision and special strengths into a competitive edge that distinguishes it from its rivals.

To say, as some business pseudosophisticates do, "We are in the business of making money," begs questions: What business? What market? What product? Where's the money, and how do we decide where to put *our* money? Developing the business without a clear sense of purpose invites that fanaticism, which, as someone has noted, "consists in redoubling your efforts when you have forgotten your aim." The company becomes a prisoner of day-to-day detail and lacks forward thrust. It is shackled to the quirky and transient demands of the day.

Try to develop a business map and some supreme values or guidelines that allow you to structure the apparent complexity and randomness of the business world within a clear, simple sense of purpose. Only then can you develop concrete business objectives and strategies and focus on the important business considerations: the concrete identity of products, services and markets; the staff needs; and the financial and administrative needs of the firm. Only then can you make highly practical, result-shaped business plans for purposeful and effective daily activities.

For 30 or so years, Peter Drucker has been America's foremost observer, writer and consultant on business management. From the start, he has insisted on the urgency of focus and definition: "Concentration is the key to economic results...no other principle of effectiveness is violated as constantly today as the basic principle of concentration....Our motto seems to be: 'Let's do a little bit of everything.' " (*Managing for Results,* 1964).

Although Drucker is writing about larger enterprises, his message is all the more applicable to the asset-strapped small firm, especially at startup. Drucker urges the manager to ask, "What business are we in and what business should we be in?"

What Business Are You In?

Neither the question nor an appropriate and concrete response is always self-evident. The owner-manager may easily become pinioned to a myopic and restricted business vision or to one that is loose and unruly—all things to all people, and anything goes. In either case, the business will be on a misguided course from the start. "What business are we in?" "Do we really belong in *that* business, is that the way we should define ourselves?" "Is that the way the public should perceive us?" Ask these questions again and again, and new and more effective ways of seeing the same business may be exploited.

For example, is the dominating purpose of a company to sell an herbal shampoo that happens to have dandruff-relieving components? Or is it in the primary business of offering a dandruff-removal product?

A professional hockey team is not simply in competition with other hockey teams, or even with baseball, football or basketball teams whose schedules overlap its own. It is in the entertainment business. An old movie-industry man, Sonny Werblin, understood this in the mid-1960s, when, as owner of the New York Jets football team, he signed up "Broadway" Joe Namath with a record bonus.

There is a relatively small but very profitable printing firm in Wisconsin that several years back was in the "calendar business." That was not only a highly seasonal but also a declining industry. It occurred to the owners that they didn't have to be calendar producers. "We are in the printing business," they observed. After some simple but careful market research, they determined there was a need for catalog producers, particularly at the quality end of the business. They pursued that business relentlessly and are widely known now as the leading catalog printers in their region. The firm's production equipment is basically unchanged, but its sales have boomed.

In New York City, some Korean vegetable and fruit retailers installed small, simple salad bars for takeout at very moderate prices. Business grew. They expanded the salad bars, adding meat salads and hot takeout foods. More sales were realized, and other Korean produce retailers followed suit. They now consider their primary mission to be takeout food retailers, "saving time and work" for hundreds of thousands of New Yorkers on modest budgets who have neither time nor inclination to prepare meals, yet demand more in taste and nutrition than frozen TV dinners.

There was a small auto repair garage that specialized in rust-proofing. Because its owner perceptively spotted a trend a decade ago toward longer car ownership and increased maintenance requirements, he entirely reconceptualized the business. It is now "The Car Preservation Center." The very name conveys a pithy vision of its business purpose. With just a little additional capital, the business now repaints exteriors, refurbishes interiors, cleans vinyl tops, and, in fact, does just about anything else needed to make an old car look new. Profits have soared.

Peter Drucker notes that rug and carpet dealers traditionally sell directly to the homeowner. One retailer redefined his business as a supplier of wall-to-wall carpeting to housing contractors. The contractors were thus able to use less expensive flooring in their buildings, thereby reducing the price of the housing.

But retailers of folkloric rugs would do better to conceive of their business mission as providing relatively inexpensive, colorful, and tasteful household decorative goods for an upscale market with limited budgets.

Lane McFaddin of McFaddin Ventures in Texas describes himself as a saloonkeeper. He is, in fact, a very acute entrepreneur. While putting in time several years back at a Holiday Inn franchise, he observed that "a bar needed 5 percent of a hotel's capital, yet contributed 30 to 50 percent of its sales." He now has a chain of nearly 50 "saloons." Yet he conceives of them not as conventional bars but as "theme clubs." One, for example, features a dance floor built around a Studebaker car of 35 years ago—the model that looks more modern than anything on the road today. Another is based on the urban cowboy theme. Common to all the "clubs," in the words of *Forbes* magazine, "is a clean, well-lighted place for a young, single and relatively affluent clientele to meet." McFaddin says that the heart of his ventures is not the sale of liquor and beer. "We're selling fun. The sale of alcoholic beverages is really a by-product." He has a nice, tight grasp on a dominant business purpose. Clearly, there is none of the "Let's-do-a-little-bit-of-everything" attitude.

Critical Factors of Success

Time and again, if you talk to the owner-manager of a patently successful small business or just observe the company in action, you will soon know that it is a business that stands for something. Ask the owner-manager about the critical factors of success for the particular venture, and it is odds-on you will hear a concise statement of the few crucial considerations that the owner believes will separate the winners and losers in his particular business area.

That handful of critical factors, those few guiding principles allow you to set a course for your business, stamp a personality on its daily affairs, and stay on that course through the inevitable tumult and uncertainty. They signal where the payoff is and how to reach it.

"The [owner-manager] establishes the personality of the business," says John Cullinare of Cullinet Software, Inc. "His most important role is to set the tone. You can write memos and try to set an official tone, but it's the philosophy you act out day-by-day that ripples through the organization." And the marketplace.

The small business owner must consider, "What is truly vital to us? What *are* the critical factors of our success?"

It's natural to think, "But it's *all* important. We *have* to have good products and service; we have to market and sell these to the public and satisfy our customers; we obviously need a good staff; and we should keep costs down, manage our assets, conserve our cash, and more."

All that is true. Those *are* make-or-break considerations that apply to *all* small businesses. But each firm is unique, and it must exploit one or two particular strengths or realize some particular internal efficiencies that will allow it to survive and beat the competition.

It won't be sufficient to define those critical factors of success in vague, general terms. "A good product at competitive prices" not only lacks operating specificity but also obscures all the hard questions involving the definition of "good" and "competitive" and what the "product" should be.

A critical factor of success in a particular business may be getting the deliveries out fast and reliably. For a discount retailer and a good portion of start-up businesses, a critical factor probably will be rigorous control of the costs. The critical factor also might be the excellence of a few key salespeople, the maintenance of technological superiority, or the reach and resourcefulness of a promotional campaign. A strategic or ideal location might be the key to success. It might be the concentrated appeal of a specialty store or the wide choice of goods in a grocery or department store. Identification of these factors is obviously a prerequisite to exploiting them.

Most often, a critical factor of success is the unparalleled excellence of the product or service. If you are driving through the Housatonic Valley in northwest Connecticut, near Torrington, you may come upon the White Flower Farm, an outdoor nursery. How beautiful it is, perched on a gently sloping and luxuriant green hill. Adjacent is a splendid white clapboard colonial house used for office space. Although the majority of sales flow from a mail-order business, former investment banker Eliot Wadsworth knows his company's knack. "I worry we'll be seen as a go-go operation, a rocket ship willing to sacrifice quality to growth. And that's just not true. Our corporate strategy is simple: We will be *the quality supplier.* Period." Therefore, the nursery comes first, and the derivative mail-order business operations second.

"Eliot has a very clear idea of what White Flower Farm is, and his standards come through consistently," says an employee. "He loves beautiful things and respects them. I don't think anyone here is confused about what we do. He wants us to be what we say we are."

A very different kind of business is a rapidly expanding East Coast pest control outfit, "Bugs" Burger. Owner Al Burger doesn't mince words describing the general competition: "I started my business because I thought it was unethical to take money for poor quality performance. I thought there should be standards and ethics in the business." Most owners in the field, he says, "are former [service] routemen who are thieves and lazy to boot. That's what you've got—a lack of scruples. And why should *their* routemen care? They've probably got their own business on the side."

The "Bugs" Burger firm sets exacting standards for its servicemen and has installed a formidable quality-control and follow-up system to enforce those standards. The company issues a simple, clear guarantee to its customers that it will eliminate *all* roaches and rodents and destroy their breeding and nesting areas. Guaranteed, unsurpassed quality and service, then, are the firm's critical factors of success. It charges at least double the fees of the competition, but revenues continue to increase.

Value, reliability, and integrity may be the critical factors of a firm's success. L.L. Bean, the Maine-based outdoor sporting apparel and equipment store that grew from a small business to a giant mail-order outfit, has traded on those elements of "customer satisfaction" for 75 years. When L.L. Bean says, "We guarantee 100 percent satisfaction," it is no empty puff. Its first mailing circular in 1912 read like this:

Notice
I do not consider a sale complete until goods are worn out and the customer still satisfied.
We will thank anyone to return goods that are not perfectly satisfactory.

Should the person reading this notice know of anyone who is not satisfied with our goods, I will consider it a favor to be notified.
Above all things we wish to avoid having a dissatisfied customer.

That's the way it is today, and because L.L. Bean delivers, several generations of satisfied customers regard it as a national landmark.

Conde Nast built his publishing empire on a new concept, "a class act," according to his biographer, Caroline Seebohm. Nast reconceptualized the whole basis for attracting larger advertising revenues by deliberately *limiting* readership to an affluent market. That was his critical factor of success.

Priorities and Objectives

To manage is to choose among all sorts of desirable or tempting objectives and activities. But no small business can undertake successfully more than a few objectives and related activities at any one time. Limited resources severely constrain a small concern's scope of operations, and thin margins of success and failure impel that constraint. It is "guns" *or* "butter," in effect, not guns *and* butter.

Establishing priorities is one of the small business owner-manager's chief responsibilities.

"We will invest in *this,* but not that; we will provide *this* market with *these* goods, and not those other markets with a full range of goods; we will set out to realize *this* objective, and really do it well, and then and only then will we push on to others." This is the nature of establishing priorities among fiercely competing considerations. To manage is to make some tough decisions and wrenching trade-offs.

In small business management, those choices are ultimately expressed in concrete allocations of resources and specific activities. Robert Sternberg, a Yale psychologist, has written that effective resource allocation is not only a key ingredient of practical intelligence, but also of "successful living in general."

How a company's resources are deployed—where and how the owner-manager and the staff spend their time, which monies are budgeted where, which products are sold to what markets—is a question of foresight and planning.

Business planning is no more effective than a vague New Year's resolution unless it incorporates clear, concrete and doable objectives of a high standard. When the owner-manager can state, or, better yet, write down realistic, specific, and possibly quantifiable objectives, they can be translated into achievable action plans. Harold Geneen, Chairman of ITT in the 1960s and 1970s, commented that running a business is just the opposite of reading a book. "You start from the end, and then you do everything you must to reach it."

How you go about defining simple, effective business objectives is one of the matters discussed in Chapter 11, "Planning for Action and Results."

Again and again throughout this book, the message of Sutton's Law is that to be effective and productive, you must: Simplify, simplify; focus, and concentrate.

There are two particular areas where owner-managers may indulgently or unwittingly invite trouble by violating Sutton's Law: discerning the vital and important from the desirable and trivial ("Frills and Fat") and using time effectively.

Frills and Fat

There is nothing as disconcerting to observe in a small business, especially a new one, as the squandering of precious assets on frills and fat.

The well-known venture capitalist, Fred Adler, recounted the following: "One of my 'laws' is: 'The probability of success is inversely proportional to the size of the President's office.' I once received a well-constructed proposal from the president of a small company, so I decided to visit the plant. In the parking lot space reserved for the president was a brand-new Cadillac. I was ushered into his office—enormous, impressive. But the plant was only twice as large as the president's office. So I asked about cash flow. 'Our projections,' he replied. 'I didn't ask for projections,' I said. 'What about cash flow?' 'Well, last month it was a negative $300,000!' 'Then on the basis of the figures I've seen, you can stay alive another three months?' 'Yes!'"

Jerry White of Southern Methodist University's Caruth Institute of Owner-Managed Business believes a preoccupation with frivolous facades is one of the top five reasons for small business failure. Scarce and vulnerable assets are misdirected where they have no payoff or productivity.

The possibilities for frills and fat are long and tempting. Here are some typical examples.

1. Huge offices, with a Mr. Big desk for the owner-manager, mock antique furniture, and wall-to-wall carpeting
2. Decorative office supplies and logo-imprinted office memorandum pads
3. A Hollywood telephone system and underutilized office equipment
4. Prestige perks—a status company car, first-class air fare, and travel privileges for the family; business lunches at Chez de Luxe; ostentatious gifts to company charities

No matter that they are "nice," or "convenient," or that "the employees appreciate this." They are not vital, nor probably even marginally productive.

There is, for example, the $600,000-a-year company with no profits and in need of basic capital improvements. It spends $4,000 on an employee Christmas party. If employee morale is truly a priority, there are many more effective and less expensive ways of enhancing it (see Chapter 6).

Unhappily, it is common to observe rampant nepotism, or,

even more dangerous, the proliferation of managers, assistant managers, and assistants to managers. All the typical vices of many prosperous big businesses are incorporated from the start, and bureaucratic sclerosis sets in. There are the complex organization charts and the rigid chains-of-command. The owner-manager builds a cocoon around personal grandeurs and forfeits contact with the customers and employees. Disguised underemployment, a dissipation of motivation, and bloated budgets abound. Complicated company manuals and rules soon emerge. The boss has a full-time secretary, whereas a part-time secretary shared with the other top people would fill the need.

Often, an owner-manager overlooks the possibility of using one competent employee to perform several functions or of hiring part-time assistance. Students can be hired part-time for errands; all the better if one can type, but dictaphone devices and outside typing services also can be used.

Start-up entrepreneurs often see expenditures as all-or-nothing propositions, when so often there is a creative middle ground. It may be more economical and effective, for example, to buy used goods and equipment or lease them. One new venturer needed some laboratory test equipment that sold for about $100,000 new. He heard of a distress sale in a trade journal, purchased one-year-old equipment for $7,000, sold it to a leasing company for $45,000, then leased it back for five years.

The Yellow Pages list a variety of used equipment and surplus merchandise dealers, as well as secondhand dealers for specific items such as "Office Furniture." Bankruptcy and liquidation auctions, advertised in the newspaper classifieds, are also a good source for finding used equipment.

As a woman starting a second business venture, after failing in her first, observed: "This time I'm going to drive an old pickup truck instead of a Mercedes. I'm going to rent a Quonset hut on the edge of town. And boy, do I know about cash flow." Simple can be beautiful for the startup entrepreneur.

Sutton's Law: Using Time Effectively

In Chapter 1, I noted that it is a fact of life in small business that the owner-manager's role is not limited to management. He or she is also a player and, by necessity, a very active one.

The founder of a small business usually brings special talents and experience in one or more important functional areas of the business, such as product development, marketing, or sales. But if he or she is diverted from making those contributions, if "there just isn't time" to attend to the products or call on the customers, critical areas of the business will go untended, unless equally experienced—hence, expensive—employees are hired to fill the gap.

An additional fact of life for small business owners is that 50 percent or more of available time is consumed by administrative housekeeping and minicrises. Routine paper work, small repairs, employment applications, employee problems, disputes with insurance brokers and tax examiners, time with lawyers and accountants—these general maintenance and support responsibilities are important in the sense that they must be done, but they don't directly contribute to the firm's productivity.

Daily brush fires consume even more time: A heating system that is out of order; an employee who quits without notice, leaving an entire job function to be plugged until a suitable replacement is found; five important customers demanding immediate attention.

You can spend entire days and weeks dodging bullets, until gradually, the immediate and pressing replace the critical and important in the scheme of company priorities. Even major decisions will begin to reflect those confused priorities.

A $10,000 investment in new equipment, for instance, may be given no more thought and attention than three other tasks in the same hour. The owner-manager pleads lack of time to make a more reasoned decision, forfeiting a possible $5,000 bargain on some first-rate equipment in the process, because

SUTTON'S LAW: SIMPLE IS EFFECTIVE 43

the day before—just to save $200—he spent too much time on an errand he should have delegated. Not having time for a high-priority decision actually cost him $5,000.

There is a popular restaurant in Chicago with a sideline off-premises catering business. The owner-manager is, of course, harried with the press of daily tasks. So is his catering director.

They "just never have had a minute" to figure out that the catering business must produce $100,000 a year to break even, which is precisely the level at which sales have hovered for several years. But the catering business makes little sense to the restaurant unless sales considerably exceed the break-even point. Up to that level, it is no more than a drain on the attention of key restaurant employees.

What is clearly needed if the catering activities are to be justified is a major outreach program to solicit new customers. But, "there's no time for that now," claims the owner-manager, who, truth be known, spends about 15 hours a week attending all catering events and working on small planning details. The positive contribution of this time to company profits is, of course, zero.

Has he or the catering director met with or at least written to the 10 or so leading party brokers who contract out several millions of catering contracts annually? Has he written to the managers of the dozen or so attractive party sites in town where most off-premises parties are given? (Several of them would probably delight in establishing at least a semi-exclusive arrangement with a reliable catering firm.) Has he sent brochures to special target customers or even advertised? "No," is the impatient and uncomprehending reply. "I just don't have the time."

Many a time-pressed owner-manager would mumble and stumble if you asked, "What are the three most important things you have to accomplish in the next month or two?" or, "What are the three most critical concerns for your business in the coming year, and what are your specific plans regarding each of them?"

Owner-managers must detach themselves sufficiently from daily housekeeping and minicrises to establish discretionary time to deal with the needs of the business that truly matter. Keeping it simple means finding or making time to do the important things.

Some entrepreneurs actually prefer "busywork," as one experienced owner-manager calls it, even though they may not be conscious that they do. For the action-motivated "doer," there is real emotional reward in performing and completing finite, limited tasks. The payoffs are visible and immediate; never mind if they are inconsequential, they seem to be evidence of usefulness. Furthermore, handling the daily routine and "fire fighting" is relatively undemanding. It may be time consuming, but it is easy and safe. By contrast, it is hard work to carefully monitor business operations, make tough choices and decisions, and engage in long-term planning with uncertain results.

Yet, if even more daily tasks land in the laps of owner-managers who plead lack of time for longer range activities, they seem to take it in stride and get it all done. *The issue is not so much a lack of time, as a lack of awareness of what is important and productive.* Preferring to do the tasks of today that can be completed today, they don't yet believe in the efficacy of going where the money is.

In other cases, it simply has not occurred to an owner-manager how just a few hours a week in quiet reflection and consideration of the purposes, priorities and activities of the business can produce disproportionately large payoffs.

A concentrated and active search for problems and solutions and a fresh point of view, revealing opportunities of real significance, can literally transform a company's performance. A two-hour consideration of new ways to cut costs by 10 percent will often yield a splendidly practical insight or two that no one had conceived of before. This in turn will yield additional and, frequently, significant profits.

Discretionary time for the make-or-break factors must be found, or better, made. Ten hours a week, maybe, or one to two hours a day is probably enough.

The best place to start is to ask:

1. What are our really basic needs, now and in the coming months? What are three proverbial "first things" that should be done first?
2. How can I, and the staff, undertake them efficiently?
3. How can I organize my time and work so I can be sure to pay close attention to and get active on the "where-the-money-is" factors?

Many businesspeople keep little signs on their desks that say something like this: "Is What I'm About to Do Really Going to Contribute to Our Success?"

Focusing on first things first in no way precludes minding the store and staying afloat through the daily crises *if* some simple tools of time management are observed.

1. *Concentrate effort and time on the critical needs and areas of the business.* That will help considerably in sorting out where and how to spend the limited hours each day and week.

2. *Delegate some of the work.* Chapter 6 discusses in detail the elements of delegation that experienced managers have found effective.

3. *Learn timesaving procedures to reduce work load and eliminate time killers.* Any well-stocked paperback bookstore win have one or more books on time management and organization. Stephanie Winston's *The Organized Executive* is helpful. If you feel besieged by more work than you can handle, the few hours spent perusing a book on time management will be easily regained in less than a week by more effective and efficient work organization.

That in itself is a profitable application of Sutton's Law: Simple Is Effective.

Managing Your Money Tip

You can use Managing Your Money to organize your time, delegate tasks, and make sure that your time is spent efficiently. Managing Your Money will alert you to phone calls you need to make, appointments you need to keep, projects you need to complete, and other things to do. Managing Your Money will even summarize all of these items in a daily Time Summary that you can print out and use to make sure you do everything you need to accomplish during a given day.

These time management functions can be accessed from anywhere in the program by holding the CTRL key and the appropriate letter, such as

> CTRL-A for Appointments
> CTRL-O for To-Do List
> CTRL-P for Phone calls
> CTRL-R for Reminders
> CTRL-T for Time summary

You can also access these selections from the Desk submenu.

All of these functions share certain common characteristics:

- To add a new entry (appointment, reminder, etc.), after you've selected the type of entry you want to add, hit F5. To elaborate on the item, move the cursor to the "detail" field (which will light up when the cursor is in it), and hit F2. Once you're done this, the field can be edited to your heart's content (hit F1 to see all of the options you have). Just hit <esc> to get out of the detail field. Once you've completed the entry, hit F10 to save it.

- (By the way, MYM is very forgiving when it comes to entering dates. The format for the date is 4/15/93, but if you enter 4/15, MYM will supply the year. If you enter just 15, MYM will supply the current month and year. And you can enter 4-15 instead of 4/15; MYM won't mind. Of course, if you point to the date field and use CTRL-D, you can choose the date from a calendar.)

- To change what you entered for an item, highlight that item's date (move the cursor up or down until you've done so) and then hit F2. Type over whatever you previously entered until you're happy with the new information. (To edit the detail field, move the cursor to the "detail" field, and hit F2. Hit <esc> when you're finished.) Then hit F10 to replace the old item with the updated one.

- To create multiple Reminders which contain similar information (such as a series of appointments with the same client), just enter one item, point to the new entry, and press F7. Everything will be the same, and you can change the date and/or time with just a couple of keystrokes. Then save the new item by pressing F5.

Tip

You need to assign the same task to your 14 employees. Use F7 to to copy the first entry 13 times, changing only the "WHO" to whom it's assigned.

- To print a list or schedule of items, press F4.

- To delete an item, hit F3, then hit F10. If you want to delete an appointment or phone call (but NOT a reminder) from your Time Summary *only*, but *not* from your appointment or phone call list, highlight the item's date while in the Time Summary, and hit F8. This will mark the item as completed and keep it from being displayed in the Time Summary, but will preserve a record of the item in its particular list. This allows you to keep a record of your completed appointments and Phone calls.

Now let's look at each of these time management functions individually.

The Reminder Pad—Crtl R. You can use this section of the program to keep your daily schedule, and keep track of important dates and projects. You can also use it to keep track of birthdays and anniversaries (although Managing Your Money will do this automatically for any birthday or anniversary for anyone entered in your Card File).

When you enter the Reminder Pad, the existing reminders are listed by date (and, within a given date, alphabetically by the first letter of the reminder). You can quickly move through the entire list with the Arrow keys and PgDn, PgUp, Home and End. The entire list can be printed by pressing F4.

Reminders may be one-time (March 6; make sure inventory is shipped to warehouse), annual (April 15: file tax return), quarterly (for estimated tax payments), semi-annual (for bond payments), monthly (pay the rent), weekly, biweekly, or half-monthly. By specifying the type of reminder, you can be sure to be reminded for every recurring task that you have to perform in your business.

You can have Managing Your Money warn you in advance of an item you want to be reminded of by specifying the number of Warning Days you require in that area in the Reminder (after you've hit F5 to enter a new Reminder or F2 to edit an existing Reminder).

The Appointment List. Appointments will remind you of any appointments you've entered.

The Phone Call Log—CTRL-P. The easiest way to enter a phone call is to begin with F7. This will enable you to select the name and telephone number from your card file Just type in the first letters of of the person's name. MYM will take the first phone number on the line, unless you TAB to another number that you want. Then press F10. Now all you have to do is enter the date that you want, add any message that you like, and specify the call's status.

If you've already set up your program to work with your Hayes-compatible modem, MYM will even dial the call for you. Just press F6.

The TO-DO List—Ctrl-0. The TO-DO function lets you keep track of ongoing projects. TO-DO items lets you enter the hoped-for completion date (the Due Date), a description of the project, the number of days in advance you to be reminded of it, the initials of the person who's responsible, and its importance.

Your list of TO-DO items may be sorted—and then printed—six ways. Select the criteria you'd like to sort the list by hitting CTRL-F and CTRL-R. (In sorting the "who," MYM assumes that the third initial is the last initial, and that you want to sort by last name. So if you only know two initials of the who, leave the first or second initial blank. Don't leave the third initial blank, or else the person will be sorted to the top of the list).

Once you've completed the TO-DO item, you can either edit the item by hitting F2 and then entering the date completed (and then saving the item as completed by hitting F10), or you can point to the item in the Time Summary and press F8 (which will enter today's date in the date completed field). If you're late, your TO-DO item won't be deleted once the completion date passes. Instead, the "negative warning days" in the Time summary will show how late you really are.

By recording your appointments, phone calls, and things to do in MYM, you can keep track of your time. Using the Time Summary daily will prompt you of tasks you need to do today (as well as things you wanted to accomplish before today, but didn't complete).

One way to use your time most efficiently is to prioritize what you need to do every day. By numbering the items in the Reminder section of your Time Summary, you can focus on the most important tasks first. And you can tell at a glance if you need to postpone appointments to accommodate important jobs that have to be done.

The Reminder selection is great for delegating tasks. Just describe the job to be done on the "Reminder" line. Use the Detail area for the name of the person you're delegating the task to, as well as other pertinent information. The Reminder will appear on your Time Summary every day until the job gets done, and you remove it. As long as it appears, you'll be reminded to check with the employee to see how he or she is progressing.

You can customize your Time Summary to include any (or all) of these items:

> Appointments
> Phone calls
> Reminders
> TO-DOs
> Birthdays & Anniversaries
> Key Dates from Insure

Just select Optional Features in the File submenu, and then select Time Summary Options. Answer "Yes" to each item that you would like to include in your Time Summary. You can also tell the program how many warning days you would like for Appointments, Birthdays & Anniversaries, and Key Dates from Insure, and whether you would like the Time Summary to display the first time you run Managing Your Money each day.

CHAPTER

4

CONNECTING PRODUCTS AND CUSTOMERS

Time and again, capable, intelligent small business venturers make two decisive mistakes.

1. They design and evaluate their goods and services in the perspective of their own values and needs, not those of their customers.
2. They fail to concentrate their efforts and to specialize in tightly defined markets with a correspondingly distinctive range of goods and services.

In short, they fail to relate their products to the wants and needs of their likely customers. This chapter is about the fundamental necessity of connecting your products and your customers.

New firms need customers to start the business. These same firms need *satisfied* customers to survive and prosper. Satisfied customers are provided goods and services *they* think have value in their lives, not what a businessperson *thinks* they should value. In the small business world, the wants and needs of the customer are supreme.

But the resources of small firms are severely limited. If small firms hope to grow, they must concentrate on relatively select groups of customers. And they must attract those customers with somewhat specialized or distinctive goods and services that satisfy their particular wants.

Almost all of today's successful midsize companies started out by rigorously targeting their efforts on narrow, specialized segments of a larger market. They found market niches that weren't being satisfied. They concentrated on likely customers and their special needs and filled those needs. The successful entrepreneur is usually a gap-filler.

Unless you are content with a relatively static market and very limited growth (a neighborhood laundry, for example), a "me-too" strategy stands the least chance of success. The larger and established businesses will simply outmuscle you. They have too much money to spend freely on product research and development, and on marketing and selling. They have too many economies-of-scale in their production or operations and can underprice the me-too upstart. They can absorb extended losses to flatten the little upstart. Specialization is nearly always where the money is in small business.

Think of three essential keys to selling a small business's goods and services.

1. Cater to the special needs and concerns of relatively narrow and identifiable groups of customers.

2. Offer relatively distinctive, reliable goods or services that fill those special needs.

3. Provide excellent service.

In short, your best chance of success in the marketplace is to sell a *differentiated* line of goods *that work,* and that are made and sold *by people who care,* to relatively small *sub-groups* of *people* who are most likely to *benefit* from the purchase.

Some Basic Examples

By way of introduction to these basic concepts, consider two examples.

There are not many Americans who consider a high-altitude trek in the Himalayas or a raft trip down a treacherous Andean river the ideal vacation. But there are enough that a handful of "adventure travel" organizations have built prosperous businesses by targeting those people and satisfying their search for adventure and the fellowship of like-minded spirits. These adventure organizations find their clients not only by word-of-mouth but by advertising in carefully selected publications whose readers are relatively prosperous and interested in wilderness activities.

A very different sort of business is the ministorage industry. You might think that kind of business would be pretty well constricted in to whom it sells and what it sells. In Troy, Michigan, however, a fellow named George Field owns a company called Your Attic, Inc., that has innovatively turned the industry on its head by distinguishing Your Attic from all the other storage businesses. Conventional wisdom had identified the typical user of ministorage space as a transient resident. But Field found a bevy of commercial customers who were eager to store their excess inventory and records at Your Attic's $10-a-square-foot rate, rather than clutter their more expensive business and office sites. Commercial tenants now account for about 75 percent of Your Attic's business.

Having targeted a new market, Field determined to distinguish the storage premises from the usual dull, look-alike Mom-and-Pop operations. He developed a farmhouse design for the rows of storage garages and exploited the farmhouse motif to draw the attention of passing motorists and to create logo displays in advertising. He maintained spotless facilities and provided 24-hour, on-site premises for a manager. Field also computerized security procedures and offered an appealing range of related services, from rental trucks to inexpensive flashlights.

Each of these businesses has expanded and prospered by targeting a narrow niche in the market and fashioning distinctive goods and services to satisfy special customers.

Politicians have known about this technique for centuries. A historian wrote that "Jacksonian Democracy (1825-1850) found a major constituency, identified its concrete needs, catered to them in its programs, won the interested voter, and so became a great political force."

Products and Customers: Chicken-and-Egg

Ideally—and that's the way it is propounded in the textbooks—the business founder has pondered and studied the overall marketplace, identified that special unfilled niche, then retreated to the drawing board to design a suitable product to fill the niche. That's hardly ever the way it happens in reality. It's more a chicken-and-egg phenomenon, a happy marriage of two essential components, the product and the likely customers.

But even though an owner-manager is likely to start with some general product concepts, *commercial* perception must begin with the customer: "Who are the potential customers? What are the particular values, wants, concerns, and problems that must shape the actual marketplace product?"

It is said that you don't reform customers, you satisfy them. Products and customers' needs don't exist apart from each other. There is a connection that must be made and respected absolutely if the small business is to thrive.

A Bad Start: Product-Driven Ventures

Many entrepreneurs really do believe at the gut level that if they build a "better" mousetrap the world will beat a path to their doorstep to buy it. "But if you say you can build a better mousetrap, you'd better make sure people need it. And you'd better be able to deliver it," says on old hand in the small business world. And you'd better make sure the customers' idea of a better mousetrap is the same as your own.

"Entrepreneurs are technically oriented," notes Paul Farrel, the owner-manager of The Los Angeles Financial News Network. "They don't appreciate that building a better mousetrap is not the name of the game. They tend to develop a product and then figure out how to sell it, instead of figuring out what the market wants and then designing it."

Businesses that are preeminently technology and product oriented are said to be "product-driven." That implies a relative insensitivity to customer needs and concerns. Business founders just plow ahead with the product before discovering the sad news that there are few buyers for it out there or that it costs too much to adapt to the public demand.

If consumers believe that a smaller widget is better, it doesn't matter that a business has perfected a terrific larger widget. If an attractive gizmo is what the customers value, it is irrelevant that an ugly gizmo is developed with technologically superior features. In fact, those technologically advanced features may be too far advanced for public acceptance, for it takes some time for people to adjust to thoroughgoing innovation, no matter how valuable the owner-manager regards these advances. If sufficient customers don't *perceive* value and utility, then there is no value or utility in a business sense. It is a very tough thing to launch a company or a product in a low-demand market.

"But just look at the number of homes or automobiles or teenagers that could use my product," thinks the aspiring owner-manager. Perhaps.

One small business spent lots of money developing a "superior" new welding torch for repairing automobiles. None was ever sold. Why? It happened that that particular torch couldn't be used on any automobile body where the upholstery was already in place.

A Massachusetts company was founded on the development of a novel system for keeping track of inventory, namely a sensitive scale device to be built into shelves on which a company's inventory was stored. Unfortunately, most inventories aren't stored so neatly or uniformly, and the system found no buyers. "The entrepreneur," says a local venture capitalist, "developed the technology, and then went looking for a market. It's not a good way to start a company."

It is not just a question of whether customers exist who will find value or quality or utility or whatever in a product. The small business must first find those customers and then sell them. One commentator notes that "hundreds of companies can produce a good product for every one who can sell it."

The product-driven owner-manager may also badly miscalculate the capital outlay and costs of developing a finished product. Similarly, production costs may be miscalculated on the basis of unreasonable expectations of initial success. As a result, the anticipated market price may be severely underestimated and buyers may prove unwilling to pay the actual market price. Often, too, the market price is based on underestimates of operating costs, including normal business overhead costs and advertising and selling expenses. The requirement for a profitable markup is ignored. Similarly, the product-driven owner-manager may have overlooked installation requirements or service requirements that eventual users of the product would regard as elemental.

Focus on the perceptions of likely customers. Only a market-driven business can truly respond to consumer demand and convert mere things into commercially valued goods and services.

The Market-Driven Small Business

All owner-managers "care" about their customers. Customers provide revenues.

But market-driven owner-managers really *do* give a damn. Customers for them are not just abstract money machines, they are people. They are live, emotion-laden people with wants, needs, and hopes. They have problems and concerns. They like to be treated as human beings; they appreciate receiving respect, friendliness, honesty, and attentiveness. Customers like it when businesspeople *listen and respond* to their expectations, needs, and concerns.

Market-driven owner-managers know a lot about their customers—who they are and what it takes to satisfy them. They also know a considerable bit about prospective customers— who they are and why they are not yet actual customers. They have a plan for reaching them.

The market-driven owner-manager knows above all that the business neither starts nor stops at the point of sale but that a preeminent advantage of a small business is the capacity to render a flow of attentive, responsive services to the customers. Attention and care begin long before the sale and continue long afterwards.

The market-driven owner-manager makes sure that everyone in the business cares equally, and he is likely to fire an employee who treats the product or the customer with disdain.

It shows. A market-oriented business radiates care and respect for customers' needs.

Think of the business establishments you patronize on a regular basis. Which ones clearly radiate this concern for customers' needs? Which don't? The bet here is that you know the answers well enough without much reflection. The bet also is that at best two out of ten sparkle with, and communicate, this respect and attention for you, the customer.

The market-driven business knows the customers and centers its business on their real and felt needs and values.

Who Are the Customers?

If owner-managers are truly serious about connecting products with potential customers, the question "Who are the customers and what do they want?" will be a daily preoccupation.

But the frequent answer—"They are the people who buy our goods, and they obviously want what we sell"—just begs the question. The owner-manager wishing to match attractive products with customer needs and to satisfy an expanding number of customers needs a more complete and richer set of answers. We will discuss how you can go about finding those answers at the end of the chapter. First, though, the questions.

Who the customers are suggests what their needs and wants are and how to reach them. Similarly, *what* satisfies the customers in a firm's market niche helps to identify who they are more precisely.

The Customer Profile

Let's start with some basic characteristics of a company's customers.

1. *Economic Bracket.* In what economic bracket(s) do they

predominately fall? Low, middle, or high income? What kinds of work do they do?

2. *Income Allocations.* How do they spend their money? On necessities, such as food? On inexpensive entertainment? On status and prestige goods? Is price really an issue? Where do they spend? Predominately in the neighborhood? Do they travel to and buy at nearby cities or relatively distant shopping malls? Do they order by phone or mail? Are their purchases based on well-considered comparisons or prior research? Are they predominately made on impulse? Is the buying concentrated at certain times of the day, week, or year?

3. *Gender.* Do men or women do most of the buying? Who makes the actual decisions to buy?

4. *Marital Status.* Are most of the customers married or single? Parents?

5. *Education.* What are their educational levels?

6. *Age.* What age groups predominate?

7. *Locale.* Where do they live?

8. *Lifestyle.* What are the customers' "lifestyles," their self-images? What kind of life do they aspire to? Is there a concern for leisure? For education and learning? For upward mobility? Is there a bias toward an "active, healthy" life? What are some of their dominant values, interests, activities, and concerns?

The curious and questioning owner-manager can add a number of similar questions based on the particular nature of the business.

Who Buys the Goods? Who Makes the Purchase Decision?

In considering who your customers are, you will want to ask who makes the purchases or the decision to purchase? Is the customer a wholesaler, a retailer, or an end-user? If more than one, which of these is the most important—is it the department store chain, which first buys the goods and then can promote or kill your goods depending on how they are displayed and sold? Who has to understand your product if the end-user is to be sold and satisfied? Are you highly dependent on informed retail salespersons? Where is the service responsibility? And where does the customer think it ought to be?

Take an "educational" product. It could be computer software or school textbooks or sporting equipment. Again, who are the buyers, who makes the purchasing decisions, whom must you influence, whom must you satisfy? Is it the state or local school boards? The school principals? The teachers? Parents? Students? If the answers to these questions are unknown or fuzzy, it is nearly impossible to develop a sales strategy.

And who isn't buying? Who are the likely or prospective or potential customers of the business? Why aren't they patronizing the business? Is it that they haven't heard of it? How do you reach them? Do they patronize a competitor? Why? If the business redefined its market niche or product line would that influence the non-customers?

Tentative answers to questions such as these are never precise, but they are very helpful because they suggest specific sales strategies and product improvements.

Finding Your Market Niche

There are few successful all-purpose shoe stores. But there are prosperous ones that concentrate on relatively narrow market niches. There are men's and women's shoe stores of different types. There are everyday shoe stores for low-income and medium-low-income customers. And shoe stores that do very well, like Church's, selling the highest quality shoes for upper-income customers. "Sneaker" manufacturers, too, make these distinctions. Gone are the days of the all-purpose Keds. There are sneakers for jogging and tennis and sneakers for leisure wear. And sneakers for schoolchildren. First, though, you need to know your target market.

Food concerns have increasingly narrowed their market segments. Many small food businesses thrive in very tightly defined niches. They know, for example, that busy "Yuppies," whether married or single, are insisting on quality preprepared foods, be it frozen or takeout. Older people, too, increasingly rely on convenience food shopping. Restaurants like humorist Calvin Trillin's "La Maison de la Casa House, Continental Cuisine," are becoming relics of the past.

Age, marital status, and lifestyle can, collectively, point to some valuable marketing strategies. A New York City wine bar, specializing in serving a large number of good value wines by the glass, promoted some special weekly wine tastings. Contrary to expectations, it was discovered in conversation and observation that nearly all the attendees were under 35 years old, and at least 90 percent were single. The realization followed: These events were not so much wine tastings as dignified opportunities for meeting people of the opposite sex with similar interests, incomes, and lifestyles. The discovery helped focus promotion and marketing of the business's wine tastings and its catering business as well.

A successful baby carriage owner-manager, Deaver Brown, has described in his book, *The Entrepreneur's Guide,* how an evolving definition of his firm's customer profile affected the entire way he conducted the business. His first definition of the company's market identified mothers, aged 18 to 34, who purchased a "wheel goods product" at department and specialty stores in the spring and summer and were thought to be mainly influenced by "appearance." Three years later, the predominate marketing targets were grandmothers and friends who were recent parents. They strongly influenced the mothers' buying decisions, by recommending convenient, functional, "all-purpose baby transports." Brown's baby carriages were then understood as all-year purchases, more likely to be made at discount and variety stores. This market-sensitive information helped shape key decisions on how to promote and where to sell the baby carriages.

What Customers Want

What all customers want from a small business can be generalized in four categories:

1. Goods and services that *work*

2. Goods and services that *benefit them,* that have some tangible or intangible value in their lives, in return for hard-earned cash or savings

3. Goods and services that are either *better* than those of the competition, or are *different,* or that no one else provides

4. *Service*

That seems simple enough. But for most ongoing businesses and their owner-managers, the importance of such factors appears obscure or not worth the effort. How do we know? Because those elements are rarely observed in the aggregate, and more often than not at least one of the four is thoroughly disregarded.

These are not trivial matters, just four more things among the hundreds the owner-manager must think about week after week. They are the heart of the business.

Products That Work

People are sick and tired of things that don't work. Ours may be the first era in America in which "new" no longer signifies "better."

The market is flooded with goods that break down on first use. There are containers that seem impossible to open and then splash the contents all over you when you finally do pry them apart. There are products with unreadable and illogical instruction manuals, or whose installation defies the talents of even the company representative. Warranties don't mean what they say they mean. Professionals of various kinds and consulting firms bill exorbitantly for shoddy, inattentive work.

Small businesses can exploit splendid opportunities for providing goods and services that deliver exactly what they claim to deliver. Customers are taking increasing notice of products that work. Such goods and services stand out.

Successful owner-managers don't take the prevailing, mediocre product standards as their goal, and they don't just *say* they care. They are preoccupied, they are obsessed, with quality and with products that work. And they make sure that everyone who works for them understands this.

When the primary motive is pride in the goods and services, the sales seem to follow. That inner pride usually flows from a sheer love for the company's products. When that care for a product is lacking and is merely something expressed in company manuals and advertisements, the owner-manager is in the wrong field. When the owner-manager is in business just for the hustle or for an alternative job to the one down at the old insurance company, it is highly unlikely that a thriving, growing business will develop. It is possible to luck out with a quick-sell gimmick, a great location for a retail business, or a quasi-monopoly situation. But luck in the small business world is nothing to take for granted.

Similarly, if cost reduction is the predominant focus, product quality will deteriorate bit by bit. The customers will sense it and so will an eager new competitor.

Products That Benefit Customers

So far, we have talked of quality and care in the broadest sense. But that is only the beginning.

People buy things for a bundle of economic, practical, aesthetic, technical, and psychological reasons. Generally, they buy not only the thing itself or a tangible service but a constellation of values, satisfactions, and benefits that coexist at different levels of consciousness.

The fact that many of those satisfactions are largely subjective in no way diminishes their persuasive influence on the buying decision. Nor are those decisions "irrational." They may appear so from the egocentric view of the owner-manager, but the only points of view that count commercially are those of the customers.

Consider the variety of motives that govern the decisions of buyers.

1. *Economic.* The dominant motives may relate to no-nonsense considerations such as price, payment terms, or resale value.

2. *Practical.* Purchasers may be strongly influenced by such factors as the convenience of shopping at a nearby retail store or home delivery. Highly functional factors may dominate: The product is reliable, durable, or comfortable. Perhaps it is easier to use than those of competitors. Many people buy pre-assembled stereo sets or a particular personal computer for just that reason. Possibly the product is valued because it saves time and labor, even though it is relatively expensive. Many household consumer goods exploit this buying consideration. Prepared foods are an example. Many customers are motivated by the expectation of better service, a subject we will examine later in this chapter. For the moment, just consider the competitive advantage maintained by McDonald's or some first-rate gas station you patronize: They are clean, consistent, and reliable.

3. *Aesthetic.* Frequently we buy a product for no other reason than the attractiveness of its appearance. The color, shape, size, design, or packaging may be the key factor in a decision to buy a particular product and not its competitor.

4. *Technical.* When technical features not found in other goods are valued, that may be the governing motive to purchase. Technical differentiation is an especially important factor in high-tech businesses where, we shall see, user-designed features generate many technological advances.

5. *Psychological.* Less tangible buying motives are the satisfactions pop psychologists write about. Some customers, for example, buy very heavily into prestige and status, trendiness and chic. Or they derive pleasure or satisfaction from individ-

ual or group identity. It may be that the psychological value sought is sexiness. Or it may be the security that an established brand name evokes, or the peace of mind that a no-hitches caterer bestows on the nervous party-giver. An underlying psychological concern might be friendship—the kind found in group travel programs—or the opportunity to meet the opposite sex, as with those wine bar tastings, or the theme bars in Texas mentioned in Chapter 3.

The motivating values and tastes, wants and needs, are as infinite as the human psyche. In isolation or aggregate, they comprise the influences on customers' buying decisions. Insight and awareness of these factors will help you enormously in defining the right market niche, positioning your goods and services in that niche, then selling them effectively.

Different or Better: Innovative Products

There is hardly a product on the market that can't, in some attractive or advantageous way, be differentiated from others. Even a seemingly drab and interchangeable commodity such as mesquite charcoal can be given a distinctive appeal by identifying it as "an exotic ingredient that adds immeasurably to the culinary value of meats and fishes."

Really successful small businesses almost invariably exploit some distinctive and communicable competitive advantage. "Something" different or distinctive need not represent total newness or innovative genius. A compelling competitive edge is usually gained by simply providing goods and services that are a little different or a little better than those of the competition. Precisely because new and small businesses are small, they can be magnificently adaptive and responsive to nuances in the tastes and needs of specific groups of customers.

A totally new product, of course, is the quintessence of a "differentiated" product. The telephone answering machine is one example. But totally new products turn out, statistically, to be high-risk ventures, and relatively few have lasting commercial value. Some are merely fads; others don't meet real customer needs.

Most successful small businesses provide something "different or better" by taking what's already there and developing some innovative features. Ways to do that:

1. *Improve Something.* For instance, add a device to that telephone answering machine so you can get your messages by remote control. Or make the product smaller: The pocket calculator is a heralded example.

2. *Develop Improved Techniques for Doing the Same Thing.* Develop new production techniques to lower costs and possibly prices. Or find new ways of delivering the goods to the market. A Boston men's clothing store, Albert Andrews Ltd., determined that most of its customers not only disliked shopping for clothes but were hard-put to find the time to shop. So Andrews goes to its customers' offices to take measurements, then stores them on a computer. Fabrics and patterns are shown to the customer on videocassettes. Then custom suits, jackets, and trousers are cut by laser beam back at Andrews' premises. The finished products are delivered to customers at their offices in about half the time custom cutting requires. Convenience, coupled with the satisfaction of custom-made quality, are the distinctive factors. But it was a series of innovative methods for providing traditional goods and services that made those factors possible.

3. *Adapt Goods and Services to Respond More Exactly to Customers' Wants and Needs.* Entrepreneurs traditionally fill specific market needs, no matter how small the product modifications may appear. They produce containers that don't break when you drop them. They develop ways of delivering goods or services more conveniently or quickly—just note the proliferation of "one-day service" businesses, from film development to car repairs to dry cleaning. They launch enterprises that offer adventure travel; specialty publishing firms produce books on exotic regions for that same market.

A New York City caterer, Sweet Feast, got started by convincing the administrative chiefs of the two Lincoln Center theaters that thousands of attendees would be better satisfied not with the traditional candy and liquor served by most concessionaires but by healthy and nutritious snacks sufficiently inexpensive and filling for the theatergoer to make a whole meal of them. A one-page proposal promising healthy foods was sufficient to land the job for Sweet Feast. "Professional concessionaires were so rigid," says a Lincoln Center official. "They knew exactly the way to do it, and that was exactly the way we did not want to do it. We preferred someone who was more oriented to our customers."

4. *Develop New Markets or Promotional Techniques for the Same Goods and Services.* Several years back, Lenox China aggressively promoted the bridal registry. A bride chooses a particular china pattern from Lenox's offerings, registers that choice at participating department stores and specialty shops, and spreads the word to friends and relatives that piece-by-piece contributions are welcome as the preferred wedding gift. The use of the bridal registry as a promotional tool is now widely imitated.

5. *Exploit User-Inspired Technological Innovations.* Most successful high-technology entrepreneurs are extremely sensitive to customer needs and the commercial necessity of differentiating their goods. They are acutely aware of the futility of battling head-on with richer, more established firms for shares of the same market, with me-too products.

They know that entrepreneurial innovation embraces far more than the creativity of a scientist, engineer, or product designer and that market needs, not technical opportunities, provide the best source of commercial success. Product development is a user problem first, a technical problem second. They value *market* information as well as *technological* information and translate that market information into goods that truly benefit the customer.

They cultivate contact with actual or potential customers and incorporate customer insights into research and development at a very early stage. A study of technological innovation in the field of scientific instruments concluded that 81 percent of commercially successful product improvements were user inspired. Actual or potential customers had either designed the innovation, built a prototype for it, or taken an early prototype, tried it out, and suggested significant changes.

For these customer-sensitive firms, the real or felt needs of the buyer control the business, from early in the development stage to well past the point of sale. User-generated ideas are their best barometer of actual, not imagined, market needs. User-oriented firms will freely change the shape, size or configuration of their products. They will change the basic model, add new materials, modify parts of the design—anything to meet customer needs in ways the competition has failed. They will push someone else's unexploited idea or adapt someone else's technology, as the Japanese have done so successfully. They discover the customers' needs and incorporate them into their products.

"Accurate understanding of user needs," according to Eric van Hippel, a professor of M.I.T.'s Sloan School of Management, "is widely regarded as the single factor assuring the success of an industrial innovation....User-dominated innovation should therefore have unusual potential for success."

Above All, Service...

Service

There is one area in which small businesses are inherently positioned to excel and to distinguish their products no matter who the competition is: They can provide truly excellent service to their customers.

The Human Element

The provision of first-rate service is a profoundly simple concept, and it is relatively inexpensive. It flows more from attitudes of mind and heart—care, concern, friendliness, courtesy, integrity, knowledge, attention, and a willingness to listen and respond—than from commercial expertise. The basic elements of good service are presented in Checklist 5.

Service is preeminently the human element, the personal touch in business. The small business is necessarily in direct, personal contact with its customers—live people with human concerns. Unlike the large firm, it does not normally deal with distant, mass markets.

Real service to the customer is the best shot you have at providing something different or better than the competition. In dollars and cents profits, that's where the money is. When a small business regards its products as a means for introducing the public to services that palpably excel and benefit customers, then the firm usually picks up steam and grows and grows.

Most Service Stinks

I've hardly ever met an owner-manager who didn't profess a pious commitment to customer service. But usually it is a meaningless, plastic commitment, a recited buzz word, especially when extra service takes more time, requires extra staff

CHECKLIST 5 Providing Good Service: The Human Element

---

1. *Attitudes*
   a. Pride in the goods and services
   b. Respect for the customers
   c. Respect for the employees (they tend to treat customers as they are treated by the boss)
2. *Actions*
   a. Friendly, personal contacts with the customers
   b. Careful, responsive attention to customers' needs and concerns
   c. Knowledgeable, prompt assistance
   d. Dependability in doing what you say you will do
   e. Avoidance of the "success syndrome"

---

training, costs more, and diverts the owner-manager from individual interests.

And yet a service-starved American buying public is increasingly maddened and frustrated. We feel abused and mugged by sloppy, discourteous, inattentive, and ignorant service. We may seem to take it for granted, but let the increasingly rare service-oriented firm appear, whether it is in manufacturing, retail, or personal services, and the word gets around.

Service pays off wonderfully in the post-1970s era. The ghastly inflation of the 1970s led many buyers to seek cheaper goods. Businesses responded by cutting costs. They cut them in foolish areas. They trimmed their sales staffs and skimped on salaries and training. Employees' pride in their work and what they were selling was often nonexistent. They frequently seethed with resentment, and they took it out on the customers.

Shoddy service continues into the 1980s, and yet there has been a manifest change in buying patterns throughout the country. People generally buy less and buy better than they used to. They seek value and lasting satisfaction. Owner-managers who don't truly comprehend that product quality embraces more than the thing sold, that it includes concern for the customers and their needs long before the point of sale and well after the sale, are highly vulnerable.

And they may never know it. They may never even question how many customers have been lost because of slipshod, uncaring, and discourteous service, or how many potential customers are never induced to buy in the first place. The time, energy and money sunk into the business is squandered because customers quietly perceive what the owner-manager doesn't—that the service is indifferent or obnoxious.

Few disgruntled customers complain or write cranky letters. They vote with their feet. They don't return. They say nothing to the owner-manager, but they pass the word on to friends— potential customers who are lost forever. If owner-managers conceived of those lost sales as money stolen right out of the cash register and translated it into lost profits, the significance of lost customers would resonate more decisively.

And if owner-managers could somehow be condemned to buy or shop at their own businesses like ordinary customers, they would probably understand what's missing and why the American public is stewing in anger and frustration from uncaring and contemptuous service.

Responsibility for Good Service Starts with the Owner-Manager

To repeat a basic theme introduced in Chapter 1, the qualities and attitudes of a small business are the lengthened shadow of the owner-manager. That individual's attitudes toward the customer, and the extent to which those attitudes are impressed on the entire staff, are what determine the quality of service.

When the owner-manager, consciously or unconsciously, regards the public as abstract sales statistics and anonymous ciphers, or worse, as necessary nuisances or suspicious adversaries, that is the face the entire business presents to the public. It all filters down from the top and out to the customer. When the owner-manager regards the buying public as people who don't know what they want, or if they do, as wrongheaded, that is the face the public sees and aggressively resists, choosing, when possible, more caring and responsive competition. And when the owner-manager treats the staff with coarse disrespect and insensitivity, that is the face the employees present to the public.

Pride, Respect, and Fear of the Competition

Where service is deficient, it comes down to three things. First, there is an egregious lack of pride in what the business is selling, no matter in what other areas the business may excel. Second, deficient service expresses a lack of respect for the customer. And third, there is a gross insensitivity to the commercial threat of a superior competitor.

Pride and respect. When they are missing, the owner-manager is contemptuous not only of the customer but of personal business prospects as well.

Some large concerns can get away with this. They hold quasi-monopoly positions in the market, and the customer has few alternatives. Public or government-owned organizations that hold monopoly positions generally provide the worst service. No hungry competitors are peering over their shoulders. It doesn't matter where you are from, you know that if the U.S. Post Office were challenged by just one competitor across-the-board it would be out of business in a month.

Some time back, the New York Transit Authority proclaimed it was at a loss to explain the great decline in the number of bus riders in New York City. A deluge of letters to the newspapers followed, suggesting that all the Transit chiefs had to do was ask the riders, or better yet, start using the buses themselves. The complaints were lengthy and angry: unreliable schedules; rude or ill-informed drivers; jerky, uncomfortable, sudden stop-and-start driving; indecipherable routing signs; and "rear doors so heavy that even weight lifters cannot open them; windows so dark that even in the daylight street signs cannot be made out; drivers at route starting points who refuse to allow passengers on until they are scheduled to leave, even if it is raining, snowing or freezing cold; long waits at stops until herds of four or five buses arrive with only the lead unit filled." It's all there—a lack of pride in the product, a lack of respect for the user, and a lack of concern with direct competition, which in this case is nonexistent.

Quality service, the small business's ticket to distinction in its market, is all so simple, and yet it clearly doesn't come easily.

Paying Attention to the Customer

Care for the product, respect for the customer, and a healthy fear of the threat of a service-oriented competitor flow from attitudes and values. But good service also requires action.

Service means *personalized* contact with the customer. This requires a smile and friendliness, and a greeting that tells the customers they are guests, not intruders. It requires courtesy. It implies those special attentions and extra efforts that make a difference. It requires apologies when you have erred and remedial action to show you mean it. It requires a contagious desire to help the customer, and not simply a mechanical, surly, and intrusive, "May I help you?"

Good service, no matter what the business, means paying attention and listening to the customer, and then responding to the customer's needs and concerns, not your own. It means answering the phone after just a few rings and not putting the caller on permanent hold. It means you don't allow the customer to suffer long waits without at least acknowledging and addressing the delay.

In my neighborhood, there used to be two supermarkets, and in most respects, one of the two was clearly superior. Better produce, more variety, cleaner, less cluttered, better lit, and so on. But the lines at its two cash registers were endless and customers frequently parked their shopping carts, frozen foods, and all, right at the line, and walked out the door to the other supermarket, which had half the customers but twice the number of cash registers. It was the second supermarket that eventually survived, while the other one folded. Every now and then, we hear about some glorious supermarket that provides free coffee or ice cream cones if the lines get long. That is the type that thrives. People know the difference, and they vote with their feet.

A consumer-oriented high-technology manufacturing firm will treat customer complaints not as a nuisance but as a source of vital market information and a chance to secure a long-standing customer relationship. A company such as that will standardize service response systems so that orders can be confirmed and traced efficiently and refunds or replacements can be delivered in time to satisfy customers. Installation service will be efficient, spare parts available, repairs and maintenance provided ungrudgingly, and warranties respected as uncompromisable conditions of sale.

Making It Easy for the Customer

Good service demands knowledgeable assistance and an eager willingness to gently guide customers until they are satisfied. It means showing customers how products work and carefully explaining the products' benefits. It means responding to customers' problems, not referring them to those nasty supervisors who deal with "problem customers."

Good service implies making things easy for customers, so they don't have to work at discovering what the business is selling, why it would be a good buy, how much it costs, and when it will be delivered.

A *New Yorker* editor once dropped a ponderous, lifeless manuscript halfway through. He later told the disappointed author, "I *could* read this, but I just don't *choose* to." And that's the way customers tend to behave unless the small business makes it easy to buy, pay, install, use, maintain, and service the product.

Do What You Say You Will Do

Good service also means doing what you say you'll do. When the plumber arrives 72 hours after the leak has flooded the basement, when the wholesaler delivers goods two days after Christmas, when monies due are not refunded, when the rare steak is brought to the table gray in the middle and the potatoes never do arrive, then these businesses will be in trouble as soon as an ambitious and customer-sensitive competitor arrives in the same market.

Make the Customer Feel Good

A renowned New York City restaurateur, George Lang, has a simple formula for a successful restaurant: "When people come in from an inhospitable world, they should step into a world where everyone likes them and wants them. A good restaurant is one that makes diners feel good."

There is a trade study that supports this obvious and neglected wisdom. About two-thirds of frequent restaurant diners complain about the service. "Only" one-third complain about the food.

"Poor service," the study concluded, "can ruin the finest meal, served in the most elegant surroundings. And an ordinary meal, presented in an undistinguished setting, can be transformed into a special pleasure through attentive and thoughtful service....Most unhappy customers won't tell you what you did wrong but they do tell other people—an average of ten other people. If you can satisfy these unhappy customers, they'll return and each of them will tell an average of five people about the positive experience they had."

The Success Syndrome

Once established, you must never succumb to the "success syndrome."

"The trendy restaurants take success for granted," says a New York critic. "That hurts many of them eventually. You see places that were hot a year ago become lackadaisical, then sales drop precipitously and they fold."

One owner-manager describes the general "success syndrome" this way: "Business is great—you think you've got more than you can handle. No time for little details. Employees slack off too, because they know you won't notice. Your customers have been seeing service slip; they're not coming back. You launch sales specials, save money by cutting payroll, skimping on services or products. You may not notice the symptoms at first, but you'll notice its effects."

No matter how technical or sophisticated the business, there remain the human element and the commercial opportunity to communicate a potent message that human beings are attending to human needs.

Learning about Your Market: Customer Feedback

The successful small business has usually worked hard at finding out who the actual and prospective customers are and how they feel about the business's goods and services.

You want to determine what the customers think is good and what is not so good, where the problems are, what kinds of resistance may be keeping customers from buying, and how you stack up with the competition. The owner-managers of successful firms try to "think like the customer." The best way to do that is to listen to the customer.

There is no such thing as a product or service that can't be made better in the eyes of potential customers. And when owner-managers actively seek answers, they often discover, as a Medford, Massachusetts valve manufacturer, Leslie Lewis, puts it, that "we weren't as good as we thought we were." Lewis, for example, found that customers had trouble getting attention from his marketing, accounting, and engineering departments and that they needed more technical support services. As a result, internal order-tracing and billing procedures were established, and key executives were made available to customers as a matter of routine.

It took the services of a marketing consultant to find out how Lewis's customers felt. But small businesses rarely need expensive marketing studies that purport to deliver scientific findings. Owner-managers who are both customer-driven and cost-conscious can uncover a great deal of useful information just by keeping their ears to the ground, listening to and watching customers, and listening to their employees.

First-Hand Information: Go to the Customers

Committed small business owner-managers find out first-hand what the customer is all about: what he or she wants and needs and whether there are gaps between what customers expect and what they get.

These owner-managers will personally prowl the sales premises, observing and listening to customers. "Retailers absolutely must run things from the store up, not from the office down," notes one owner-manager, David Shakarian of General Nutrition Corporation. "The store is where the important things are taking place, not the management office."

What he sees and hears may not be "scientific," but if the owner-manager is objective and relentlessly curious, his findings may be more valuable and carry more emotional nuance than an expensive research study. For one thing, customers know what's "right," and it's best to seek insights and information right at the source, first-hand. Checklist 6 provides a brief outline for listening to the customers.

If you are looking for compliments, that's what you will probably get, and they will be one-dimensional and, possibly, hollow. And if you already "know" what the customer wants, you won't learn anything.

An art dealer in New York City was asked by an Australian for some help in buying some paintings. The Australian explained that he was a bachelor, had a nice modest house, and now wanted to decorate it with paintings that enhanced the look of his house but were "personal." He said he had to like whatever he bought, but he wanted to know that it was in "certifiable good taste." Those were his simple specifications.

The art dealer, however, was convinced that the paintings had to be viewed as an investment, as well as an aesthetic exercise. The Australian insisted, "No, just something I like, which you tell me is also good art." But the dealer showed him lots of good investments, the Australian argued that they didn't appeal to him, around and around they went, and nothing ever came of it. It was only weeks later that the art dealer discovered the Australian had meant what he said. He owned one of the largest brokerage houses in Australia, made over $1 million a year, and in truth hadn't the slightest interest in art as investment. The dealer simply hadn't taken the client at his word. She had substituted her own values for his and she lost the sales as a result.

CHECKLIST 6 Seeking Customer Feedback

---

1. *Find out who the customers are:*
    a. Where are they from?
    b. What are their ages, gender, marital, and parental status?
    c. How often and when do they purchase related goods and in what quantities?
    d. Who else do they patronize?
    e. How sensitive are they to the price/quality trade-off?
    f. What are other appropriate considerations, discussed earlier in this chapter?
2. *Observe customers' reactions* to the goods and visual displays and their interactions with salespeople.
3. *Ask customers:*
    a. Why they purchased a certain product
    b. Why they didn't purchase other products
    c. What the decision criteria were
    d. About your firm's and the competition's strengths and weaknesses terms of:
        (i)   Product and service quality
        (ii) Prices; payment terms
        (iii) Sales methods and operations
4. *Probe for the customers' underlying attitudes and concerns:*
    a. Listen carefully to key words and emphatic statements.
    b. Be sensitive to pauses or artificial tact that disguise potential criticism.
    c. Ask what problems they have, if any, with the goods and service.
    d. Actively solicit suggestions for improvement; look for the reasons behind those suggestions.

Getting the Customers to Think Out Loud

Discovering what makes the customer tick and how the customer relates to a company's goods and services is a matter of sensitive questioning and even more sensitive listening.

It is frequently useful to get customers to relax and "think out loud" about their needs and preferences. For years, grocers shied away from offering fresh fish, despite a lot of market studies that showed a significant demand. It seems, though, that when fish was wrapped in cellophane, shoppers didn't believe it could be "fresh." It looked fresh only if displayed on ice. So the key criterion was "freshness," and until it looked fresh, it wasn't fresh. Operational, applied criteria are what you listen for.

A few good listeners some years back discerned that buyers of sunglasses were more interested in the fashion and appearance of sunglasses than in the optical instrument itself. Sunglasses, they discovered, helped people fulfill fantasy roles. The people who first understood this had a considerable advantage over the competition. They had listened well, after asking some truly inquisitive questions.

Similarly, research shows there is massive customer resistance to otherwise acceptable products when salespeople don't know or won't explain how a product works. Try to determine if this is the case at your company. If so, it is a significant obstacle to sales growth.

Questions to customers must really probe, one after another, without intruding on the customers' goodwill. The first answers are rarely the revealing ones. If the customers didn't like the steak, to take a simple example, was it because they don't like steak in general? Was it overdone or underdone? Was it the sauce? Too small a plate? The side orders? The surly waiter? The price? Perhaps they really wished they were at the place down the street where they receive the warm welcome. Or are they worried about the calories and wish there had been some fish or chicken? And while I'm at it, wiping ink off my fingers as I write this, I'm reminded there is a certain kind of ball-point pen whose ink invariably smudges upwards onto the fingers. Why hasn't the manufacturer bothered to learn about and then remedy this product defect?

The Staff Is a Source of Feedback

It is enormously useful to train the staff to "think like the customers" and systematically pass along customer-sensitive information and insights. The employees are the "troops" out there on the front line. Systematic sales force feedback is not only inexpensive but highly practical. The sales staff is in direct touch with customers daily.

Pretesting New Products

New products can be pretested the same ways. While it is joked that, "What we need is a brand-new idea that's been thoroughly tested," the fact is you can go pretty far with some do-it-yourself market research.

One business venturer discovered a nut-coating process in Malaysia and decided to found a "gourmet" peanut business back in Connecticut. His business plan was just fine, he was told, except it hadn't been put to a market test. So he distributed the nuts in dozens of bars, soliciting comments. Some thought the peanuts looked like a cereal, and a few thought they looked like dog food. Therefore, the appearance, but not the taste, of the peanuts had to be significantly altered. Without the modifications, the owner notes, "the product would probably have died."

Another company, DioLight Technology, in Pontiac, Michigan, developed a light bulb that will last nine years, used 24 hours a day. Initially, the owner-manager thought of it as a consumer product and investigated the market for an appropriate niche. He happened to look around some office buildings and some hospitals as well, and began to notice 24-hour exit signs in large buildings. After a rough calculation of the number of large buildings with substantial needs for long-lasting bulbs, he decided the appropriate market for the product was the industrial and institutional market. Ninety-five percent of DioLight's $1-million annual sales of this bulb are made in that market.

Ask Friends to Help

Some owner-managers solicit friends, posing as shoppers, to act as "spotters" and report back what they see and how they are treated. An auto dealer picked up some valuable information. For one thing, he discovered that the poisonous breath of a particular salesperson was costing the company substantial business. He also learned that the premises, paradoxically, appeared both "pricey and disorganized." And it was reported that the service people "beat up on a guy when he comes in over a warranty. And in the evenings, they probably congratulate themselves on how well they're doing." How the owner-manager responds to these observations may determine his future.

Analyze the Evidence

Analyze the evidence all around you; look at the sales data to determine:

1. Which products are selling and which aren't?
2. Which salesmen are selling more than their share, what is their message, what are they playing to?
3. Which territories are hot?
4. Where the customers are coming from?
5. What's working best—direct sales, mail orders, telephone orders?
6. How large are the orders?
7. Are they made by cash or credit?
8. What percent of inquiries result in actual sales? Develop ongoing data on the lost sales.
9. Is the company losing customers? Is repeat business down? Check the books. Find out why. Solicit objective and honest comments from some former customers. It might hurt the ego but it should help the business.

See what you can make of this data. Can you find some practical significance and insights?

A grocery store that uses a customer suggestion box gets useful feedback. The customers apparently anticipate that their ideas will be treated seriously. One customer observed that the tuna salad "is more like a soup."

So the store cut back on the mayonnaise. Another customer suggested that the strawberries be removed from the relatively large boxes so people could buy as few as they actually wanted. Most groceries would wink at such a seemingly naive idea. But the suggestion was followed and sales of strawberries tripled.

Check out the accounts receivable files. You may well find a pattern of complaints or disputes that indicates needed changes. A restaurant owner-manager can similarly observe what's left on the plates after customers have finished. That might be a source of unspoken complaints. Perhaps the portions are too big, or no one is eating the onion rings because they're soggy.

Trade journals are also a good source for industry-wide buying practices and trends. Similarly, many suppliers are a fund of useful customer buying information. Ask them.

Focus Groups

Some owner-managers have organized small groups of customers, including dealers. These are usually called "focus groups." The groups are limited to 6 to 12 actual or potential customers who appear to be representative buyers in the company's business area. The point is to elicit useful comments and suggestions of any sort at all about the company's goods and services—what's good, what's not so good, and what positive changes can be made.

Focus groups are also a useful way of gaining information about business rivals—who the competition is, what they do well, what their weaknesses are—and how the company can exploit both the weaknesses and strengths of the competition.

A San Francisco construction company, Clearwater Building, Inc., discovered in a focus group of architects and designers that what bothered them most about construction companies they had contracted were the bad manners of workers, the dirt they tracked across the carpets, and their beat-up trucks. They said their "high-class" clients vehemently objected to all that. Clearwater promptly repositioned itself in the market as the contractor for high-class projects. Among other things, their workers were trained to be impeccably courteous and to roll rubber mats over carpets before they stepped on them. Estimators were required to wear ties and jackets. New trucks were purchased and maintained with regular washes. Clearwater's sales increased fivefold.

Customer wants and felt needs must be respected and met. That's where the payoff is, because the more you know about your customers, the better you can design and deliver goods and services that will satisfy them.

Managing Your Money Tip

You can use Managing Your Money to mail questionnaires to your clients and customers. To do so, you first have to have entered your customers' names and addresses in the Card File (it's in the Desk submenu, or just press Ctrl-C). Once you've done so, while you're in the Card File, press F4 and mark the names you want to mail to. (To mail to everyone, press F8. To mail to one set of addresses, and customize your mailing, press F6 and follow the instructions.) Press F4 again, and select "Labels" for the type of "report" you want to print. Follow the instructions (press F1 for more detailed instructions) to accommodate the kind of labels you're using.

You can even use Managing Your Money to print personalized letters to your clients. All you have to do is use Managing Your Money's substitution codes. When you print the letters, Managing Your Money will drop the appropriate information from the Card File into the letter at the place designated by the substitution code. Here are the codes:

[da]	Today's date	[a1]	1st address line*
[a2]	2nd address line*	[ti]	Title (Mr., Ms., etc.)

[fn]	First name	[mi]	Middle initial
[ln]	Last name	[ci]	City*
[sa]	Salutation	[st]	State*
[zi]	Zip code*	[po]	Position**
[co]	Company**	[wh]	Who
[ph]	Phone	[cy]	Country
**	Prints for marked address	**	Prints for Work address only

So a typical form letter might start out like this:

[da]

[ti] [fn] [ln]
[po]
[a1]
[a2]
[ci], [st] [zi]

Dear [ti] [zi]:

In an effort to serve you better, we're conducting a survey . . .

CHAPTER

5

MARKETING THE PRODUCTS

Products don't sell themselves. Companies have to reach out to potential buyers. They must make their goods and services accessible. They must communicate a very persuasive message, too, that the goods and services will benefit these customers.

Small businesses can find and sell customers by the seat-of-the-pants. It is far better, though, to start with a plan: A formulation of the approaches and actions needed to achieve some challenging sales objectives. Most successful concerns develop a coherent market plan that pulls together all the relevant market considerations and identifies the strategies and actions required to achieve high but realistic sales goals. What you need to create a marketing and sales plan is the subject of this chapter.

The Market Plan

You, the owner-manager, are ultimately responsible for the marketing and sales of your goods and services. It is your company, and a business without sufficient customers is no longer in business.

Don't let the words "market plan" scare you off. You have no need for one of those massive, bound volumes the big businesses prepare, or those hyperoptimistic, projection-oriented plans contained in investor prospectuses.

A marketing plan for a small business is essentially a pithy statement of assumptions about the market environment in which the company does business and the objectives and actions that flow from those assumptions.

It is possible to develop the plan in your head. But for reasons described in Chapter 11, it is more effective to write it down in a few pages, even if you have to make revisions from time to time.

As we shall see, there are a number of elements to consider in developing an effective plan to market your goods and services. All of the components of a marketing plan interconnect.

What pulls them together into a cohesive and harmonious plan is your identification of the firm's likely customers and your understanding of the customers' needs, values, and perceptions. The identity and demands of likely customers constitute the linchpin of the marketing and sales plan. All the other considerations depend on a clear sense of who your customers are and what you have to sell in order to satisfy them.

Checklist 7 summarizes the basic elements of a market plan, including:

I. The company's sense of purpose;
II. Market analysis;
III. Pricing;
IV. Sales channels;
V. Sales promotion;
VI. Sales goals and action plans.

We will now take these up one by one.

I. The Company's Sense of Purpose

A market plan does not usually develop in a logical, linear process. It evolves rather naturally, as the various pieces come together organically.

But behind this mosaic, there must be careful, informed consideration of what your firm is all about, where it is, what it is trying to do, and how it will go about it. The first step, then, is to articulate your sense of your business's identity, mission, and strategic objectives and priorities as they relate to your customers and your goods and services. Those questions and considerations are set out in Chapter 3.

II. Market Analysis

A second major element of a market plan is your analysis of the market environment in which you do business. This analysis flows directly from the basic issues discussed in Chapter 4. Your assumptions about your likely market, the impact of

CHECKLIST 7 A Simple Checklist for a Small Business Market Plan

---

I. *The company's sense of purpose.* Consider its mission and strategic objectives as they relate to customers, products, and service.

II. *Market analysis*
   A. *Customers*
      1. Actual and potential customers; the market niche (distinguish between buyers and end-users)
      2. Demographic and other characteristics
      3. Needs and values; tangible and intangible motives for buying
   B. *Goods and services*
      1. How they are "differentiated"
      2. How they satisfy customers
      3. Quality, design and appearance
      4. Scope and quality of service
      5. Customer feedback
      6. Improvements needed
      7. Costs of producing and delivering
   C. *Competition*
      1. Position in market
      2. Strengths and weaknesses
      3. Implications for your company

III. *Pricing.* See checklist of considerations on page 90.

IV. *Sales channels*
   A. Direct sales
   B. Sales staff
   C. Distribution system
   D. Marketing or sales reps

V. *Sales promotion*
   A. Concentrated sales message for greatest impact on potential customers
   B. Promotion at "home" by word-of-mouth; product and service quality; the appearance of premises and staff; direct contacts with customers
   C. Quality sales literature, targeted to most likely customers
   D. Resourceful attention-getters
   E. Advertising
   F. Public relations

VI. *Sales goals and action plans.* See Chapter 11 on developing specific business goals and associated activities to realize them.

---

the competition within that market, and the goods and services you must provide to satisfy likely customers are the core of your "market analysis."

III. Pricing

Another key element of a coherent market plan is your pricing strategy. The prices you set result from weighing all other marketing considerations: the customers' perceptions of their needs, benefits, and anticipated satisfactions; the costs of producing and delivering the goods; the company's image and promotional message developed to attract customers; the relative strengths of your product and your competitors' products and the prices charged by your competitors; the relative sensitivity of your customers to different prices; practical alternatives to changes in pricing; and the impact of price changes on your sales volume and profits.

There is no easy, precise formula for pricing goods and services. In fact, each product presents a unique pricing decision, and determining pricing levels is more an art than a science. But it is not a random or impulsive exercise. That certain "feel" that ultimately governs the setting of prices must be based on a conscious deliberation and weighing of all the relevant factors and the likely effects of alternative pricing strategies. Only then can you arrive at a best *estimate* of the optimal prices you can charge. Price setting is a pragmatic search for what works best to achieve your company's overall market objectives and, hence, to maximize profits.

The prices first charged to customers will probably be "wrong"—hopefully not radically wrong, but enough so the company should be willing to change some prices incrementally, experiment piecemeal with modified prices, and monitor the impact of the new prices.

You should seek all the help you can get, but you can't delegate pricing decisions. Only the owner-manager can see the operation in its entirety and integrate and coordinate all the considerations that go into setting prices. Key members of the staff will be understandably biased about pricing levels. That is particularly true of salespeople, whose natural goals are sales, not profits. They will nearly always pitch for lower prices and damn the costs, the company's image, or whatever. The accountant or financial people, on the other hand, are apt to invoke simplistic formulas for price setting. They cannot be expected to integrate all the other business and marketing factors into a coherent pricing policy. Product managers may know much about the goods and services, but they, too, lack direct responsibility for pulling together all the objectives of a business.

Checklist 8 summarizes some basic pricing considerations.

CHECKLIST 8 Some Basic Pricing Considerations
Before setting the prices for your goods and services, consider the following:

---

1. The goal of price setting is to maximize the profits, not the sales, the mark-up profit, or any other business factor.
2. Normally, prices are not the dominant influence on buying decisions. How the customers perceive value in differentiated goods and services is usually the decisive factor, and price is only one of many possible constituents of perceived value. Therefore:
   a. Don't be overmodest and set your prices too low.
   b. Don't be misled by your sense of "what the market will bear"—this simplistic guideline obscures several important issues.
   c. Don't be entirely governed by what your apparent competitors charge—their goods and services may not be truly comparable to your own.
   d. Be wary of standard "cost-based" price formulas—these, too, obscure a number of issues and potential pitfalls.
3. The prices you set must be consistent with the image you are trying to project for your goods and services.
4. Some products are more price sensitive than others.
5. There is an interaction between the prices and the sales, costs, and profits—you have to make a best-possible estimate of how these factors will interact in your business.
6. Other pricing considerations include the issues and alternatives to price changes, discussed on pages 98 to 99.

The Customer's Perception of Value

The key determinant in setting prices is the value that customers perceive in the goods and services. A substantial portion of growing and successful small businesses, and nearly all those that eventually move on to midsize status, compete on the basis of superior product value or superior service and not on low prices. These businesses know that when their goods and services are seen by customers as offering something different or better than those of the competition, price is no longer the decisive factor of success. These firms can often charge a handsome premium over competitors' prices, even when their own costs are lower.

Some small businesses, however, sell goods or services that have no intrinsic distinctiveness. Therefore, they usually must set prices no higher than, and often lower than, those of the competition. Sometimes, a business's one competitive edge over its rivals is its low prices. Discount houses, such as certain drugstores or factory outlets, prosper on the basis of low prices and no-nonsense, no-frills, low-cost operations. They pursue high sales, rapid turnover of inventory, and cash-on-the-line payment terms. It takes very efficient management to produce satisfactory profits from their thin cost-price margins.

The preceding chapter described the numerous values, both tangible and intangible, that customers find in differentiated goods and services. Until owner-managers really understand that it is these values and satisfactions that govern most buying decisions, they are liable to make some potentially serious pricing mistakes. The following are among the common errors.

1. *Overmodesty.* Sometimes, owner-managers are simply too modest to charge appropriately in the start-up stage of a business. "Who are we to charge more?" they ask themselves. Personal-services firms, such as architects or public relations consultants, are especially prone to such overmodesty. These businesses not only fail to charge what they could, but they depreciate the perceived value of their goods and services in the process.

Similarly, start-up businesses often establish low "penetration" prices to attract first-time customers. This strategy frequently backfires. The low prices obscure the quality and value of the goods, and many customers buy for the low prices alone. When the prices are subsequently raised to levels that yield adequate profits, many of these customers go elsewhere. They are more price conscious than value conscious.

2. *Overemphasis on the Effect of Low Prices.* More often, owner-managers see prices as the sole barrier to customer purchases. They regard their low prices, therefore, as the main incentive to attracting long-term buyers and as the principal way of competing. They see prices and sales in a nearly one-to-one relationship.

But price is normally a key factor in the buying process only when value is not an important consideration, and the goods and services are otherwise undifferentiated (potatoes), are frequently purchased (beer, soap), are basic and entirely functional (tissue papers), or are purchased by educated, discerning shoppers (usually, ironically, high-income people). Oranges may be closely scrutinized for the price, but electric juice squeezers are usually not. Plain string may be a price-sensitive commodity; shoelaces are not.

By overemphasizing price as the dominant determinant of sales, owner-managers underestimate the vital importance of the perceived value and satisfactions customers find in the goods and services. Nothing has intrinsic value until people perceive value. Overly price-conscious owner-managers ignore those "a little better, a little different" features of their goods and services that satisfy the customers.

When a low price is what the firm emphasizes as its basic message to consumers, it obscures special product or service features that could be the critical competitive advantage. Profits are sometimes seriously diminished because of unnecessarily low prices and the failure to communicate the real strengths of the products.

3. *Setting Prices on the Basis of "What the Market Will*

Bear." Another frequent mistake that flows from underemphasizing the customers' perception of value is placing inordinate emphasis on pricing at what you think "the market will bear." This might seem to be a wonderful guideline, but in actuality, it is too general to be useful. How do you determine *what,* for *how long,* and in *what quantities* the market will "bear" a given purchase price? Because customers buy today at a certain price level doesn't mean that they wouldn't buy more at a lower price or the same amount even if the price were higher, or that they will necessarily buy at the same price in the future.

Too often, owner-managers observe paying customers and suppose that the fact that they're buying confirms the "rightness" of prices. But that kind of thinking ignores the possibility that customers may make purchases because at that moment it is convenient and that they may decide never to return or buy again because prices are too high for the value of the goods.

4. *Setting Prices on the Basis of What the Apparent Competition Charges.* Another frequent pricing mistake is the abdication of price setting to the competition, as if somehow "they know" or have better judgment. If the product or service offered is a me-too item, then your pricing decision is limited, and you can't safely set prices higher than the competition even if your costs are perilously high.

But you should consider how comparable your goods and services actually are and look hard for dissimilarities that could prudently dictate different prices, including higher ones. If a consumer appliance retailer located at a popular and convenient shopping mall regards the discount dealer in a marginal area of town as "the competition," it seriously underestimates the premium many customers will pay to shop at the mall. That same retailer may also offer first-rate repair and maintenance services, credit terms, or friendly, comfortable surroundings for which customers will likewise pay a premium.

5. *Basing Prices Solely on Costs.* When owner-managers

are insensitive to the relative value and satisfactions that *customers* perceive in the goods, businesses often charge prices determined solely on the basis of the costs of the goods. Obviously the prices must be sufficient to cover all costs and expenses of producing and delivering the goods or there will be no profit. "Cost-plus" or "mark-up" pricing formulas can indicate minimum prices below which losses result, but they can't determine how high a price customers may be willing to pay.

Customers normally don't calculate or even care about cost unless they sense pure greed. They are concerned with their own benefits and satisfactions as they subjectively perceive them and the amount of money they are willing to pay for those benefits and satisfactions. If you think about it, you most likely are willing to pay a tidy premium for a good dish of pasta at an Italian restaurant, even if you know that the pasta costs the restaurant less than 75 cents in direct costs. However, some patrons of posh Italian restaurants are infuriated by $20 pasta dishes. It isn't so much that they have consciously calculated the costs; they just feel ripped off. Nor does it matter to them that the same restaurant makes little profit on a veal chop. They simply aren't willing to pay more than $20 for that veal, period.

Cost-plus pricing formulas are also a rigid vehicle for arriving at a judicious package of prices which yield acceptable profits for the entire business. Restaurant owners have to earn higher profit margins from such items as pasta dishes or coffee, for example, to compensate for low or nonexistent profit margins on veal chops and other high-cost items that customers, in effect, demand to see on the menu.

Further, cost accounting for each product is usually a far more exacting and precise exercise than many owner-managers realize. Most markup price formulas calculate only the direct costs of the goods sold. They do not include the labor, the rent, the utilities, and all the other overhead expenses, or the taxes, repayment of loans, and other expenses. A business may mark up its products by 50 percent above its direct costs—a good yield, generally—but still fold, because the other expenses, when added to the direct costs, exceed the sales revenues. Most markup or cost-plus price formulas are based on industrywide averages. For a business whose costs are higher than average, relying on formula pricing can be fatal.

Furthermore, what does a company do if it finds innovative ways of improving efficiencies and significantly reducing its costs? Using a cost-based formula, it would pass on 100 percent of the cost savings to the customer. That might not be necessary or wise. And, to further illustrate the rigidity of cost-based formulas, what about cost savings that are the result of perfecting the design of a company's product? If the company lowered its prices, it might detract from the product improvement. A price *rise* might be wiser in that case, since it would emphasize the added value, notwithstanding the lowered costs.

Cost-plus pricing may look appealing because of its apparent simplicity and precision. But it is really more simplistic than simple unless it also manages to incorporate other basic marketing assumptions and objectives.

So, first and foremost, before you set the prices or change them, look at the issue from the customers' point of view: What do they value in the products and how much is that value worth to them? To repeat, that requires that you know something about your customers—their incomes, their ages, the ways they usually order and pay for the goods, and all the other attributes discussed in Chapter 4. You need to know what they want or need from the goods and services they are buying and whether low or competitive prices are extremely important to them, not a factor, or somewhere in between.

Then you can factor in the following considerations.

a. *Image.* If the image you wish to attach to your goods is a no-frills, no-nonsense image, then obviously low or competitive prices are required. If your goods are luxury or vanity goods and your market target is high-income consumers, it is equally obvious that low prices would sabotage the very image you are trying to project. Fine-tuning the prices of products that fall in between is a tricky and imprecise exercise, but you have to give it your best shot.

b. *Price Sensitivity.* One consideration will help you in this fine-tuning process. All other things being equal, certain products are more sensitive to price changes than others. There is a cartoon that shows a man selling lemonade on a desert island. "All I need is one good customer," he says. Scarce products will be bought with little attention to price. Similarly, where demand for any other reason is nearly absolute, price has little influence on the buying decisions. Cigarettes are a good example.

A New York City wine bar that specialized in serving many wines by the glass found, after careful study, that French wines in general, and certain better known or more easily pronounced French wines in particular, sold just as well with perceptible price increases. "Daily wine specials" likewise carried moderately higher prices without a loss of sales. Sales of California wines with comparable costs, however, suffered when prices were increased.

Some products may simply be "hot" at a given time for whatever reason and will be relatively insensitive to moderate price differentials.

c. *The Relation between Prices, Sales Volume, Costs, and Profits.* Generally, changes in price will affect to some extent the number of sales you make. Higher prices will probably mean fewer sales, lower prices more sales, although there is no exact one-to-one relationship. That raises what has been called the "vital price-volume issue." The crux of the issue is this: Will those higher sales at lower prices and lower profit margins produce more or less aggregate profits than those lower sales at higher prices and higher profit margins?

Checklist 9 gives a very simple, hypothetical example of the various interactions at work, depending on the particular price you charge for a particular good. The figures used are used for illustrative purposes only. But note that:

(i) The $15 price produces the maximum profits, even though the $10 and $6 prices yield more unit sales and the $6 price yields more aggregate dollar sales. Maximizing the profits is your goal.

(ii) In some instances, a high profit margin per unit sold results in greater total profits (Scenario 2 versus Scenario 1); in other instances it results in lower total profits (Scenario 3 versus Scenarios 1, 2 and 4).

(iii) In some businesses, higher unit sales yield production efficiencies that lower the costs per unit of production. This phenomenon requires a whole new set of calculations. You have to know your costs, even if costs are not the dominant factor in pricing.

CHECKLIST 9 **The Price-Volume Issue: An Illustrative (and Hypothetical) Example**

	Price ($ per unit)	Cost ($ per unit)	Profit ($ per unit)	Units Sold	Aggregate $ Sales	Total $ Costs	Total $ Profits
Scenario 1	10	5	5	1,000	10,000	5,000	5,000
Scenario 2	15	5	10	700	10,500	3,500	7,000
Scenario 3	20	5	15	200	4,000	1,000	3,000
Scenario 4	6	3[1]	3	2,000[2]	12,000	6,000	6,000

[1]The assumption here is that at some critical level of production, say, 1,800 units, production efficiencies lower the average unit costs of production. Any such efficiencies depend, of course, on the particular business.
[2]I have exaggerated the likely general impact on sales of a price reduction to illustrate some general relationships among all the variables at work.

The pricing task is not as daunting as it may seem, and you shouldn't shy away from estimating the consequences of different prices. But the results can be surprising, and incremental experimentation is the best way of learning what prices work best.

Take the following case, in which a substantially reduced price on one product nearly doubled gross profits. A wine consultant tried to persuade a restaurant manager to lower the price of his Dom Perignon champagne. It cost the restaurant $30 a bottle, but the restaurant charged customers $110—a normal markup for champagne.

The manager said not many people drank the champagne. The consultant replied, "Not many people drink Dom Perignon anywhere. It's too expensive at the price people are charged." The manager agreed to test a price reduction and to display the bottle with the new price, $55, clearly marked.

The results? Whereas the restaurant formerly averaged sales of six bottles a week, the figure at the new price climbed to 35 bottles a week. Gross profit at the higher price was $480; at the reduced price, it was $875. While unit profits at the $110 price were $80, the unit profits at the reduced price were only $25. Yet *gross* profit nearly doubled at the lower price. Snob appeal has its price, but sometimes the price is too high. It may be that simply displaying the bottle significantly increased sales. And it is also possible that a modestly higher price would increase gross profits. The manager will never know without experimenting.

One problem with lowering the prices noticeably is that the competition frequently follows suit. Price wars are usually terminated before there are any fatalities, but at best such wars have multiple losers, including the company that originated the price reductions.

    d. *Specific Questions to Consider before Changing Prices.*

       (i) The depth of customer loyalties to you and to your competitors; the extent to which those loyalties will affect the impact of a price change

      (ii) Whether or not your customers are relatively informed and compare prices before buying (if they aren't, the price changes may have little or no effect on the number of sales you make)

    (iii) The effect of a price change on the customers' perceptions of the value and quality of the goods

    (iv) Whether a reduction in the prices will necessitate a reduction in the quality of the goods and services to reduce the costs

    (v) Whether the price changes can be made incrementally; whether reduced prices should be advertised or if raised prices should be publicly justified

  e. *Some Alternatives to Changing Prices.* Often, when profits are disappointing, owner-managers think first of changing prices. This is frequently a mistake. You should consider alternatives to cutting or increasing prices that may be more effective in boosting the profits:

    (i) Cutting costs by establishing greater internal efficiencies

    (ii) Improving the product in some telling way or providing better service

    (iii) Advertising more or engaging a public relations firm

    (iv) Finding new distributors, retailers, or sales representatives (it may be here, not in the pricing, that profit problems need to be sorted out)

    (v) Trimming low-profit products and concentrating more on profit contributors

    (vi) Modifying payment terms and not the price itself

Finding the "right" prices does not require strategic, mathematical, or intuitive genius. What it requires is a knowledge of your customers and your market objectives, a careful weighing of a number of strategic considerations, and a willingness to make ongoing reevaluations and appropriate modifications of the prices.

IV. Sales Channels

Another integral part of the market plan is determining the particular sales channels through which you intend to reach your target markets. The sales of most small businesses are made directly in relatively small or local markets. Many small manufacturers, though, target more diffused or distant markets and sell through third-party intermediaries or middlemen.

Direct Sales

If you are a retailer and sell your goods and services on your own premises, or if you are a manufacturer and sell to nearby customers, you will most likely sell the goods personally or through direct-hire salespersons.

Personal or direct sales require the elemental qualities of friendliness, courtesy, and responsiveness to customers' needs discussed in Chapter 4. Similarly, you must instill in the sales staff the knowledge and skills to sell your particular products. They must know how to focus on the strengths of the goods. It is difficult finding the right salespeople, but it is worth the effort. Recall the old 20/80 rule: 20 percent of the sales staff will sell 80 percent of the goods. That implies that one good salesperson is not only worth four barely adequate ones but is also less expensive.

Salespeople who roam the market may also need your direction in targeting the most likely prospects. The 20/80 rule applies here, too. A salesperson who randomly cold-calls a long, indiscriminate list of prospects is squandering scarce time and resources. Who are the hot prospects, who are the big-order prospects, who represents the greater likelihood of repeat business, and which contacts can multiply sales by producing other likely customers?

As the business grows, it may seek wider and more distant markets. You may decide to reach those customers directly, through personal sales efforts, or by establishing mail or telephone-order sales operations. You may also sell through middlemen.

Third-Party Intermediaries

If you are a manufacturer, you will likely sell through other wholesalers or retailers. And if you wish to reach a wider market and expand your sales, the more economical way to do so will probably be to sell through independent distributors, or sales or marketing representatives and brokers who know the market in your field and work on commissions.

One computer software expert says, "The issue today in

the computer software market is not how can I sell a better mousetrap, but how can I make more people aware that I have one. The computer software business is drifting away from a cottage industry. Clever designers may be hanging out in the hills designing new computer software, but more and more are seeking out specialists who will distribute and market it for them."

Finding good sales reps or brokers who are experienced in and knowledgeable about local markets, have good relationships in these markets, and aren't already selling competitors' goods is not easy. It takes a lot of time to find reps who will devote sufficient energies to promoting the goods of upstart or small businesses, but it is worth the patience and effort.

A consumer marketing pro, Wilson Harrell, suggests you start in a city's Yellow Pages under "Brokers," "Manufacturers Agents," or "Sales Agents and Representatives." He then advises that you make a few phone calls to retailers and some of those brokers for the sole purpose of finding out which are the ten or so largest and which represent your competitors. After winnowing the list down to likely prospects, make a simple comparison shopping test, he suggests. Visit a number of retailers in the area and observe how a particular broker's products are displayed. If they are prominently displayed, that is only part of the test. How do products of the broker's smaller firms fare? Does the broker seem to push these equally, with similar results? Harrell has found this test as good as any in selecting the right broker, but he insists that the broker must then be courted, massaged, and conceded a generous commission to induce him to work for an unheralded, newcomer firm.

V. Sales Promotion

All companies promote their business, even if the effort is limited to talking with customers. Some firms excel in promotion, though, and this skill contributes significantly to their success. Products, to repeat, don't sell themselves, no matter how good the owner-manager thinks they are.

The small business is seemingly at a great disadvantage in telling the public about itself and touting its goods. It has no broad network of superstar salesmen. The excess cash, if any, is scarce. The company can't buy customers through carefully orchestrated and massive advertising campaigns.

But here, again, the very smallness of the small firm provides some distinct advantages. For within the narrower scope of its market and operations, it has much more direct contact with customers, and an owner-manager can personally control and direct those contacts. The owner-manager also can control to a greater extent than in a larger business the conduct of salespersons, the public appearance of the premises if it is a retail business, and the ingenuity and quality of promotional and sales efforts.

In other words, the small business can really concentrate its marketing and sales creativity and intelligence on a relatively narrow market. Happily, there are a number of relatively inexpensive promotional tools in the small business's sales kit.

The promotional knack is found in the special knowledge and sensitivity to the needs of the company's customers displayed by a determined small company. It is also found in the analytic powers, creativity, resourcefulness, and dogged determination that characterize most successful owner-managers.

A resourceful and relatively inexpensive campaign to publicize and promote goods and services will depend on all the circumstances unique to a given business. But any purposeful and focused campaign will evolve from the assumptions and information derived from the market analysis.

To repeat, it all flows from your knowledge of your customers. You must know who and where those customers are. What are their concerns and needs, values, lifestyles, problems, and pleasures? How much do they spend, where do they spend it, when and how often? What are their priority concerns? Is the likely customer a household customer or a business customer?

Some years ago, for example, Avis Rent-A-Car made a crucial and savvy decision to concentrate its promotional efforts on the business renter and not on the casual driver.

How can these customers be reached; what are the different ways of attracting them; what's the cost; which alternatives would appear to yield the greater coverage or impact at different levels of expenditures?

The Basic Sales Message

Before you can plan a promotional campaign you first have to develop your basic sales message. What should the company tell the likely customers about itself and its goods and services? No doubt there are a lot of attractive selling points you would like to communicate. But the question is: Which key attributes should you emphasize that will best convey your message and make the greatest impact? An effective sales message is a focused message.

You may be a retailer with a convenient shopping location, some interesting or distinctive products, low prices, easy payment terms, and favorable warranties. You may be proud of a number of other impressive business attributes. But you have to hone in on one, two, or, at most, three decisive strengths and advantages that will resonate in the minds and imaginations of your potential customers. And you have to repeat the same basic message again and again before it begins to take hold in the public mind.

The Promotional Campaign Starts at Home

The small business promotional campaign starts at home, so to speak. Word-of-mouth is the best promotional tool for generating new business. The campaign begins with quality products and service. It extends to those direct, personal contacts with the customers that, I have insisted, must be cultivated in all small businesses.

Visual appearances are a distinct part of the promotional message. If salespeople are unkempt, if the premises are cluttered and faded, if a restaurant menu is spotted, disorderly, and has typographical and spelling errors, the business will communicate a damning message of sloppiness and mediocrity. One New York restaurant critic, Seymour Britchky, says that a relatively foolproof pretest of an establishment's food is the appearance of the menu. He observes that if it reveals a lack of attention and care, those same qualities invariably characterize the food and service.

Are the displays scruffy and outdated? Is the neon sign outside missing two letters in the business's name? Are the premises, both inside and out, clean and freshly painted? Are the delivery trucks presentable? Do the drivers and deliverers look neat and clean? Do the people who answer the telephone convey courtesy, knowledge, and responsiveness, or just plain sour resistance and impatience?

Direct salesmanship, whether by the owner-manager, key employees, or well-trained sales personnel, is the opening wedge to a growing market. The basic sales message must be known and communicated with knowledge and enthusiasm.

Sales Literature

The company's sales literature, such as the brochures, flyers, catalogs, newsletters, manuals, and periodic mailings, is an extension of direct sales. If the recipients are carefully selected and targeted, the literature can be a very cost-effective sales tool. But these materials, too, must look attractive: Clean, well laid out, and zippy. They must communicate a focused message and say it quickly and to the point, or the message will be lost on the way to the wastebasket.

For example, I discussed in Chapter 3 a Connecticut nursery, White Flower Farm, which has built a growing mail-order business in spite of its primary emphasis on direct sales. Distant customers rave not just about the quality, packaging, and service provided by White Flower Farm, but also about the

sales catalog itself. This catalog would excite the most confirmed city-dweller to active visions of gardening. There is no
hype, just a contagious love of plants, a sense of great integrity,
and a desire to inform and assist potential customers. Catalog
customers' comments read like this: "When I received the
catalog, it made me feel so good...." "I like to read anything
when the English language is used well. The photographs are
absolutely gorgeous. I feel I have learned quite a lot from the
catalog...." "I also like the helpful hints...." "What's important
to me is they go out of their way to set things straight." A little
extra pride in the product and the corresponding sales literature, respect for the customers, sensitivity to customers' problems and concerns, and unconcealed enthusiasm can make a
palpable difference.

Using Your Ingenuity

Between small promotional budgets and large ambitions,
many small business owner-managers seem capable, no matter what the circumstances, of a creative flair in attracting new
customers. They invent enticing buying incentives such as
special payment terms, volume discount bargains, and trading
stamps. They design eye-catching, mind-grabbing window
displays or clever internal display fixtures for the "impulse"
buyer.

They institute public service tie-ins. A Pennsylvania pizza
restaurant promised to contribute 50 cents on every sales
dollar, up to $1,000, to the local fire department for some
needed equipment. The fire department, in turn, distributed
related flyers and posters. They even put them in the windows
of fast-food competitors.

For little money, small businesses can dramatize the benefits
and pleasures of their goods. A Cadillac dealer in a Chicago
suburb gave coupons that entitled holders to the free use of a
Seville for a day. It handed to railway commuters copies of the
Wall Street Journal featuring a front-page insert called *The
Village (Cadillac) News*. "They loved it," the owner-manager

recalls. "It sold 45 automobiles." Three young owners of a New York City exercise studio dress in formfitting leotards and stand for an hour a day by the nearest subway stations handing out flyers.

In 1967, Wilson Harrell paid $30,000 for a marginal company that produced a first-rate spray cleaner. By cultivating U.S. military contacts and hiring local celebrities to make his sales pitch (for which he gave them small blocks of the company's equity), he boosted sales to 5 percent of the market. At that time, Procter & Gamble, according to Harrell, "got ready to roll out their own spray cleaner. It didn't take a genius to realize that, with their marketing muscle, they could blow us completely out of the water. I couldn't outspend or outpromote them, so I had to out-think them." Just a few days before Procter & Gamble launched its new product in some preselected territories, Harrell flooded those markets with exceptionally low-priced, giant-size, four-months'-supply bottles of his spray cleaner. Shoppers greedily bought the bargains, leaving Procter & Gamble with large promotional expenditures and no customers. Their sales results were so poor, in comparison with marketing research projections, that Procter & Gamble dropped the product. Harrell later sold his company to Clorox for $7.5 million.

Advertising

The first impulse of many owner-managers is to spend large funds, if they are available, for an advertising campaign. Expensive advertising may work—it takes large amounts of new sales to break even on advertising expenditures—but it may not work. Much depends on how carefully the media are selected and whether the advertising communicates the sales message in a pithy or visually convincing manner. But before embarking on a $10,000 advertising campaign, the results of which may be uncertain, you should consider other potentially more effective and cheaper ways of promoting the business. A public relations campaign is one.

Public Relations

Many cash-strapped small business owner-managers have found that publicity or public relations campaigns are far cheaper and more effective than advertising. The object is to get your story in the press or other media. Sometimes, that requires home-designed press releases or profiles and stories planted by friends in the media.

Often, though, it is necessary and worthwhile to hire a public relations professional with the contacts and experience to generate the right media exposure. A good public relations consultant can operate his or her business out of a telephone booth. One or two well-placed calls to the right journalists can produce wonders that no amount of expensive advertising can equal. If the public relations firm doesn't have the contacts, though, your $1,000 or so monthly fee will go down the drain, and you will have nothing more than a 3:00 A.M. spot on the local FM radio station to show for it.

Managing Your Money Tip

Earlier, on page 83, we discussed how to use Managing Your Money to mail questionnaires to your clients and customers. You can also use Managing Your Money to mail press releases for your business. To print labels, you first have to have entered the recipients' names and addresses in the Card File (it's in the Desk submenu, or just press Ctrl-C). Once you've done so, while you're in the Card File, press F4 and mark the names you want to mail to. (To mail to everyone, press F8. To mail to one set of addresses, and customize your mailing, press F6 and follow the instructions.) Press F4 again, and select "Labels" for the type of "report" you want to print. Follow the instructions (press F1 for more detailed instructions) to accommodate the kind of labels you're using.

You can even use Managing Your Money to print your press release. Just select MYM-Write from the Desk submenu (or press Ctrl-W), press F5 to start a new document, and type away. When you're done, just press <esc>. To print the document on your printer, press F4, place an "X" opposite "Printer", and press F10.

Follow-up calls might make your promotional effort more effective. Want to put together a list of people to call? Select Phone Calls from the Desk submenu (or press Ctrl-P), press F5, F7, and the first few letters of the last name of the person you want to call. When the information is filled in to your satisfaction, press F10 twice. A reminder to make this phone call will be entered into your Time Summary (which you can access by pressing Ctrl-T, or selecting Time Summary from the Desk submenu).

VI. Sales Goals and Actions Plans

A coherent marketing plan that pulls together all the pieces—the market analysis, the connecting of products and customers, the pricing, the sales channels, and the sales promotion—will conclude with specific, challenging, but realistic sales objectives and a concrete, step-by-step action plan to achieve them. Some thoughts on this end-process appear in Chapter 11, "Planning for Action and Results."

With useful market information, a marketing and promotional strategy, and specific sales goals and related action plans, you will be far better positioned to reach out and sell likely customers than you would be on a day-today, hit-or-miss basis.

CHAPTER

6

BUILDING AND MANAGING THE STAFF

Bob Rouark owns a Long Island, New York, auto parts manufacturing company. Each day when he arrives at work, he writes on a pad, "We can do together what I can't do alone." He says it sounds corny, but he believes it is a healthy antidote to his natural disposition to go it alone.

Successful ventures are collective, team efforts. Other than your own vision, energy, and managerial capability, productive employees are perhaps a small firm's most important asset. Building and managing a productive staff are make-or-break conditions of success or failure in small business.

In this chapter, we will focus on the key elements of building and managing the staff:

1. Determining the specific job needs of the company and the associated work performance and results you expect from the employees;
2. Hiring employees so you match their talents and experience with those needs and expectations;
3. Delegating effectively substantial authority to the employees;
4. Motivating them to improve their productivity.

Benefits of a Good Staff

There are few things in small business quite so satisfying as managing employees who do what you expect them to do and do it very well. Whether you hire an employee to perform specific tasks or undertake major areas of responsibility, performance that meets high standards is both economically and emotionally gratifying. Some of the reasons are these.

1. *Your business is in good part the sum of the work of the staff.* You alone responsible for hiring and managing the staff. But good employees make good managers. When they don't perform what has to be done to meet the business's objectives, you are in serious trouble.

2. *First-rate employees fill the gaps in your own experience, interests, and skills.* They allow you to concentrate on the

things only you as owner-manager can do and the things you do best as well. They spare you concern that key areas of the business are being neglected or attended to inadequately.

3. *Similarly, they save you and others valuable time and money.* You don't have to monitor their work as carefully, redo their work, or clean up after them. You can concentrate on productive work, not on damage control.

4. *Productive work is contagious.* Good employees set examples that others tend to follow. Cooperative, result-oriented employees help establish energetic work environments and high staff morale.

5. *Good employees go that extra mile.* They initiate valuable ideas and the associated activities that improve the profits.

If all that seems obvious, it nonetheless takes most owner-managers several years before they really appreciate the yields of a good staff. If you ask them what valuable lessons they have learned since they started the business, one of the first they mention is likely to be: "Don't cut corners on the staffing. Hire good people and make sure you spend a lot of time developing them."

Inexperienced owner-managers tend to recruit and pay at lower levels than they should. They only gradually upgrade their staff as they come to value the contributions of truly productive employees. There are several reasons for this.

1. They exaggerate their own capacity to do all the important work themselves.
2. They underestimate the make-a-difference contributions of good employees.
3. They are, as it turns out, foolishly cost-conscious. They hope to "get by" with very ordinary employees. They either invest available funds in less productive areas or else distribute them to themselves. Although their overall goal is "cost-effectiveness," they overemphasize the "costs" of a good staff at the expense of "effectiveness." Cutting corners on staff costs is a false economy that, in the end, undercuts effectiveness.

4. They haven't adequately identified the needs of the business and matched those needs with the associated talents required to realize them.

An experienced owner-manager comments, "The head has to be a lion tamer, but if he's going to succeed he's got to have some pretty good lions." One person who understood that was Andrew Carnegie. These words are on his tombstone:

Here lies a man
Who knew how to enlist
In his service
Better men than himself.

It doesn't take long to recognize the symptoms of a weak, poorly managed staff. But take a look at Checklist 10 for a foretaste of the consequences of managerial neglect of this vital area of the business.

As paragraph 2 of Checklist 10 indicates, employees have legitimate grievances of their own. Your responsibilities for managing a productive staff do not end with hiring "good" people. You also must, as we noted earlier:

1. Identify the concrete objectives of the firm that have to be achieved by the employees;
2. Delegate effectively;
3. Motivate the staff to identify their work with the objectives of the business.

Hiring Productive Employees

The goal is quite simply to hire employees who will be productive when and where it really counts. That means you must first identify the job needs of your company. Only then does it make sense to look for candidates and interview the more promising ones. It is usually a good idea to formally hire an employee only after a suitable trial period.

CHECKLIST 10 Symptoms of Weak Staffs

---

1. *From the Owner-Manager's Perspective*
   a. Assignments are performed halfheartedly and seldom completed satisfactorily the first go-around; responsibility is shirked.
   b. Work is careless.
   c. Obvious problems are ignored or taken for granted.
   d. There is lack of cooperation with fellow employees; only the minimum is undertaken.
   e. There is a tangible lack of pride, spirit, and pleasure in the work.
   f. Dishonesty and sabotage of company objectives are common.
   g. Service is poor; customers and products are treated with disrespect.
   h. Lateness and absenteeism seem uncontrollable, turnover among the better employees is high, and the staff is filled with time-savers.
2. *From the Employees' Perspective*
   a. Pay and incentives are low.
   b. The work environment is disagreeable.
   c. Management won't listen:
      (i) The boss makes little contact with employees and seems indifferent to or contemptuous of their ideas and work problems.
      (ii) The staff is not consulted on company policies and work assignments.
   d. The boss doesn't seem to know what he expects of the employees; therefore they never "get it right," no matter what the circumstances.
   e. There is a lack of pride in the business; employees do not identify with company objectives; they pursue their own short-term interests.

Identifying Needs

Before considering any live candidates, consider the following questions:

1. Is there a real job need?
2. What kind of need is it?
3. What realistic, specific results do you expect from a well-qualified employee when you fill that job?
4. What qualifications best meet those needs?

1. *Is the job need a real one?* Robert Townsend, author of

Up the Organization, wrote, "To keep an organization young and fit, don't hire anyone until everybody's so overworked they'll be glad to see the newcomer no matter where he sits." The issue is whether a well-qualified candidate would make a real contribution to the productivity and profits of the firm. Often, though, we hire to satisfy underlying motives relating more to prestige and convenience than to productivity. Most owner-managers of young businesses simply cannot afford a full-time secretary. The money is much better spent on developing and promoting the product, improving the compensation of key employees, and on a score of other purposes. But a secretary is often justified as essential, even though a number of alternatives would meet the need for secretarial services. For example:

a. The typing could be done by a typing agency.
b. An existing employee with typing skills could be paid extra to do, say, five hours of typing a week.
c. A part-time or full-time secretary could be hired and shared by everyone in the business.
d. A temporary secretary could be retained for overload periods.

Keep an eye out, then, for convenience hiring that adds nothing to the muscle and productivity of the business. Staff assistants and personal assistants, in particular, should be looked at skeptically. Watch out, also, for what the economists call "disguised unemployment." That refers to underworked employees who could, if necessary, complete their work in a fraction of the time presently alloted to it.

2. *What is the specific job need?* There is a danger that the owner will fail to consider the *specific* job need and will hire on the basis of some fuzzy job description.

Here's an example. An owner-manager wants to "boost sales." He advertises for someone with "a strong record in sales." But what is the specific business objective: to open new markets, market new products, or increase the sale of existing products in the same market? Is the specific need a marketing expert, a sales manager, or a salesperson? Further, if a salesperson is required, is the need for an independent sales representative or agent, or rather for a direct-hire salesperson?

If the company needs a "product manager," is the real need for technological proficiency or for cost effectiveness? In the words of the old A&P advertisement, is the need for "Mr. Quality" or "Mr. Quantity?" It may be, for example, that the essence of the job is to organize and train a technical staff, in which case the owner-manager would be particularly concerned about candidates' skills and potential for organizing and training other people. Or perhaps the principal need is a person skilled in marketing or sales. It is up to you to consider and define the exact job need before you proceed to the hiring stage.

3. *What results do you expect from a well-qualified employee?* Another way of looking at the "need" issue is to consider what kind of performance would justify the hiring of a candidate, after the fact. What will you require of this employee, not on paper, but in practice, day-in and day-out? What will that person have to do to be considered a good performer? What specific results would you gladly reward if achieved?

4. *What qualifications best meet those needs?* When you have carefully considered the issue of job needs, you can then consider what it is you will look for in specific candidates. Referring back to the example in paragraph 2, if the need is for a sales manager, you clearly will be looking for someone with the ability to organize, manage, and motivate a sales staff. Those qualifications are quite different from those you would seek in either a marketing manager or a sales representative.

The goal, of course, is to match specific needs and specific qualifications. That is far from easy in practice. You will have to make a number of trade-offs. For instance, as you develop priority qualifications, you will have to consider length and relevance of experience. Those, in turn, may have to be weighed against character, resourcefulness, human-relations skills, and all the other intangibles. You will have to determine, for example, if priority should be given to maturity, reliability, and exactitude, as in a bookkeeping job, or to boundless energy, innovation, and learning potential, as might be desired in a product-development manager. In the first case, a premium might be on age and on proven, though not extraordinary experience; in the second case, the premium might be on youth and unproven promise. None of those considerations can be determined in the abstract. You must define your needs and priorities.

Filling Job Needs: Interviewing and Hiring

When you have a good sense of what the job need is, what results you are looking for, and what the relevant qualifications are, you have strongly increased the possibility of hiring the right person.

The primary task is to identify the candidate's strengths and determine if they are the same or similar to those needed for the job. The key question is whether there is a reasonably close fit between what the business needs done and what the candidate apparently does well.

In examining the candidate's past work record, it is important to know not only what those jobs required and what the candidate achieved but also whether that particular experience is truly relevant to the job for which the candidate is being interviewed. It is the candidate's *next* job, not his last one, that is the focus.

The life of an interview is in the details, not the frequently stereotyped and self-serving generalizations of the candidate. Good questions begin like this: "Tell me about that," or, "What if…," or "Give me some examples of that." Similarly, "How would you go about…" and "In that situation, what first steps would you take to…"

Many interviewers find it revealing to ask candidates to pose whatever questions they have about the company and the job. The answers can reveal a basic vacuity and lack of interest. Or, they can demonstrate a probing, spirited mind and imagination, and a sense of priorities.

Most owner-managers find that the assessment of intangibles is less direct and usually more difficult. You must generally intuit and sense such capacities as inner motivation, initiative, pride in performance, stature, stability, directness, intellect, honesty, attentiveness, and so on. That is one reason why a second interview for a short list of candidates is usually advisable. You can corroborate your first impressions and get a second reading.

Similarly, it is why references must be checked, no matter how unproductive an exercise that often is. Many times, a person does not reveal emotional or behavioral problems until exposed to the steady pressures of a job situation and fellow workers. Those will not be picked up in an interview, but if you are fortunate, you can learn about them from prior employers. It is usually best to go to the candidate's immediate supervisors, although there is little guarantee that even partially useful information will be communicated. The fact is, few employers are disposed to undermine an unsatisfactory ex-employee or one on the way out, especially if they are anxious to detach the employee from their payrolls as soon as minimum decency will allow. And after a year or two, the applicant's shortcomings are decently overlooked, in favor of some nice generalities.

When checking references, what you have to do, beyond confirming the candidate's basic employment data, is to read between the lines. What is *not* said by past employers may be far more revealing than what is said. Checklist 11 below lists some questions that may be useful in penetrating the dissembling or selective silence of a past employer. They are the kinds of questions that tend to be answered directly, or about which the ex-employer is unwilling to utter even a little white lie.

A Trial Period

Frequently, an effective and fair procedure is to take on new personnel for a trial period before formally hiring them. If your

CHECKLIST 11 Checking the References: Some Questions

1. "Knowing what you do, I take it you would immediately rehire this person for the same job?"
2. "The person sounds like a valuable employee. I gather you have unqualified respect for her?"
3. "The candidate sounds downright perfect! No weaknesses to speak of, I guess?"
4. "I take it you would recommend this person to your favorite brother if he were recruiting for the same position?"
5. "How would you rate the candidate on a scale of 1 to 10?"
6. "Is there anything more you want to tell me? Is there anything I need to know that I haven't asked about?"

standards are not met, dismissal under these circumstances, while still difficult, is nonetheless far less damaging to both the company and the individual.

An adequate trial period may be one day or three months, maybe more. But the time period should be specified precisely in advance. The applicant then understands that what is offered is an opportunity to earn the job and not a secure entitlement. The applicant's performance will determine the outcome.

To be effective and fair, this procedure requires two things: (1) you should specify with great care exactly what kind of performance will earn the job; (2) you owe the applicant useful feedback several times before the trial period ends. Ideally, the information gleaned during the trial period will be sufficiently germane to make it obvious whether or not the applicant should be hired.

Delegating the Work

You cannot really manage your staff without delegating effectively significant portions of the work.

Why You Have to Delegate

Those owner-managers who can't or don't delegate either preside over permanently small enterprises, or else their companies grow chaotically and progressively develop one problem area after another. In either case, the owner-manager is probably settling for a barely adequate, but certainly not a dynamic and productive, staff.

Sooner or later, if your firm grows beyond the embryo size, you must accept the need for reorganization and some specialization. You then must delegate much of the daily work you formerly assumed yourself. To grow profitably is to delegate effectively.

By effectively delegating some of your former workload to the staff, you will reestablish your two primary roles: first, to lead and manage; and second, to do those things you do best and those that have the largest impact on the firm's profits. Effective delegation allows you to concentrate your time and energies where they count the most.

Delegation also lets you develop the full potential of the staff. It requires you to train and encourage the employees to assume more responsibility and to make valuable contributions to the business. It helps you keep those people from departing in frustration.

If you don't delegate, you will be a prisoner of detail and work overload. You will have no free time to observe, reflect, and plan. You will be swamped by a morass of papers and problems. You will be besieged by employees who aren't doing what you hoped they would do and who, in turn, are handing all their decisions and problems over to you. You will end up doing part of nearly everyone else's work and probably doing it poorly.

Some Reasons Owner-Managers Fail to Delegate

If the principles and imperatives of delegation are so obvious and compelling, why do so many owner-managers fail to delegate or do it so halfheartedly? Clearly, it is difficult to share responsibility. Many, many owner-managers, as we observed in Chapter 2, become preoccupied with control and perfectionism. They feel acutely uncomfortable and even remiss in relinquishing authority to anyone else.

Here are the words of one owner-manager, who reluctantly delegated direct responsibility for his firm's export sales, which he had built into a substantial division of the firm: "I'm sorry to let it go. It won't be done as well as I did it several years ago. But it will be done better than I've done it for the last two years. If you're involved in a growth situation, you must prune your areas of activity."

Here's another owner-manager's lament: "It's a temptation to check every invoice and make sure we got 15 drums or 50 drums or 500 drums and that we paid the right price. I could spend seven hours a week doing it, and I wouldn't find $300 of damage, if I found that. So it really isn't worth it. But it's very difficult to keep your fingers out of things you did as you built up the business."

Another owner-manager claims, "Sure, I'd like to delegate more, but the staff just isn't up to it. Better to do it myself." Don't be so sure. Part of that may be the sheer vanity that "owner knows best." Maybe that owner-manager has never really attempted to delegate or has done it poorly. Maybe he expects more of an employee than he does of himself and is intolerant of anyone's performance except his own.

And maybe the staff "isn't up to it." But what does that mean? A 100 percent performance, when a good 80 percent is all that is needed for the tasks in question? Or are the employees not "up to it" because of ineptitude? If that's the reason, the owner-manager has hired the wrong people. Or are they "not up to it" because the owner-manager hasn't properly trained and developed the staff? But effective development is part of the very process of effective delegation.

Nothing in the concept of effective delegation, nothing whatsoever, implies a diminution of owner-managers' ultimate responsibility for the destiny and performance of their firms. There is an old military maxim that commanders who delegate authority never shed final responsibility.

How to Delegate Effectively

How the delegation is managed largely determines the results. Checklist 12 contains a checklist of the basic elements of effective delegation.

CHECKLIST 12 How To Think about Delegation

As a first step, think of the traditional journalists' questions:

1. *What* is delegated, *what* is not delegated
2. *Why* it is delegated and *what* results are expected
3. To *whom* it is delegated
4. *When* it is to be completed
5. *How* it is to be done
6. *When* and *what* is to be reported back to you
7. *How* you must monitor the delegated work, retain oversight, and provide evaluation and feedback

Boiled down, the elements of effective delegation are these:

1. Specifying what responsibilities are delegated and why
2. Deciding to whom the task is delegated
3. Specifying, if appropriate, how to do it
4. Establishing deadlines
5. Providing authority and resources to do the job
6. Communicating the delegation
7. Monitoring the delegation

Let's look at those elements more specifically. Whether the delegation relates to an area of responsibility, a project, or a simple task, the following factors are involved.

1. *Specifying What Responsibilities Are Delegated and Why.* An effective delegation of work sets out the specific goals,

expectations, priorities, and results you want accomplished. Vagueness and indecisiveness are the enemies of effective delegation. They occur because owner-managers haven't bothered to think the matter through and focus on what's significant and important. They vaguely hope the employee will do the thinking, planning, and policy making for them. They are then bound to the employee's subjective interpretation of what is needed.

Take a frequent type of assignment: "Go and solve that damned Keystone Company problem." Is the owner-manager asking for action?—because a run-with-the-ball employee will do just that. Or is it a request for a plan? If that is the interpretation, the owner-manager will get that—a plan. Or does this person really want, say, three to four options to mull over? If that is what is really wanted, or would be wanted if satisfactorily considered, then that is the task that has to be clearly delegated.

Unless the delegation is obvious, it is usually useful to explain how the work relates to the policies, plans, or problems of the company. If the work is important, that fact should be made clear.

Many owner-managers feel it is useful to place employees in "the big picture" starting on the first day of the job. They don't want to duplicate those silly extensive orientation meetings of some large organizations. But they do meet with new employees and discuss some of the more potent facts about the company. Owner-managers can then relate employees' job responsibilities to the larger context, and hope that this imparts meaning, excitement, and an initial clarity to the employees' work.

Since effective delegation avoids vagueness, it also must be realistic and obtainable. It is frequently appropriate to discuss the work with the employee and gain his or her active assent.

Can the work be done? If the employee thinks not, why not? Is there an attitude problem? Or is there a regrettable lack of confidence? Those issues must be dealt with differently. Perhaps there are good reasons why the work can't be done as expected. You ought to know about them and revise your objectives and tactics accordingly.

Perhaps your standards are simply much higher than those of the employee. Then it is time to lay down the law that what is expected is not only possible but also what you insist on. But if an employee's reticence stems from lack of experience, it suggests that you need to take some time for training and development.

Some delegations will not be carried through because they are patently ridiculous or onerous, and the employee feels the more sensible tactic is silence or inaction. A law partner in New York City, famed from his crisis days in the Kennedy Administration, was notorious for handing out assignments at exactly 5:30 P.M. Fridays that were due Mondays at 9:00 A.M. and regularly required about 20 hours of work. One owner-manager incurred hilarious disrespect among his staff over his requests for pompously complex charts of abstruse information that made no sense to anyone and could never be used to any effect.

2. *Deciding to Whom the Task Is Delegated.* Some owner-managers believe the work should be directly delegated to the least senior employee who is capable of doing it. Others believe in a more hierarchical delegation, to a "department head" or similarly positioned person, who will then be responsible for its execution but may in turn re-delegate the activity. The choice is a question of style, although most small businesses flourish in an atmosphere of organizational informality and with a minimum of structure.

Otherwise, there is no issue unless more than one employee is fingered. "I want you guys to handle this one," is an invitation for confused inaction. Responsibility has to be delineated, and the particular persons responsible must know exactly what is expected of them.

3. *Specifying, if Appropriate, How to Do It.* There is thorough agreement that you should delegate *what* is to be done but not dictate *how* it is to be done. General George Patton

used to say, "Tell people where to go but not how to get there, and you'll be amazed at what happens." Of course, you will need to pass on any relevant background information—problems, company standards or procedures, useful sources—and provide appropriate teaching and training. Without that training and information, you may heedlessly place the employee in a no-win situation.

Otherwise, encourage the employee to think the matter through and develop the habit of resourceful work and problem-solving skills. To employees who passively seek a blueprint for action, you can simply ask, "What do you recommend? How do you propose to go about it?"

4. *Establishing Deadlines.* Deciding *when* the job should be done is one of the essential elements of effective delegation. This is frequently accomplished by setting milestones for the completion of significant portions of a task or project. Some owner-managers, having established what needs to be done, will ask the employee when he or she can have the work completed. If the employee responds with an acceptable deadline, the owner-manager will indicate, "All right, that's what I'm holding you to."

5. *Providing Authority and Resources to Do the Job.* You must make clear what authority is delegated and, just as important, the limits of that authority.

What specifically is expected? A decision or an action? Must this be approved? If authority for purchasing is delegated, the ceiling on that authority, if any, should be specified: "Up to $2,000—anything more requires my approval"; or, "No equipment is to be purchased, only rented, and I want to review with you the first of these contracts before you sign"; or, "Get me, please, all the comparative data, and the terms and conditions for renting a medium-sized delivery van."

Check-signing authority typically contains limitations: "Up to $1,000 and on such-and-such matters I alone will sign."

It is vital that sufficient authority be delegated to carry out the work efficiently. If, for example, an employee's work interconnects with the work of other employees, it may be necessary to grant authority to direct them. If the work requires a stream of purchases, failure to grant purchasing authority would tie the employee's hands.

The delegation should contain an injunction to report potentially serious problems—in fact, one of the firm's few rules should be: "There shall be no surprises." That is sometimes referred to as the "red-flag rule." The point is, as problems or trouble or changed circumstances of importance develop, they should be relayed promptly to you for our attention and action. Too often, the employee may try to cover up a serious error or take sole responsibility for working out some looming disaster. You have every right and need to know of such situations immediately and to assume responsibility. The view here is that failure to report a true red-flag problem should be a firable offense.

Likewise, you should convey to the employee any reporting responsibilities: "Get back to me if this or that develops"; "Give me a one-pager every week on your progress and any problems"; "Let me know when Stage I is done, and remind me then to set up a meeting with you, Helen, and Ed"; "If you don't have a proposed solution by March 1, get back to me and be prepared to give me the relevant facts, the most promising options you have been considering, and what the problems are."

When delegating, you should also be sure to make available whatever resources are appropriate to do the work efficiently, including the people, money, materials, and facilities.

6. *Communicating the Delegation.* A delegation must be communicated clearly, so that there is a meeting of the minds about what is to be done. It is easy to make an assignment which only the owner-manager thinks is crystal-clear. You shouldn't take it for granted that the delegation is understood as intended, and then get angry as hell if it was not.

Encourage employees to seek clarification and ask questions regarding what is to be done, what the expectations are, and any matters relating to the background of the delegation. The employee shouldn't have to guess at the "true intentions" of the instructions or feel like a fool for asking.

If you give instructions orally see that employees take notes or ask them to repeat their understanding of what is required.

The delegation must be made public when the authority and work affect other employees. A "no-one-told-*me*" from some other employee can sabotage the delegation.

7. *Monitoring the Delegation.* It is not enough to pick good people, tell them what's wanted, and then let it rip. Too many things can go wrong in too short a time. Employees can carry the ball too far or in the wrong direction or simply not do anything. Delegations, whatever their nature, are not self-executing. You must know enough about the work to make sure it is proceeding as you want. Reporting requirements are not sufficient to determine if instructions are fully executed. "I've taken care of that," can mean anything.

You have to develop a hands-on trouble-detector system, based on your own observations of the work and reliable sources of information. Checklist 13 briefly outlines things you should monitor.

The monitoring and oversight function also allows you to perform two other uniquely managerial responsibilities.

1. Evaluating the employees—their work habits, attitudes, skills, reliability, and effectiveness
2. Providing frequent and direct feedback to the employees

It is useless to conduct those formal once-a-year personnel evaluations favored by the big organizations. Not only are they dishonestly inflated, but they lack specificity and come too long after the fact to be of any help to anyone.

The evaluation and feedback should be related to concrete work situations. They should be provided face-to-face. Further, if the comments are sufficiently direct and forthright, they stand a better chance of being interpreted as constructive. Focus on specific work problems so that criticism won't be

CHECKLIST 13 Monitoring Delegated Work

---

1. Is the work on schedule?
2. Is it moving in the right direction?
3. Is it on budget?
4. Has the assignment been interpreted correctly?
5. Are there unforeseen problems or circumstances that you can resolve or that require redefinition of the assignment?
6. Are there internal personality or turf disputes that you must broker?
7. Are any additional resources needed—personnel, money, facilities, authority?

---

construed as a personal attack. Attacks on the person simply generate defensiveness.

Too Little or Too Much Delegation

Recurring problems in delegating the work involve too little or too much delegation.

The owner-manager who refuses to delegate any real work responsibility must do a lot of the work, handle almost all of the problems and decisions, and deal with relative trivia or matters which could be handled perfectly well by others.

When, however, the delegations are so broad that they are bereft of standards of performance, limitations on the employees' authority, or satisfactory supervision, the owner-manager has forfeited ultimate responsibility for the performance of the staff and the business itself: "I delegate everything, so nothing ever gets to my desk," in the words of a *New Yorker* cartoon.

In a typical example, the owner-manager just plops a new employee in a general job description, as it were, points to the work quarters, and that's that. No work context and background; no priorities; no clarification of responsibilities; no attention to the employee's authority and availability of resources; no training or supervision. Under those circumstances, it is not at all clear what the owner-manager cares about and, therefore what the employee should care about. It is not even clear that the owner-manager does care. Not bothering to determine and convey goals and expectations really *means* not caring.

That owner-manager, at the end of a year, may express disappointment with the work results of the employee and consider replacing the person. But the results are the owner-manager's. Final accountability cannot be delegated.

Motivating the Staff

An age-old question among managers is: "How do you motivate employees to improve their performance and identify their own goals with those of the company?"

Compensation

A traditional way of motivating employees is to pay them well. Harold Geneen, former chairman of ITT, allegedly observed, "I've got my executives by their limousines."

Small businesses, though, have no "limousines" and are frequently limited in their ability to pay the prevailing wages for talented, experienced employees. They cannot simply "buy" talent and motivation.

The smart owner-managers, however, will go the extra mile to assure that their few first-rate, key employees are paid at least the going rate and, hopefully, more. "If you pay 20 percent over the going rate," says one, "you'll get double the person." And that person will be much less likely to leave as soon as someone else waves some bigger bucks.

As for the other job slots, let's just observe that cheap is expensive. If you can't somehow allocate the monies to pay the going rate, you are likely to hire weak, unproductive employees. If, for example, the going rate for an experienced, competent bookkeeper is $20,000 a year, pay it. For $16,000, you will "save" $4,000—but very likely regret it for several years.

It is odd, though, how many owner-managers will balk at the extra $4,000, when they don't hesitate to spend $4,000 extra on, let's say, a particularly deluxe delivery van that catches the eye. That deluxe van won't yield an extra dollar of profit or save an hour of work, but a competent bookkeeper improves efficiencies and save monies in innumerable ways that you can only appreciate after you have experienced the work of a poorly trained and careless bookkeeper.

Fortunately, base salaries are not the only form of compensation. If a really excellent job performance has produced extra profit, that extra income can be shared. Sharing the proceeds of increased productivity not only provides a concrete reward for excellence but also provides incentives for all the employees to achieve above-standard performance.

Profit-sharing comes in many packages. There are employee stock option plans, known as ESOP's. You can divide a portion of the company's annual profits on a pro rata basis among all the employees. Or, you can provide unequal distributions to the star performers. You can give discretionary Christmas bonuses or provide immediate bonuses to reward a particularly good piece of work. Token grants of $10, $50, or $500 may be given for valuable ideas or critical one-shot contributions. A special lunch, a gift of theater or sports tickets, or something else with meaning to the employee can also be given to reward good performance.

Each owner-manager must determine what kinds of monetary awards the company will make, in the context of its particular needs and its tax circumstances. Each owner-manager must decide whom to reward, at what times, and for what work standards. But bonus or incentive payments which are easily earned or which are more truly an entitlement have no effect on superior performance. Better to classify them as base pay. Average or good work should be covered by salary. Incentive or bonus pay should be reserved for excellence.

Managing Your Money Tip

Writing checks come payroll time can be a headache. Managing Your Money's Quick List can automate the process.

First, select Quick List from the Money submenu. Then press F5 and "S" (or select "Spend Money", and press F10) to add a new account. Fill in the information for the employee who's on your payroll. When you're done, press F10.

Now you'll have a list of all your employees. Come payday, just place an "x" under the "Mark" column opposite each employee you want to pay, and enter the amount they'll be paid under the "$ Out" column. (If they're paid the same amount each check, you won't have to do this last step.) Then press F10. Managing Your Money will set up the paychecks for printing, and account for them in your books.

To print the paychecks, make sure your printer is set up for printing checks. Select Print Checks from the Money submenu, and press F10 to print the payroll checks.

Job Satisfaction and Enrichment

The fact is, small businesses are usually at a disadvantage in providing short-term monetary incentives. However, they are very well-positioned to motivate employees by tapping into some powerful but intangible sources of work incentives. The operative concepts are "job satisfaction" and "job enrichment."

Nearly all employees experience job satisfaction and corresponding motivation when their bosses:

1. Set exacting examples;
2. Provide considerable autonomy and responsibility for doing the work;
3. Provide recognition for that achievement;

4. Provide real opportunities for learning, participation, and achievement.

In such circumstances, it is the work itself that motivates the employee. Let's see how you can set those conditions in motion.

1. *Setting a Personal Example.* Whatever the organizational psychologists may say, there simply is no one management style that consistently reaps the best performance from a staff. There are distinctly calloused bosses who are effective, and there are nice guys who are effective. Most owner-managers who build productive staffs are somewhere in between.

Whatever the style, you shape the work environment by your own values, your own actions and expectations, and the living example you set, day after day after day.

When you set high standards at the outset and make it clear that you are dead serious about them, you go a long way down the road of job motivation.

The care you take to monitor the work of employees and to assist them when necessary shows convincingly that the work matters and that the employee is an important person to you. When you combine those standards with personal work habits that demonstrate a pride and attention in doing the important things and doing them well, you set a contagious example and challenge for all the staff.

Those calloused but effective owner-managers may appear dictatorial and abrasive, but they are not aloof. They *do* concern themselves with the legitimate interests and performance of their staff. Within the framework of their own high standards, they are honest, fair, and reward achievement. There is none of that adversarial mind-set that is the curse of so many businesses. And effective nice-guy owner-managers set rigorous standards and enforce them. They identify with employees' interests for just so long as those interests are compatible with important company objectives.

When you can show employees that there is a nice coincidence between their individual interests and the company's, there is mutual gain.

In the restaurant business, many waiters and waitresses do not pursue their obvious best interests with any savvy. They never quite calculate that the courtesy, friendliness, and helpfulness that the house asks for—and the resultant return business and higher average sales per customer that the house depends on—are in their own interests. Larger guest checks and more business mean more tips. Once they truly understand that they have, in effect, a concession—a personal profit motive in the success of their assigned tables—their performance invariably improves. If it can be shown to one waiter, say, that an increase of three dollars in his average customer check would create $8,000 a year more in tips, then both he and the restaurant gain significantly.

Leadership is an inspiring force. Employees want owner-managers who know where they are going and how to get there, who make tough decisions, and who admit error when appropriate. In short, they want bosses who manage.

2. *Providing Delegation.* When work is properly delegated, the employees will experience both autonomy and responsibility for their own work. When the owner-manager's controls are loosened, employees can initiate plans and activities for the work. They must anticipate obstacles and persevere in solving problems independently and resourcefully. They are accountable for the results. If they have done the work reasonably well, they experience a personal feeling of achievement.

They certainly will not be working in a vacuum but will come in contact with the firm's customers, products, or some other mainstream concerns. They will increase their knowledge about their work, the business, and about themselves as well. That is the stuff of job enrichment, and it motivates employees.

3. *Recognizing Achievement.* Monetary rewards for excellent work are not the only way of recognizing achievement. The employee, like all people, feeds on the good opinions of others. The proverbial pat on the back is one of the most

elemental forms of motivation. "I would live for two months on one good compliment," said Mark Twain. Almost any display of appreciation should do the trick. When those compliments are issued publicly they have even more effect.

4. *Encouraging Ideas for Improvement—Listening to the Staff.* Employees like to contribute new and potentially valuable ideas and suggestions. They experience real satisfaction when these are converted into improved results. They feel they belong. They believe rightly that they are valuable employees, who are given respect and consideration.

"Always talk to the troops," said General Patton. "They know more about the war than anybody. Make them tell you all their gripes....They will not trust you if you do not trust them. Always remember in talking with the troops the most important thing to do is listen."

You have to spend time with the employees and get to know them. You have to work actively to elicit their ideas and knowledge. An old factory hand has it right: "Don't let your employees tell you what you *want* to hear. Let your wife do that. Make 'em tell you what you *have* to hear." Listening to this openly and tolerantly produces just that sense of trust and participation referred to by Patton.

By asking questions, you not only elicit potentially valuable information and productive recommendations for improving the business. You also provide a major stimulus of work satisfaction and motivation to do a better job. Checklist 14 gives a list of questions you can pose to your employees. Try it.

CHECKLIST 14 Questions To Elicit Employee Contributions

---

1. What would you do first if somehow you became the owner of the business tomorrow morning?
2. What changes in your job area would you consider if you were me?
3. What is the best use of your time? Your knowledge and abilities? How are they being wasted, if they are? What could you be doing that you're not doing?

CHECKLIST 14 Questions To Elicit Employee Contributions (*Continued*)

---

4. How can we help? What do we do or not do that hinders you the most?
5. What should I know about your work that I don't know? What do you need to know about the business that you don't know?
6. Give me three ideas tomorrow on how Ave might get such-and-such done.
7. What do you believe is the underlying cause of this problem?
8. What do the customers say to you, reveal to you, about the product(s)— about price and quality, about service, about the competition? What three comments do you hear most frequently?
9. What seems to you to work well here? Why? What doesn't work so well? Why do you suppose it doesn't?
10. What sorts of annoyances and minor screw-ups do you see here time and again? What consistent foul-ups, product defects, customer gripes, lack of information, or needed decisions do you have to put up with on the job that prevent you from achieving what you think you ought to?
11. What opportunities do you see that we're really not exploiting? What problems do you see ahead that we're not aware of? What would you do about them?
12. Are there any areas of your work where your job isn't clear enough or where other people don't know what you're expected to do or that you're authorized to do it?
13. Tell me more about those two years you spent before you joined us and what you learned about such-and-such that we could possibly apply here.

The joint achievements that result are perhaps the best motivators of all. When the right people know what you expect of them and are motivated to give that extra effort to achieve it, you have taken a major step to success in small business.

CHAPTER

7

MANAGING THE ACCOUNTING AND FINANCIAL CONTROLS

One of the primary causes of small business disaster is the failure to keep appropriate, accurate, up-to-date accounting records and controls *and*—to use them to manage the business.

The lack of an effective accounting system is not just an accounting problem—it is a management problem. Without adequate records and financial controls you cannot understand your business. You are flying by the seat-of-your-pants, and a crash is almost inevitable.

True, you may be able to "get by," even though the firm's record keeping and controls are chaotic or months behind. *If* the firm is very small and sales are sufficient to absorb a lot of seemingly invisible waste and provide an adequate pocket of cash, you may appear to know "well enough" what's happening. But you shouldn't kid yourself that you are *managing* the business.

If an effective accounting system is not established right from the beginning and consciously utilized as a basic management tool, its neglect will haunt the business for years to come—*if* it stays open that long. Without the numerical data and internal controls that a good accounting system provides, you will be stumbling around in a pitch-black business world with no perceivable order, significance, or pathways. If you don't understand your costs, you may be promoting goods and services or bidding on projects that yield no profit. You won't know which of your products are selling well and which are lagging. You will have, at best, only a hazy idea of where your money is going and how much cash you have on hand in relation to your liabilities. You won't be able to receive any of the signals telling you if your assets are being dissipated in creeping inefficiencies or even in fairly substantial theft. You may well be oblivious to a serious cash crunch looming ahead just when you must pay large suppliers' bills, a hefty insurance premium, and substantial tax assessments you inadvertently neglected along the way. When the lights do go on, it may be too late.

This chapter focuses on the importance of a practical accounting system for small businesses, on what it takes to put one in place, and on why a first-rate, hands-on accountant is indispensable to the survival and success of your firm.

In fact, management information and tools provided by an effective accounting system are so vital to understanding, directing, and controlling the firm that they are dealt with in detail in several chapters of this book. Chapters 4 and 5 demonstrated the importance of basic marketing data in determining sales and costs. A substantial portion of Chapter 10 ("Understanding the Business Inside Out") relates to understanding and using the numbers produced by the accounting system to improve the business. Chapters 8 and 9 discuss controls and policies that can help you preserve and secure available cash when you need it and avoid the pitfalls of rapid expansion. Clearly, a well-designed, functioning accounting system that tells you what you need to know when you need it is critical to all aspects of the business.

Yet, many owner-managers regard the accounting function and data as "necessary evils"—and pretty boring at that. They leave "the numbers" and the internal controls to the "back-of-fice" people and the accountant. "Just show me the sales figures, the bottom line, and anything else you think is important," they say.

Eventually, however, they understand that they have overestimated the complexity of a good, workable system and underestimated its contribution to their management performance.

When an effective accounting system is in place and functioning efficiently, you are well on your way not only to understanding what's going on in the firm and controlling your scarce cash and other assets, but also to avoiding dangerous run-ins with the tax authorities. Further, you will have clean, professionally prepared books that depict to bankers and investors the firm's true status and value.

Although most basic accounting terms used in this and other chapters are defined as we move along, a glossary of some key terms is provided at the end of the chapter.

Reasons Accounting Function Is Neglected

Setting up an accounting system that can serve as a valuable management tool is the joint responsibility of the owner-manager and the accountant. But sometimes, for whatever reasons, owner-managers actively ignore the accountant and establish minimal, improvised, and joyously amateurish books of their own. At an extreme is the old lemonade stand system: A cigar box for cash and the back of an envelope for expenditures. Only barely refined, it is the system used by a number of small companies, especially start-ups.

More typically, however, owner-managers fail to appreciate the functions and process of an effective accounting system. They are not so much disdainful as simply insensitive to what they neither know well or feel comfortable with.

Most owner-managers come to the small business world with an ignorance of and a subtle emotional aversion to the numbers game. Their backgrounds are usually in the product and service or marketing and selling areas. The accounting and controls functions are regarded as nonproductive.

Many of these owner-managers assume, too, that they are so intimately involved with the business and so close to its daily operations that there is little of importance they can learn from, or do with, the numbers. But the truth is, they find the numbers game intimidating.

Overcoming the Aversion

When Supreme Court Justice Louis Brandeis was a young lawyer he had a number of small business clients. He soon realized that bookkeeping and accounting were "the universal language of business." He resolved to master that language so he could understand the business background of his client's legal problems and provide the kind of counsel for which he later gained a national reputation. It is even more essential for you, as owner-manager, to gain a similar mastery.

In Chapter 2, at Checklist 3, I briefly listed some ways you can familiarize yourself with the vocabulary and functions of the accounting process. That knowledge will take you far in overcoming any distaste or lack of familiarity you have for the numbers. Once you've eliminated the mystery and ignorance, you will probably find that there is little more to accounting than some organization and simple arithmetic and that your acquired knowledge and ease with the numbers can contribute mightily to taking control of your business in an area where the consequences of neglect can be fatal.

You can save yourself much time and confusion by reading a book or two on accounting and bookkeeping early in your small business experience. One excellent and accessible work is Benjamin Graham's and Charles McGolrick's *The Interpretation of Financial Statements*. In addition to helping you "interpret" the numbers, it lays out basic accounting vocabulary and methods in simple, clear language. The sooner you absorb the fundamental terms and processes, the more likely you are to be aware of the vital uses of the accounting function.

You will find it helpful, too, to familiarize yourself with the fundamentals of bookkeeping technique. Keeping the books is an in-house task, and if you understand what is involved you will demystify the process and be a step closer to mastering the management tools and information at your disposal. *Bookkeeping and Accounting* by Joel L. Lerner is very good on the nuts and bolts, without being overly technical or complex.

Inadequate Accountants

By the end of this chapter, it should be very clear how invaluable the contributions of a really good accountant are, assuming you lack years of small business management experience. Checklist 15 gives a brief summary of the ways good small business accountants can help you succeed in your business.

As in any profession, however, there are second-rate or irresponsible accountants who have little intention or capabil-

CHECKLIST 15 How a Good Accountant Contributes to Your Business

---

A good accountant will:

1. Help set up an appropriate accounting system and show you how to make the most of it;
2. Help organize and supervise in-house staff in the keeping of books to avoid unwitting chaos;
3. Provide timely, accurate, and useful financial statements so you can understand what's going on;
4. Make sure appropriate financial controls are in place so you don't squander cash and other assets;
5. Help detect theft before it cripples the business;
6. Prepare accurate and timely tax returns that give you full advantage of all legitimate savings and help in advance with both business and personal tax planning;
7. Provide, as an experienced hand in small business operating problems, valuable advice on running the business.

---

ity of providing the kind of service that small business clients need and deserve. Be aware of some of the problems.

1. *Many small business accountants have a large number of clients and only a limited number of hours each month for your business.* They may pop in a few hours each month, collect the raw numbers, take them back to their offices, and then, in a two-step process, "post the general ledger" and produce the income and balance sheet statements (the "financials"). At year's end they prepare the business's tax returns, and, if agreed, they will file other ongoing monthly or quarterly tax reports. If the firm is hit with an audit or tax assessment for a past year, the accountant will intervene with the authorities, but that's about it.

2. *A number of accountants don't really believe in the efficacy of financial statements as a management tool, whatever they may say.* The financial statements they prepare may include significant errors or deceptions perpetrated by your

in-house staff. With appropriate diligence, those would have been identified and corrected. Furthermore, the financials may be delivered so late they are mere curiosity items.

Often, they are not organized to provide the information you really need to manage your particular business, but instead contain general categories of numbers that obscure the underlying and significant business phenomena. Some accountants produce canned, computerized formats that are applied to all their clients' businesses, whether hairdresser or auto parts manufacturer. Or, they may provide only an income statement, omitting the equally useful balance sheet statement.

The financial information you need to manage your business will be reviewed later in this chapter. But bear in mind that your accountant is not performing even his minimum responsibility if he fails to provide timely, accurate, and useful numerical information in the financial statements. And if you don't know exactly what's going on and where your money is going, there will be a lot of unpleasant difficulties ahead. The numbers are only a start, but you can't manage without them.

3. *Many accountants are too little concerned with the adequacy of their clients' accounting systems and the effectiveness of the staffs who work with them.* Their view seems to be that the bookkeeping is entirely your department and if "garbage in produces garbage out," that is your problem. It is your problem, but one that calls for considerable help.

4. *Few small business accountants have the interest or inclination to help establish basic accounting controls based on the numbers.* Cash management, inventory, payables, receivables, cost controls, and so on—they may regard none of this as part of their function, whatever they may have agreed to before you hired them. Further, many don't have time for, or don't like, the operations side of the business. If that is also the underlying attitude of the owner-manager, the firm runs a double risk of sooner or later disappearing in a bog of financial and administrative disorder.

5. *Similarly, while an experienced accountant can be an*

invaluable source of practical business advice, not many actively make practical operating and financial recommendations. Either they haven't had the time or bothered to learn the businesses, needs, and problems of their clients, or they are afraid of losing an account by pointing out, even tactfully, the follies and ignorance of the owner-manager.

6. *Many small business accountants do not provide truly professional tax preparation or informed and reflective tax planning.* Those omissions can affect both the firm and the owner-manager's family, since the accountant invariably prepares both business and personal returns. Careful and considered planning requires not only a thorough knowledge of both business and individual tax law, but likewise a sure understanding of both the business's affairs and needs and those of the owner-manager and her family.

Tax problems may be given short shrift. Assessments by tax agencies for back taxes may not be researched properly or dealt with on a timely basis. Tax problems may not be presented or defended persuasively and effectively before the relevant agencies. Negligence such as this has cost many an owner-manager his business.

Unquestionably, good small business accountants are indispensable. Their contributions to the health and vitality of the firm are endless—and you may take them for granted. But a mediocre, careless accountant, lacking the time or inclination to go beyond the perfunctory, is a menace to your business. The direct or indirect monetary damage he can inflict is often a huge multiple of the fees you pay him.

Hiring and Using a First-Rate Accountant

Owner-managers will probably work with an alarming number of professionals—an architect, a lawyer, a banker, and so on. At any given time, all of them are important to the firm. But for small businesses owned and managed by persons with little or no accounting, financial, and tax background, the choice of an outstanding accountant will dwarf the selection of any other professional in terms of long-term effect on the business. That is particularly true at the start of the firm's activities.

The choice of an accountant is one of the most decisive appointments you will make. The quality of that choice is often a direct or indirect determinant of your firm's success or failure. If the accountant you wish to hire charges a few hundred dollars a month more than other candidates, hire him anyway. A really good accountant will save you the difference many times over. Just as you wouldn't economize in the choice of a physician, you shouldn't economize in your choice of an accountant.

As we saw in Chapter 6, the first requirement for hiring effectively is to identify the needs of your firm.

Locating Several Candidates

Checklist 16 sets out some considerations that should help you in narrowing the search for an accountant.

CHECKLIST 16 Finding the Right Accountant

---

1. *Hire an Outside Accountant on Retainer*
   a. You don't need a full-time accountant until your sales reach several million dollars a year.
   b. Independent accountants serve as a check on the accuracy and integrity of the in-house operations and staff.
2. *Hire a Certified Public Accountant (CPA)*
   a. CPAs generally are the best qualified accountants—they have passed a rigorous examination and are publicly licenced by a professional board of accounting peers.
   b. Only CPAs can provide third-party investors—venture capitalists, bankers, private investors—with "audited financials."
3. *Hire a Small Accounting Firm*
   a. Large or "Big Eight" firms only make sense if your firm is highly specialized

or publicly regulated and narrow commercial and tax expertise is required (a real estate development firm, for example).

CHECKLIST 16 Finding the Right Accountant (*Continued*)

---

    b. Otherwise, a small firm is generally a more promising source for a small business because:

        (i)   It probably has more small business experience;

        (ii) There is a better chance of a continuing professional relation with the same accountant;

        (iii) The fees are usually substantially lower;

        (iv) Smaller firms are less likely to make a heavy pitch for extraneous or cumbersome "extras."

4. *Look for Prior Experience with Small Business Clients*

    a. Accounting needs, financial and operating problems of small businesses are substantially different from those of large ones; the CPA should have both knowledge of and a feel for those needs.

    b. You want someone who *likes* small businesses.

    c. It helps, but usually isn't decisive, if the CPA has prior experience in your particular area of business: A top CPA can learn the peculiarities of your field relatively quickly and is good whatever the field.

5. *Get Personal Recommendations*

    a. Personal recommendations are the most practical and usually the best sources for locating particular CPA candidates.

    b. Ask fellow owner-managers, your lawyer, banker, insurance broker, friends for recommendations.

    c. Find out the exact basis for the recommendations:

        (i)   Integrity;

        (ii) Professionalism, competence;

        (iii) Small business experience.

    d. Be careful that a recommendation isn't based on limited contact, where work done was on a special one-shot project or was limited exclusively to tax services.

    e. Find out:

        (i)   How long the CPA has worked for your source;

        (ii) What specific work was performed and why it was good;

        (iii) How well the CPA understood the client's needs;

        (iv) Whether the CPA was involved in internal controls and gave advice on operating problems;

Interviewing the Candidates

Checklist 17 contains questions to ask the various candidates. As I suggested in Chapter 6, though, interviewing candidates for any position is as much a matter of chemistry and feel as it is a precise and objective exercise.

So much depends not only on the answers to your questions, but your own intellectual and emotional responses to the candidate's answers.

For example, is the candidate intellectually and professionally competent?

1. Did you feel the CPA was sharp, to the point, quick to focus on an issue and responsive to that issue?
2. Informed?

CHECKLIST 17 Interviewing Accountant Candidates: Some Questions to Ask

---

Ask about:

1. *Background, technical interests, and expertise*
   a. Does the candidate have a specialty?
   b. Is he/she a member of the American Institute of CPAs' section on close-held companies?
   c. How does he/she stay abreast of developments in the tax field?
   d. Ask one or two technical questions relevant to your business to get a feel for the candidate's knowledge and capacity for clear thinking, for example:
      (i) What kind of inventory system should your company use?
      (ii) Should your company be a "Sub (S) Company" (the corporation's profits and losses are passed directly to the owners, avoiding double taxation)?
2. *Clients*
   a. How many?
   b. How much time the candidate devotes to each; how much time he/she spends with the owner-managers themselves.
   c. What kinds of clients—predominately small businesses? If so, what fields of business?
   d. Services he/she performs for them.
3. *Views regarding a CPA's scope of responsibilities to a small business client*

CHECKLIST 17 Interviewing Accountant Candidates: Some Questions to Ask (*Continued*)

4. *Specific views regarding the CPA's responsibilities or opinions regarding:*
   a. Establishment of an appropriate accounting system;
   b. A suitable accounting system for a small business like yours;
   c. Supervision of in-house employees who work with the system;
   d. Which financials should be provided;
   e. How regularly financials should be delivered and how soon after end of period reported;
   f. Internal financial controls—working capital, theft prevention;
   g. Cash management, cash flow preparation, and analysis;
   h. Tax services;
   i. General business advice, CPA's obligation to disagree with dangerous or unworkable policies/practices.
5. *Where a company like yours is likely to get in trouble:* What is the CPA's responsibility for preventative measures? (In the words of one owner-manager, if manure hits the fan, you want some of it distributed to the CPA.)

Also ask about:

6. *Who in the accounting firm will do the actual work:*
   a. The candidate?
   b. Someone else?
7. *How many hours per month* he/she supposes are necessary for your account
8. *The fees*—be specific:
   a. A monthly/annual retainer? How much?
   b. What does this include?
   c. What specific services are not included and how much is charged for them. For example:
      (i)   Annual tax preparation;
      (ii) Back tax problems with tax agencies;
      (iii) Periodic tax compliance reporting;
      (iv) Detailed advice about establishment and administration of internal controls.
9. *References*
   a. Try to get a list of his/her clients so you can call them randomly.
   b. Ask the same questions about references you asked of persons who recommended the accountant [see Checklist 13, (5)(c-e)].

3. Precise and careful?
4. Responsible?
5. Did you feel comfortable with the candidate's definition of his or her services and responsibility to the firm?
6. Or, was the CPA rambling, evasive, and good with the shovel?

How is the chemistry?

1. Did you feel comfortable with the candidate as a person?
2. Did he or she strike you as quietly assured?
3. Did you understand what the candidate said or were you left with a fuzzy sense you wouldn't be able to paraphrase what you heard?

Ultimately, however, you will have to depend on your own inner sense that the candidate is "right" or that, on the contrary, you would be making a mistake in hiring the CPA, even if you can't precisely say why. Those nagging, won't-go-away doubts must be respected.

Appendix 1, at the end of this chapter, contains Checklist 18. It can be utilized in drafting a Letter of Engagement with the CPA, detailing exactly the commitments of both you and the CPA. This will also serve to remind you of the basic elements of an effective accounting system.

You can, of course, terminate the relationship if you believe the CPA's work is inadequate. It is not easy or convenient to change accountants, but it is better done before the chickens come home to roost. Few problems can be as costly and threatening to the small business as an indifferent and careless accountant.

Sooner or later, slapdash mediocrity will not only encroach on your valuable time and erode your good nature with worry, frustration, and anger but will also endanger you and your firm financially.

An Appropriate Accounting System

A "good" accounting system is whatever the particular business needs and not what any other business needs or thinks it needs. It's a little like Abraham Lincoln's response to the question, "How long should a man's legs be?" "Long enough to reach the floor," he replied.

Therefore, soon after retaining a new CPA, you should have an extended discussion to determine what you need—the specific accounting information and financial controls to help you understand the business and safeguard and use your assets productively.

You should brief the CPA on the history, operations, financial status, and problems of the business. Describe your personal financial condition and your sources, if any, of future investment capital or emergency funds. Let the CPA know what data and controls you think you need to manage the company.

A hands-on CPA will, in turn, have a number of questions for you. If yours is an established firm, the CPA will want to see the books, the financial statements and tax files, and whatever controls are already in place for cash, inventory, payables, receivables, as well as security measures. He or she will review your insurance policies and the organization of your files to assure necessary records and papers are retained for tax purposes. The CPA will meet with the bookkeeper or internal accountant to discuss their work and capabilities.

Jointly, you and the CPA should then determine what you need in a cost-effective accounting system so you will get the reliable, timely, useful information and accounting controls you require to manage the business. Small firms don't need and can't afford the complex systems and accounting exotica found in big organizations. You shouldn't get data you don't need and don't have time to digest. And you shouldn't spend two dollars to save one.

The basic requirements of an appropriate accounting system relate to the following matters, which we will now take up one by one.

1. Books and records
2. Internal staffing needs
3. The question of whether and when to automate the system

4. Financial statements
5. Internal controls
6. Taxes

The Basic Books and Records

One owner-manager makes the following comment: "We kept books and financial statements from Day One. You have to know where your money goes. Some of the companies that have gone out of business essentially kept their bills and invoices and everything else in one big box. You need a structure to keep control of the details while you're doing something else."

It is one of the CPA's first jobs to establish or approve that basic "structure." The structure consists of certain basic books and ledgers. There are prime journals, or "books of original entry," for total sales and cash receipts and for cash disbursements and check disbursements. In addition, a company normally maintains subsidiary books or ledgers for such transactions as capital purchases, accounts receivable, accounts payable, and the payroll. Together, these books record in detail the increases and decreases in the business's assets and liabilities and its income, expenses, and capital. The expenses are posted on the basis of code numbers established in a "chart of accounts." Which of these various journals and ledgers are needed and how they are to be kept are decisions made by the CPA and should be explained to you.

In addition, there is always a "general ledger." It is the keystone of the system. The general ledger is a composite of all the accounts, a record of all the company's financial transactions in summary form. It forms the basis for the financial statements. If you haven't done so already, take a close look at your firm's books or examples of such records in one of the counting or bookkeeping texts referred to earlier in this chapter.

The basic books and records also include the financial control procedures and records that the CPA can help install, such as the inventory control system. The accounting system may also include whatever other systematic and organized compilations of numerical information are jointly deemed desirable for management purposes.

Managing Your Money Tip

You can use Managing Your Money to manage your business' finances. Managing Your Money is suitable for self-employeds, doctors, dentists, and salespersons.

- Money can handle accounts payable and receivable, with aging. It will print customized invoices, checks, and sum everything to tax categories in Schedule C for your small business.

- You can use the Quick List transactions feature to pay employees and suppliers each week (or other period you choose). Whenever you want, you'll be able to call up summaries of your expenditures by budget category or employee. This will make your accountant's job easier and faster.) You can even get the kinds of cash flow projections that can keep a small business from unexpected shortfalls that put them entirely at the mercy of their bank. In fact, MYM will allow you to generate frequent reports and balance sheets to keep your banker happy. (Send them monthly and he'll figure you're the most organized debtor he has. Print a graph or two and he'll have you borrowing at two under prime, just like GE.)

In-House Staff

The CPA will organize or construct the essential structure, but it will have to be kept current and administered by either you or one or more in-house employees, depending on the size and needs of your company. If the business is a classic "out-of-a-garage" operation, you will probably keep the records yourself. You must be well advised and supervised by the CPA lest you lose interest or generally ignore important requirements or pieces of the system. If you do, you will have an awful mess on your hands before long.

When the company grows beyond embryo size, it is likely that the books will be maintained by some other employee, who may spend 5 to 10 hours a week on them, depending on the needs of the firm. The CPA should have direct responsibility for training and supervising this employee and reporting to you problems or deficiencies that are beyond a CPA's control. You in turn have a responsibility to secure the CPA's assurances on this matter. Otherwise, months later you may find yourself in the aggravating position of hearing the CPA evade responsibility for some costly mess by saying in effect, "How do you expect me to get my job done when the books you keep down there are pieces of junk and the work I get is invariably late?" In this situation, both the owner-manager and the CPA are "to blame," but remember that only the owner-manager suffers the consequences.

As the firm grows, it will need to hire a trained bookkeeper. Frequently, this person will be employed part-time and eventually will take on full-time responsibilities. It depends on the particular firm, of course, but many companies employ a part-time bookkeeper when annual sales reach roughly $300,000 to $500,000. Generally, a full-time bookkeeper is useful after about $1 million in sales.

Whatever the hours or responsibilities, don't hire an untrained bookkeeper. As I noted in Chapter 6, cheap is expensive. You may save some weekly payroll expenses if you use one of the untrained employees in your firm to keep the books, but you are likely to deeply regret that move later on. Hire someone with experience, training, and maturity. As the firm grows and the paperwork expands, you simply cannot afford someone who is inexperienced and lacks the careful and patient temperament of a valuable bookkeeper.

Typically, the bookkeeper does at least the following:

1. Posts the journal entries
2. Reviews and processes the firm's payables so you don't have to review their accuracy
3. Keeps on top of the accounts receivable
4. Either prepares the payroll or forwards the necessary data to a payroll service
5. Prepares the various periodic tax and other statutory reports

A "full-charge" bookkeeper—one who has had considerable experience with all aspects of the accounting system—will also post the general ledger at the end of the month.

As the company continues to grow, it normally hires an in-house accountant who is trained to perform a heavier and more sophisticated workload than a bookkeeper. With further growth, a comptroller or financial director is hired. These latter positions call for considerable planning, analysis, and judgment, as well as a knowledge of capital markets not normally associated with internal accountants.

Automation

There is little question that the blessings of the computer can benefit almost all small businesses. There is a real danger, though, that many owner-managers will be oversold on the magic and benefits of prematurely automating the entire accounting system. The greater the size and complexity of the business, the greater the benefits of full-scale automation in relation to the costs. Where the critical point comes is hard to say in the abstract, but $500,000 to $1.5 million in sales per year probably defines the boundaries, depending on the firm.

Prior to that point, it is usually wise to rely on a basic manual system and utilize certain outside computerized services or internal "subsets" of computer programs. For example:

1. An outside payroll service is a very cost-effective substitute for preparing the weekly payroll checks and making

the calculations for gross compensation less social security and other employee benefit withholdings.

2. Many retailers find automated point-of-sales systems extremely useful and cost-effective in controlling their inventories and in providing detailed daily information about what is selling and who is selling it.

3. Many small firms have successfully computerized the accounts receivable and billing procedures.

In the survival and early growth stages of your business, a manual system is appropriate because it delivers what you need and is cost-effective in relation to a fully automated system. As your business grows and the paperwork increases, your CPA can show you or your staff how to use a "one-write-system" to record several bookkeeping transactions in one uniform manual exercise. This will allow you to avoid the difficulties in converting to a fully automated system until it really makes good sense.

Here are some of the problems in adopting an automated system from the start or converting from a manual to a full-scale automated accounting system.

1. The capital costs are substantial.

2. Installation itself can be problem-ridden, laborious and costly.
   a. You must code the system correctly before it functions.
   b. Then you must test and debug the system.
   c. You must train your personnel to operate it.
   d. If your employees are not experienced or fully trained, human error is inevitable, and the consequences of those errors will likely become your number one immediate business problem.

3. Finding the right software package is difficult. The software may not produce the information you need in the form you need it. It may provide excess data in some areas and insufficient data in others.

4. If you modify or "tamper" with the software, you lose the benefits of the manufacturer's warranty and services.

If you are planning on rapid expansion of the firm beyond the critical size and complexity mentioned above, proceed with great care. Install the automated system before the advent of a surge of growth, while there is time to debug it and assure that the staff is well trained to operate it. Otherwise, both the growth and the new system may overwhelm you.

Managing Your Money Tip

> As you've seen, Managing Your Money is quite suitable to handle the bookkeeping needs of many smaller businesses. If you need more versatile software, consider Great American Software's One Write Plus. This bestselling program is a complete one-write accounting system that is powerful, easy-to-use, and inexpensive. Perhaps best of all, One Write Plus avoids almost all of the problems of automated accounting named in points 1, 2, and 3, above. To order, call MECA at 203-256-5000.

Even if you feel at ease with computers, it is well to seek a variety of opinions regarding the specific needs of your business. Beware of salesmen's pitches for the obvious reason that they are biased. Your CPA may be a good source of advice, but look for a broader spectrum of opinion. Owner-managers of businesses similar to yours are a good source, but they may not acknowledge all the particular problems they have encountered, and they are not in a good position to make comparative analyses of alternative systems.

One way to begin is to check with the trade association for your business and get the names of programs widely used in your field. You can also review the technical references at a large retail computer store. They will contain both the pros and cons for a variety of software packages. Narrow your list down to five or six programs and ask for the names of some of the purchaser-users of those programs. Give them a call and ask if they are satisfied and why. Ask them, too, what support they have received from the manufacturers and what the problems are.

Exercise a muscular skepticism and ask "dumb" questions. You may discover, for example, if you own a wine bar and stock over a hundred beverages, that the expensive inventory control system proposed to you breaks down at precisely the point and for the same reason your manual system is vulnerable. Whatever the system, it is no better than the daily count of bottles at the bar itself and a comparison of those counts against the specific sales figures of the day, sale by sale, beverage by beverage. Since the computer is incapable of this step, and since the software program is therefore no more reliable than your present manual procedures, you would be throwing good money away for a relatively useless program.

The issue is always one of cost-effectiveness: Does the automated system produce sufficient benefits to make it worth the costs, the time, and the risks? The more informed opinions you seek and the more questions you ask, the more secure will be your final choice. A book to consult is Jack Bender's *A Layman's Guide to Installing a Small Business Computer.*

The Financial Statements

The CPA reviews the accuracy of the company's books and then prepares the financial statements. These statements should always include the "income" or "profit and loss" statement and the "balance sheet." They may include, as needed, a "source and application of funds" statement (the source of your cash and where it was expended) and a cash flow projection.

The financial statements are frontline sources for understanding and managing your business. They provide signals of problems and changes in the business that indicate that follow-up action is required. If you have a portfolio of stock market investments, you probably check the financial papers each day to see how they are doing. Yet many owner-managers only look at their own financial data every two or three months. Think of your own company as a highly volatile and risky growth investment that requires careful and constant monitoring. How you go about this is reviewed in detail in Chapter 10.

To help you understand the business, the financials must be:

1. Timely;
2. Consistent;
3. Organized so the numerical data is useful.

1. *Timely*. One venture capitalist comments, "A company behind in its financials by two or three months is a firm that lacks a handle on its business. It may be out of control. It is not being managed." Southern Methodist University's Caruth Institute of Owner-Managed Business found that the average bankrupt small business had not had financial statements for seven months at the time of its demise.

The CPA should submit financials no later than three weeks following the end of the prior month. Even then, a trouble area reflected in one of the financial statements (for example, a cost of goods sold problem) may have been underway up to six or seven weeks earlier. The phenomena behind any disturbing numerical data must be confronted as soon as possible, before a brush fire gets out of control.

Look at it this way. If an income statement for the month of May is received June 22 and shows that your firm's cost of goods sold are up substantially, you will not be able to analyze the situation and implement a remedial program before late June or early July. The problem may already be eight weeks old, yet you won't get the first indeterminate results of your remedial actions until the July statements, received August 22. You may not know with confidence that the corrective action was successful until September 22. Now, if the financials are consistently received two months later than necessary, this uncertainty is stretched out to November 22, about 26 weeks after the initial emergence of the problem. A lot of damage can occur in that time if the first-shot diagnosis and corrective program are not on target.

Managing Your Money Tip

> Managing Your Money is excellent for reporting your net worth. MYM will print an up-to-date balance sheet in any one of three styles and, if you have a graphics card, bake pie charts at each level of detail. You won't have to reenter any data MYM can extract from elsewhere. All of that can be summoned with a single keystroke—F6.
>
> To see your net worth report, select Net Worth from the main menu. To print a net worth report, Select Your Net Worth from the Net Worth submenu. Press F4, and select the style of report (bank-style, corporate, etc.). Then press F10, and select whether you want to display the report on your screen, or print a copy on your printer. Then press F10 again. For more information on this menu selection, press F1 for help.

2. *Consistent.* One of the uses of the financials is to allow you to compare the performance of the firm in one month with prior months so you know where the changes are. That means each month's results must be calculated on the same basis, or you will have to reconstruct the statements yourself to find out how they compare.

Let's suppose your CPA uses the "accrual" method of accounting and matches expenses with the income they produce in the same month they are incurred, whether or not actual sales receipts or payments for the expenses are made that month. The CPA should stick with this method consistently. If, for example, the CPA records a large, prepaid semiannual insurance premium in the month you paid it rather than amortizing it (spreading it equally over six months), your income statements win seem out of whack until you unbundle them and put the apples back with the apples and the pears with the pears.

3. *Useful.* You should work closely with the CPA to structure the income statements so that they provide you with the numerical data you need in a useful, readable format.

Significant categories of data should be grouped together and segregated from different kinds of data. When the CPA uses the same format for all clients, you will not get the numerical breakdowns that are relevant to your business. For example, a canned format may lump all "marketing" expenses in one line item. This may be acceptable if you have few marketing expenses. But if you spend considerable funds on sales commissions, sales literature, advertising, and other promotional efforts, you need breakdowns on these.

It may be the case that your "Repair and Maintenance" (R & M) expenses are a significant factor in your business and that in-house labor contributes to a substantial portion of those R & M expenses. You can't keep track of the R & M, however, if the related labor expenses are included in your overall payroll expenses. The situation is further confused if the CPA includes substantial equipment rentals under R & M, when those expenses are best understood in isolation. Chapter 10 discusses the kinds of breakdowns of numerical data that will help you understand what's going on.

Similarly, as the firm grows, it will be useful for you as an active manager to have separate breakdowns of income and expenses for substantially different major product groups, especially if those products incur different magnitudes of expenses. You may need a multicolumn income statement with, for example, one vertical column for Product(s) A, another for Product(s) B, and a third column representing the consolidated results of the firm.

Here's a simple example of why you usually need separate allocations of income and expenses for distinctly dissimilar activities: Suppose a small business has two separate product lines and makes an annual profit of $50,000. That may be the significant point for the tax collector. For the active owner-manager, though, what is truly significant is that one of the product lines yields a profit of $100,000, while the other yields a loss of $50,000. If the income and expenses of the two product lines were integrated, the owner-manager would never perceive that one product line was a great success and the other a major problem. It is essential to break out the specific expense items that contribute to the $50,000 loss before corrective action can be undertaken. But you have to work closely with the CPA to determine exactly how best to allocate the various expenses—especially the labor and overhead—to the separate products.

Internal/Financial Controls

Make sure that both you and the CPA give close joint attention to the accounting controls you need to generate more cash and manage your assets productively. The decisive controls in a small business relate to:

1. Cash;
2. Inventory;
3. Accounts receivable;
4. Accounts payable;
5. Theft.

Since these controls are all essential conditions of effective cash management, they are dealt with in detail in the next chapter.

Taxes

A CPA who is weak or inattentive in the tax field can leave you and your firm dead in the water, and you may never know the cause unless someone more observant shows you the alternative tax options or tax requirements that were unheeded or ignored. Three, four, or five years after the allegedly taxable events, you may find yourself spending hours and hours a week dealing with ancient tax matters. The tax authorities are like wolves at the door once they have caught the scent of vulnerability. No matter how honest your reporting, indifferent and shoddy tax counsel and preparation can tear apart the business.

Good CPAs understand both your firm's and your personal financial condition. They know the various tax rules and regulations sufficiently well to plan your business and personal affairs to be consistent with tax opportunities. If you are not well served in this area, you will be astonished to find the number of perfectly legitimate tax savings you and the firm may be entitled to.

The CPA as tax planner can determine:

1. The proper legal organization of the business;
2. The best ways of contributing capital to the firm;
3. The best alternatives for financing the business;
4. The best ways to distribute profits;
5. When to accelerate or postpone income;
6. When and how to incur expenses;
7. The best methods for applying depreciation and valuing inventory.

Tax planning is no place to cut corners with an indifferent CPA.

The CPA must also know and advise you which periodic taxes are owed to various city, state, and federal tax authorities. That includes state sales taxes, the seemingly endless employee benefit taxes, as well as social security withholdings for yourself, property taxes, and so forth. The CPA should have primary responsibility for:

1. Preparing the tax returns or showing you how to prepare them;
2. Telling you when to pay them;
3. Reviewing and defending against assessments for back taxes.

Handling these tax requirements should quickly become a part of your firm's administrative routine.

However, if you are not aware of tax requirements or for any other reason fail to pay taxes promptly and accurately, it can seriously upset your business several years down the line. Assessments, including huge penalties and interest charges, will be issued.

Managing Your Money Tip

> The Tax submenu allows you to track the tax position of your business. Schedule C will estimate the taxable income or loss form your business. To print a report, just press F4 and follow the instructions.

Assessments for past taxes are bound to be levied against a small business at some time. Some are correct, but some are ill-founded. A dedicated and tactically skilled CPA can be decisive in successfully defending against such claims. But if the CPA fails to take prompt action in researching and defending against an assessment, the matter may drag along inconclusively for several years. If the firm turns out to owe the back taxes, penalties and interest may double the amount due, and the business may find itself in an awful cash emergency. Worse occurs when the owner-manager or the CPA casually disregards official notices to pay and discovers one morning that the tax collectors have placed a lien on the firm's bank account or boarded up the business.

A hands-on CPA will also advise you which records you should retain in your files and for how long, for tax audit purposes.

The point is that a first-rate CPA can save you thousands and thousands of tax dollars by careful and knowledgeable attention to your affairs. A poor one can cost you your business.

The general lesson—one better learned sooner than later—is the necessity of hiring CPAs who will systematically familiarize themselves with the operations and financial situations of their clients and diligently apply their wide expertise to helping the clients make a go of their ventures. Your obligations as owner-manager are:

1. To hire such a CPA;
2. To work closely with the CPA to determine jointly which accounting tools and data you need to understand and control your firm;
3. To apply those tools and data to manage the firm effectively.

APPENDIX
I

CPA ENGAGEMENT LETTER

Before the CPA is formally retained, it is customary for both the CPA and the business to sign an "Engagement Letter" setting out the mutual expectations of the parties. This "letter" is useful in making explicit jointly shared expectations and undertakings so that there can be no after-the-fact misunderstandings about who is to perform specific work tasks.

Checklist 18 outlines some key responsibilities that can be included in the engagement letter.

CHECKLIST 18 Responsibilities, Functions, Assistance of a CPA

---

1. In cooperation with owner-manager and in-house staff, overall responsibility for contribution and effectiveness of accounting function, based on ongoing familiarity with needs and activities of the business.
2. Preparation of monthly financial statements:
    a. Income and balance sheet statements;
    b. Cash flow projections and source and application of funds statements as needed;
    c. (a) and (b) above to be delivered no later than third week of each month;
    d. Financials to be based on appropriate review of accuracy and integrity of the company's books.
3. Active advice and assistance regarding:
    a. Establishment and maintenance of in-house accounting books;
    b. Adequacy of overall accounting "system";
    c. Hiring, training, supervision, and evaluation of in-house personnel working on accounting matters;
    d. Establishment and supervision of financial controls, as needed, including those related to:
        (i)   Cash
        (ii) Theft
        (iii) Inventory
        (iv) Purchasing and payment procedures
        (v)   Accounts receivable and payable policies and procedures
        (vi) Payroll procedures
    e. Insurance coverage;
    f. Audits or spot audits as appropriate;

g. Personal and company tax planning and preparation;

CHECKLIST 18 Responsibilities, Functions, Assistance of a CPA (*Continued*)

---

h. Periodic compliance reporting, tax and other;
i. Defense against tax assessments;
j. Active recommendations to owner-manager regarding:
  (i) Increased effectiveness of accounting function and owner-manager's related responsibilities
  (ii) Cost reduction
  (iii) Forecasts or projections
  (iv) Computer systems
  (v) Productivity improvement
  (vi) Financing
  (vii) Business planning
  (viii) Benefits/compensation
4. Mutual understanding between owner-manager and CPA about specific responsibilities for posting of general ledger, reconciliation of bank statements, and any other accounting matters not always performed by a CPA.
5. Statement of fees, hours.
6. Allocation of duties between CPA and others in CPA's firm—provided that CPA has prime responsibility to client for all matters listed above.

APPENDIX
II

GLOSSARY OF KEY
ACCOUNTING TERMS

Most accounting primers for managers include a far more complete glossary—consult one of them for additional definitions.

ACCOUNTANT. A person who prepares and maintains the financial records; an accountant has received more training than a bookkeeper and has a far larger scope of responsibility (for example, the accountant prepares the financial statements on the basis of the accounting books kept by the bookkeeper). (See CPA.)

ACCOUNTING CONTROLS. Organized numerical information which allows a manager to keep track of and control a company's current assets; for example, an "inventory control system." Also referred to as "internal" or "financial" controls.

ACCOUNTING SYSTEM. Refers to the entirety of the process whereby a business keeps track of all its financial transactions and establishes financial controls.

ACCOUNTS PAYABLE. Amounts owed by a company to outside suppliers. They are part of a firm's "current liabilities."

ACCOUNTS RECEIVABLE. Amounts owed to a company by its customers. They are part of a firm's "current assets." (See "Aging.")

ACCRUAL(S). Refers to: (1) accrual method of accounting, whereby revenues and expenses are matched and recorded at the time a transaction occurs, not when cash is exchanged; (2) accrued expenses which are charged against current earnings even if not yet paid.

AGING. A process that classifies accounts receivable by age. Accounts receivable long overdue are considered "aged" and not worth their book value.

AMORTIZE. To charge a fixed portion of an expenditure against earnings over a period of time. For example, a $600 prepaid insurance premium is charged at $100 per month for six months.

BALANCE SHEET. A statement of a company's assets, liabilities, and capital at a specific time. Assets equal liabilities plus capital.

BOOKKEEPER. A person who keeps the accounting books or the records of financial transactions.

BOOKS. A company's records of financial transactions.

BREAK-EVEN. The point where sales revenues equal expenses. Break-even analyses show the interrelations between fixed and variable expenses and sales, in determining profit.

CASH. Available, spendable money.

CASH FLOW. The amount of cash generated by a business over a period of time. The difference between total inflows and total outflows of cash; and, hence, not the same as accrual accounting.

CONTROLS. see "Accounting controls."

COST OF GOODS SOLD. The direct cost of all items sold during an accounting period. Usually calculated by taking the opening inventory, plus inventory purchases in the accounting period, minus the closing inventory. It is usually expressed as a percent: the cost of goods in relation to the sales.

CPA. A certified public accountant is a trained accountant who, following a professional examination, has been certified as qualified to perform accounting and auditing of a company's books.

CURRENT ASSETS. Cash or other assets readily converted into cash; generally comprised of cash-on-hand, inventory, and accounts receivable due within one year.

CURRENT LIABILITIES. All obligations which are payable within one year.

DEPRECIATE. To periodically charge against earnings the loss in value of a capital asset over a long-term period. Hence, a machine costing $10,000, with a useful life of ten years, might be depreciated on a straight-line basis at the rate of

$1,000 per year; the $1,000, in turn, would be allocated into 12 monthly portions.

EARNINGS. See "Profit."

EXPENDITURE/EXPENSE. Whereas expenses are costs which are charged against current earnings, they do not necessarily involve related cash disbursements until some future time (see "Accrual"); expenditures represent actual cash outlays, although they may involve no related charge against current earnings.

FINANCIAL CONTROLS. See "Accounting Controls."

FIXED EXPENSES. Those expenses which do not change with different levels of production or sales; for example, the rent (see "Variable Expenses").

INCOME. See "Profit."

INCOME STATEMENT (profit and loss statement). A statement of net profit or loss in a specific accounting period.

INTERNAL CONTROLS. See "Accounting Controls."

LIQUID. Pertaining to available cash or assets readily converted to cash.

OVERHEAD. Usually synonymous with fixed expenses, though does not include certain fixed costs associated with the production or sales (see "Fixed Expenses").

PROFIT. The amount remaining after subtracting expenses from revenues (a "loss" is therefore the excess of expenses over revenues).

RECEIPTS/REVENUES. Pertain to sales; but receipts are the actual cash amounts received by customers; revenues include both receipts and amounts due in the future.

SMALL BUSINESS. There are no really good definitions of "small" businesses. Most have annual sales of less than $5 million, and fewer than 75 employees. The Small Business Administration uses these very ample criteria: manufacturers—fewer than 500 to 1500 employees; wholesalers—fewer than

500 employees; retailers—less than $13.5 million annual sales. Perhaps the best working definition is a functional one. Businesses are small so long as the owner-manager can personally control the entire concern and sheer size has not yet dictated a substantially decentralized management structure.

VARIABLE EXPENSES. Those expenses which change with different levels of production or sales; for example, the cost of goods sold (see "Fixed Expenses").

WORKING CAPITAL. Current assets minus current liabilities, hence, the net current assets. Generally, the cash plus inventory plus accounts receivable (current assets) minus accounts and taxes payable (current liabilities).

CHAPTER
8

MANAGING CASH
AVAILABILITY

The poet did not have small business in mind, but Lord Byron, a consistent debtor, wrote that "Ready money is Aladdin's lamp." And that is the message of this chapter. Cash is king in the small business game.

Survival precedes success. And the one, absolute precondition to survival of your firm is the availability of ready cash when you really need it. Out-of-cash means you are out-of-business.

Many small businesses and most new ones are afflicted by insufficient cash and capital. More than one-third of owner-managers questioned in one survey said that undercapitalization was their biggest problem at the outset of the business. And many small businesses continue to have cash shortages for years thereafter.

A cash crunch can be a symptom of a deeper problem. Often, it is not simply the consequence of an ailing business but a specific case of inadequate cash management. Cash management means control of the business's cash availability, based on an understanding of, and planning for, its timely cash requirements.

Cash management is a make-or-break condition of survival and success in small business. In the words of the famous venture capitalist, Fred Adler, "Happiness is a positive cash flow. Everything else will come later....There is no such thing as an overfinanced company."

Why Cash Is King

Before discussing the specific elements of effective cash management in the small business, let's briefly consider *why* ready cash availability is such a decisive factor in so many small business ventures.

Cash Is Scarce in Small Businesses

Cash shortages are endemic to small businesses; almost all experience a scary cash problem at one time or other. Big businesses, by contrast, are generally cash rich, have access to cash, or can sell valuable assets or portions of the business to generate it. But small businesses have little or no access to traditional capital markets. Nor can they sell a subsidiary or division to raise new funds. The founder of a small business has usually sunk nearly all savings into the new venture and has already put an arm on family and friends, as well. Seldom do bankers come to the rescue: The firm either has no track record or it is not a bankable one. And it is difficult to go to the well a second time to cajole new funds from original investors.

Raising sufficient capital to finance a new venture adequately is hard enough, but there are inevitable start-up losses, as well as the misguided plans and surprises that visit the fledgling firm. Those require additional cash.

Further, you may have to raise additional monies to generate growth. That growth, as we shall see in the next chapter, may in turn require more cash. There never seems to be enough cash.

Big businesses can buy experts to design and implement sophisticated accounting controls and cash management. But seldom can a small business afford such experts. And rare is the owner-manager with substantial sensitivity or experience in using basic cash management tools. An unfortunate irony of small business life is that the smaller the firm, and the more meager its resources, the greater the need to manage the productivity of its scarce financial assets, and the more difficult a job it seems to be. But manage them you must.

Out-of-Cash, Out-of-Business

Cash, or liquidity, is the oil that lubricates the entire business. If the tank runs dry, nothing further can happen unless investors or bankers replenish the flow—at the price, of course, of diluted equity or future debt.

There is a quiet finality about an irreversible negative cash position. It is the most unforgiving of small business insufficiencies. Moreover, it is usually accompanied by some painful "buts" and "but fors": "But we were actually making a profit when we ran out"; or, "But for that unexpected cash crunch, we were on our way and our hopes were high. We just ran out of cash. And that was that."

Behind the Eight Ball

Cash scarcity need not bring a firm to its knees, or few would ever survive. But serious cash shortages will cause some extremely disagreeable and inhibiting problems, especially to a cash-strapped start-up business. Here are some of the common problems.

1. *Confidence and morale are eroded.* Mere survival is the object. "We were so undercapitalized that it was one continual crisis," recalls one owner-manager.

2. *The constant danger, recognized or not, is that a day of reckoning will suddenly arrive.* There is no money to pay the staff; a critical supplier will no longer extend credit and ceases deliveries; the tax collector knocks for the last time, boards the doors, and that's that. It happens all the time. It is simply the suddenness and the finality that stun.

3. *There are no contingency funds* to meet the unpredictable emergencies that seem to haunt upstart businesses.

4. *The business cannot buy time.* It cannot sustain expenditures that could pull it out of an otherwise temporary trough. The shortage of cash robs the owner-manager of the time required to think, act, and talk his way out of difficulties. The business cannot buy time until sales increase sufficiently to cover expenses.

5. *There is little margin for digging in and overcoming mistakes.* Most small businesses are fortunate if they can squirrel away cash reserves to meet the fact-of-life emergencies and to cushion inevitable error and misjudgment. Unlike big businesses, they usually cannot absorb monumental gaffes or carry years of losses to make a go of a shaky venture. Such a policy

in big business is called "bold." But small businesses can be crushed by the loss of a key customer or overly optimistic expansion plans. Unlike many big businesses, they are undone by internal inefficiencies and bloated payrolls.

6. *A cash crunch precludes improvement* and expansion-oriented profit programs. There are no funds for adequate advertising and promotion. The firm cannot afford to properly market a good product. In its haste to get to market, it is incapable of sustaining adequate research and development, engineering, manufacturing, or tooling costs. It cuts corners and skimps on the product; goods or services of inferior quality sour the business's public reputation.

7. *Similarly, the owner-manager is unwilling or unable to assume calculated risks* that are normally essential to generate growth and future stability.

8. *In desperation, the owner-manager may raise prices beyond the market's willingness to pay or slash them to cut-rate levels,* below the level most customers would pay anyway.

9. *The staff is underpaid,* and funds are unavailable to hire quality people in one or two key slots.

10. *Taxes are unpaid,* and penalties and interest are incurred for future months.

11. *The business cannot take sensible volume discounts from suppliers.*

And on and on. Serious cash shortages produce continuous crises, and that is not why you are engaged in a business venture.

Profit Is Not Cash

There are several misconceptions about what cash is and isn't. Above all, you should understand the vital distinction between profit and cash. Many owner-managers believe that simply because a firm is in the black it necessarily has the funds to meet its obligations. That is not correct.

Cash is something tangible, something in hand, and if it is not immediately green, it can be converted to cash pretty quickly. Cash is not merely a promise, like an account receivable. It is readily available. Cash is not just any asset of value, like inventory. It is liquid, meaning that within just a few days it can be converted to actual cash.

You can't pay your bills and meet your obligations with illiquid assets. It takes ready cash. Accounts receivable don't pay bills; inventory doesn't pay bills; neither equipment nor bricks in the wall will pay bills. Only cash.

Obviously, sales themselves don't necessarily yield sufficient cash to meet all the obligations of the business. In the first place, expenses may exceed sales. Furthermore, small businesses are notorious for failing when sales are growing, and the entire next chapter is focused on the peculiar problems of growth, many of which are special cash problems.

It is astonishing to many owner-managers that a great number of small businesses fail even though they are profitable. Profit, to repeat, is not the same as available cash, and the failure to understand the difference can be ruinous.

Look at it this way. "Profit" is an accountant's abstraction, a convenient symmetry whereby a price to be paid by a committed customer ("revenue" or "income") is matched against the commitments made by the firm to effect the sale ("expenses"). In short, profit equals revenues minus the expenses incurred to produce those revenues. But the actual way we transact business does not reflect the accountant's elegant abstractions. Revenues are not the same as cash receipts. Expenses are not the same as actual cash expenditures. They occur at different times.

Vital time gaps usually occur between the transactions in this chronology: (1) the time when a firm expends cash to produce or make available goods or services; (2) the time when a customer orders or buys those goods and services, at which point revenues and related expenses are booked by the accountant; and (3) the time when the customer may actually pay for the goods or services. The expenditures made at (1) are disbursed before the profits are booked at (2). And the profits may be booked well before the firm receives customer payments at (3). *In short, the profits are booked after the expenditures, but before the customers' payments are received. There is an outflow of cash before the corresponding inflow.*

In fact, the cash disbursements for labor, inventory, overhead, and other expenses necessary to produce or provide goods and services may precede by two to three months or more the actual cash receipts in payment for those goods and services, especially when liberal credit terms are extended. For a potentially decisive period of time, there are significant outflows of cash, but no inflows. An accountant's profits may exist, but not the cash necessary to pay the current bills.

A business's disbursements for the purchase of materials and goods must be made out of cash surpluses or must be externally financed. Many, many companies cannot meet current cash needs from either source. There is profit but no cash—a situation that has caused the demise of many a concern.

Profits are often reflected not in increases in the company's "cash-on-hand" but rather in increases in other nonliquid current assets, namely increased accounts receivable or inventory. "Working capital" (the ratio of current assets to current liabilities) will improve, but it won't result in cash to pay the bills. A healthy working capital ratio can be dangerously deceptive when the favorable ratio conceals low cash and high inventory, high accounts receivable, or any other nonliquid current assets, such as prepaid semiannual insurance premiums.

Consider some other ways in which profits may not generate equal amounts of cash available for current operations.

1. *Profits may be reinvested in the business.* This may result in a substantial and sudden decrease in the firm's cash. But that decrease will not be reflected in the ongoing income statements, which simply allocate (amortize or depreciate) the disbursements over 12 or more months. It is frequently argued, moreover, that after-tax profits may be illusory in many young

businesses, since those profits may only barely sustain the ongoing operating needs of the business and are not sufficient for significant repairs and maintenance or adequate for future improvements and expansion. They are most likely not available for distribution to owners.

2. *Similarly, pretax profits do not yield equal amounts of cash.* Obligations for corporate income taxes take a further bite out of the available cash. Receipts allocable to sales taxes, of course, may never be considered a part of available cash.

3. *Profits, too, can be taken right out of the business* and will no longer be available for the firm's cash needs. Obvious examples are: dividends; loans or advances to the owner-manager, other owners, or employees; and loan repayments to creditors.

4. *Theft not only decreases the profits* otherwise available for cash needs *but also reduces available cash* even before the theft is reflected in the income statement.

5. *Profit and positive cash flow over an extended time period—say, three to six months—may not reflect serious cash problems within that time period.* Sales receipts, for example, may be seasonally low at precisely the same time heavy obligations to tax authorities, large suppliers, or the insurance company come due. When the crunch is not anticipated, there is crisis.

Owner-managers frequently do not analyze and plan cash flows and needs until too late. Only then do they understand that the ultimate responsibility for managing cash availability is theirs alone, though they may need considerable help from their accountants in evaluating the cash situation.

One businessman and author, Deaver Brown, says a small business is like a dingy in a squall—one big wave can sink the entire vessel. But successful owner-managers are careful, knowledgeable, and shrewd navigators. They are *managers* as well as entrepreneurs or day-today administrators. One of the areas of the business they *manage* is cash availability. That responsibility starts before the business opens.

Cash Management: Understanding and Planning the Cash Flow

Responsibility for cash management begins with calculated estimates of cash inflows and cash disbursements. Stanford Business School Professor Steven Brandt wrote in *Entrepreneuring*, "If you can't do a cash flow projection with confidence, you don't understand the business you are trying to start. If you won't do a serious cash flow projection that others can critically review, you are kidding yourself about wanting to succeed in the big-league of entrepreneuring." This observation is equally valid for any ongoing business with even a remote cash shortage problem on the horizon. Cash flow analysis and planning is a basic tool of small business management. If you ignore it, you imperil your chances of survival and success.

The term *cash flow* means simply the balance or difference between incoming cash (receipts) and outgoing cash (disbursements or expenditures) at the end of a particular time period. If the entire business were transacted through checking, the cash flow would be the difference between checks deposited and checks written.

The cash game is not so much a matter of magnitudes as it is of timing and balancing the inflows and outflows. What this means is that you must anticipate as accurately as possible your future cash needs, and you must assure yourself that cash will be available to meet those needs on a very timely basis.

Take a look at the cash projection format in Checklist 19. It shows, without the plug-in numbers, what cash inflows and outflows and a subsequent cash position might look like for a typical operating company. The goal, of course, is for the final line, (5), always to be positive. If it isn't, and you have planned in advance, you will have time to take a number of actions, including cutting costs, raising funds to meet the deficit, or extracting cash from nonliquid current assets. Advance planning gives you time to *manage* the situation.

CHECKLIST 19 Cash Flow Projection (format for six months)

	Jan	Feb	Mar	April	May	June
Cash in						
Cash Sales	___	___	___	___	___	___
Credit Receipts	___	___	___	___	___	___
Other	___	___	___	___	___	___
1. TOTAL IN						
Cash out						
Inventory Supplies	___	___	___	___	___	___
Rent	___	___	___	___	___	___
Utilities, Phone	___	___	___	___	___	___
Payroll and Related						
Taxes Administration	___	___	___	___	___	___
Marketing & Sales						
General Supplies and						
Rentals Taxes						
& Licenses	___	___	___	___	___	___
Insurance	___	___	___	___	___	___
Professional	___	___	___	___	___	___
Other Operating Expenses						
Capital Expenses	___	___	___	___	___	___
Loan Repayments						
and Interest	___	___	___	___	___	___
Loans, Advances, Distributions						
to Owners, Others	___	___	___	___	___	___
2. TOTAL OUT						
3. Cash flow for month,						
(1) minus (2)	___	___	___	___	___	___
4. Starting cash position	___	___	___	___	___	___
5. Ending cash position,						
(3) plus (4)	___	___	___	___	___	___

Best Estimates Required

Nothing magical or arcane is involved, just knowledge and consideration of the business, thoroughness, a lot of objectivity, and hard realism. There is no room for roseate projections of sales receipts or "best-of-all-possible-worlds" estimates of expenses. A Milwaukee banker, Frank J. Pipp, says, "I don't care if the projections are done on a computer or with a pencil. But the numbers must be on target and based on hard facts." They must also be founded on well-reasoned and considered assumptions.

The estimates required are not easy, especially for a new company without a past record on which to base the estimates. But your best estimates are better than no estimates, and these best estimates must be constantly revised. Work with your accountant. He is able not only to guide you through the process but can also serve as a useful check on your own thoroughness and realism. But the accountant should never be given sole or final responsibility for cash flow projections. You yourself must finally judge or analyze the activities and direction of the business.

The farther into the future you are planning the business—capital improvements, sales growth, compensation, distributions, and so forth—the farther into the future you must do a cash flow analysis. Six months seems appropriate for many new or growing businesses.

Managing Your Money Tip

You can use Cash Forecasting to display your current and future cash positions, based on your budget, so you can spot trouble well in advance. To see your Cash Forecast, select Forecasting from the Money submenu.

The Forecasting screen is divided into three sections—your current cash; the cash Managing Your Money projects you'll have at the end of this month; and your cash at the end of each of the next 11 months. (If you've turned on the 5-year-forecasting Money Option on the FILE submenu, F6 will take you to see that too.)

If you want to exclude a budget item from your cash forecast (such as a savings account you're keeping for your kids, or any account whose balance doesn't really affect the amount of cash you can lay your hands on), include "XXX" anywhere in its name ("1st Federal XXX"). The item will still figure into your net worth, but it won't show up as ready cash.

For more information on this menu selection, select Fore-

Be Realistic

Owner-managers frequently overestimate sales and underestimate expenses. They either don't really know their business, haven't given the matter much thought, or are victims of overoptimism. An extreme example is a particular owner-manager who in the third month of operations still insisted on analyzing his business on the basis of a preopening model of sales—a highly abstract and optimistic model, at that—rather than the actual sales figures reported by his accountant.

Not only are sales usually overestimated but so are sales receipts. The likelihood of delinquent or bad accounts receivable is glossed over. What's needed is to estimate carefully the percentage of receivables that will be paid within one month, two months, or more, and allocate credit sales receipts accordingly. Further, the delivery times of goods that trigger payments are frequently underestimated, resulting in an overestimate of sales receipts in an earlier period.

In any event, actual sales of the fledgling company may be assumed to be smaller than planned, and actual expenses greater. A retail business that, after three years, takes sales of $5,000 or $6,000 a day for granted may wait six or more months at the outset for a $1,000 day.

Examine Your Assumptions

The assumptions that underlie the various estimates must be exposed and articulated. The timing of inventory replacement expenditures, for example, must be analyzed. How often and when must the inventory be replaced? When must the cash disbursements for new inventory be made?

Seasonal Variations

Seasonal variations in sales and expenditures must be factored in. There are few small businesses whose expenditures and sales take place on a straight-line basis. Their timing and magnitude vary from month to month and within the month, as well. Monthly, quarterly, and annual tax payments are irregular. Promotional expenses, insurance prepayments, professional fees, inventory replacements, loan repayments—these may come due in different amounts in different months, and they may come due in appallingly large bunches. Seasonal sales may vary enormously, too. Consider the retail store or consumer manufacturer with a splurge of December holiday sales, followed by a January-to-March draught.

Contingency Funds

Contingency funds should be factored into the cash flow analysis, either in "Starting Cash Position," or as a special line item under "Cash Out." Murphy's Law will frequently, without question, seem enacted for your business alone. Depending on the nature of the business, a start-up venture generally banks on contingency funds for from six months to two years.

Compensation

Another factor to consider is your compensation. Even if you plug in a number for salary, it is usually advisable not to count on a salary or any other source of income from the business for at least a year, and sometimes two years. This is a fact of small business life, and you may overcome it, but you probably shouldn't plan on it. Further, if compensation is projected, provision must be made for personal income taxes on the compensation.

Start-up Businesses

The pre-start-up business must not only prepare an operating cash flow analysis for its opening months of operation, it must also draw up a budget of all preopening capital requirements. All the considerations of thoroughness and realism discussed above apply. Preopening capital requirements include not only the obvious expenditures for plant and equipment, lease-hold improvements, and fixtures but also for preopening rent and wages; opening inventory; office and business equipment; general supplies; legal, accounting, architectural and contract-ing expenses; promotional expenses; and a large, large con-tingency fund for overruns—around 33 percent or more.

Cost overruns don't "just happen," but that's the way it always seems. If you don't build into your capital budget a substantial contingency reserve, the odds are very strong you will be severely undercapitalized from Day One of business. And similarly, sufficient capital funds must be raised to meet the normal and expected cash flow deficits of the first long months of operations. In the first month's cash flow analysis, there must be substantial cash in "Starting Cash Position." Without it, chances are the business is doomed, unless you have ready access to additional funds.

Cash Management: Asset Control

A significant aspect of cash management is the preservation and squeezing of further cash from the business's already scarce resources.

There is opportunity to produce vital, extra cash in almost every corner of every small business. The productive control of the firm's working capital, in particular accounts receivable, accounts payable, and inventory, is often as decisive a factor in small business survival and success as adeptness in the product and sales areas. One experienced small business accountant estimates that cash management inefficiencies can rob a small business of 25 to 30 percent of potentially available and vital cash. Those amounts can make or break the enterprise.

Cash management as asset control means, more specifically:

1. Accelerating the receivables;
2. Stretching out the payables;
3. Reducing bloated or slow-moving inventories;
4. Preventing theft and fraud.

Accounts Receivable

Most small businesses do an appreciable amount of credit business. You would do well to begin a cash management regime by examining and controlling your accounts receivable. Where there are substantial credit sales, there are very likely not only accounts receivable problems but also sizable opportunities.

The problem of large receivables is not only that they are illiquid and can't be spent to pay bills and produce more profit. There is also the "opportunity cost," representing interest that could be earned on cash receipts, but not on a mere accounts receivable book asset.

Take a simple example. A company cleans up its accounts receivable procedures and reduces the average outstanding amount due from $200,000 to $100,000. Not only does the firm free up an additional $100,000 a year for productive or delightful purposes, but the $100,000, if not expended, will earn, at 7 percent, an additional $7,000 a year. Or, if ploughed back into the business, it may save even greater borrowing costs. Furthermore, fewer accounts receivable mean fewer future bad debts and write-offs, as well as less employee time on processing and collecting the receivables.

An effective accounts receivable control program starts with accurate and timely record keeping. Accountants frequently speak of records that are so fouled up that it is nearly impossible to identify deliveries, billing, and payments.

Not only must invoices be sent promptly and without delay but shipments and payments must be posted promptly. A simple system is also needed to keep monthly track of which receivables are current, that is, due in 30 days or less, and which have been due for 30 to 60 days, 60 to 90 days, or more than 90 days. This process of sorting out the receivables by age is known as "aging." Any accountant can set up a standard file that makes this breakdown. Be sure to note if only partial payments are tendered and, if appropriate, establish a dispute file for follow-up.

A credit and collection policy must be established and strictly enforced. You must articulate credit terms from the start. Who is to receive credit? You should probably clear credit for any new accounts of consequence prior to, not after, delivery. When is the customer to be billed? If not on delivery, what is to be considered a billable event? There is, for example, "milestone billing" upon the completion of a specific event, such as passing a critical design review, or "progress billing," which allows the business to invoice costs as incurred, on a periodic basis.

Many businesses have customary payment terms that respond to such issues as:

1. When are the payments due? Is the policy "Cash on Delivery" (COD)? Within 30 days of billing?
2. Are incentive discounts applied to payments within 10 days of billing?
3. Is there a charge for lateness? Will this charge apply to good customers? Large customers?

Spell out the terms in clear and well-designed invoices. This will preclude a lot of after-the-fact weaseling by foot-dragging customers, and will bear the stamp of authority.

You need a policy regarding collection, too. Oversized re-ceivables are sometimes the consequence of nothing more than lax and soggy collection methods. Some customers will pay only under pressure, and many just need some tactful but to-the-point reminders.

The first question is, what percentage of total receivables has been due for more than 30 days? The task is to reduce that fig-ure. Analyze it: Are there just a few laggard customers who contribute to most of the over-dues? Should they be the focus of attention, or is there lateness across-the-board? The answer will help determine collection tactics. But don't wait until the receivables are 60 to 90 days past-due. Send reminders after 30 days. Start using the phone. Find out where the problems, if any, are at the customers' offices. Who is the best person to con-tact—the president, a department head? Or is it a clerical prob-lem? State that you are calling to remind them of a 40-day over-due payment, that cash receipts are important to your firm, and ask when payment can be expected. Follow up on that day.

If lateness becomes so extended that you have lost the customer's business—or won't want to maintain it in any event—give the over-dues to a collection agency. Ask your accountant or fellow business associates to advise on proven local collection procedures.

Managing Your Money Tip

It's time to talk about accounting techniques. There are two basic ones: cash and accrual. In cash-basis account-ing, you earn income when you receive cash and incur an expense when you pay it. In accrual-basis accounting, you account for income when you sell an item, even though you may not be paid for several weeks. Similarly, you account for expenses when you incur them, not when you pay for them.

Managing Your Money is set up for use by individuals, and individuals are, in accounting terms, cash operations. However, accrual accounting on Managing Your Money can be accomplished. Managing Your Money supports accounts payable and accounts receivable, which makes it unique among best-selling personal financial software products.

To use accrual-basis accounting in Managing Your Money, select Optional Features from the File submenu. Then press "M" (or select "Money options"). Select "Yes" for Accounts Payable and Accounts Receivable. Press F10 to save your selections.

When you incur a Payable (that is, receive a bill or invoice from someone else), you'll "spend" money as you normally would, except it will be "By:" Receivable (instead of Check, Cash, etc.) No money will be deducted from a Money Account. Instead, an account payable will be posted for the Money Account you selected. Until you pay it, the Payable will show up on your Net Worth statement as a liability. To pay the invoice, go to Payables in the Money submenu, mark the Payable you intend to pay, select the means you wish to pay by, and press F10. The amount you paid will then be deducted from the Money Account, and your Payables will no longer reflect the amount of the Payable.

Similarly, when you issue an invoice for product or services that you sold, you have created a Receivable. So you'll "receive" money as you normally would, except you'll receive it "by" a "Receivable." When you designate the transaction as a receivable, Managing Your Money will do two things. First, it will create an invoice number field. Second, it will create an entry under Receivables in the Money submenu. If you go there, you'll be able to print the invoice by pressing F6. To see a report of outstanding invoices, press F4, highlight "Printer," and press F10. Even though you will not have been paid, the receivable will show up on your Net Worth statement as an asset. When you are actually paid, mark the Receivable, and press F10. The amount you received will be added to the Money

Account, and your Receivables will no longer reflect the amount paid to you.

Accounts Payable

Accounts payable are the flip side of the company's receivables. Whereas your asset control program aims at accelerating payment of the receivables, the task here is to stretch out the payables as long as possible without alienating your creditors. Determine when suppliers really want or expect payment. It is frequently long after the formal terms. Use credit cards. If the business is going through a cash crisis, be candid with the main suppliers and ask for a tide-over period. That works surprisingly frequently.

Inventory

Runaway inventories are frequently the biggest threat to cash liquidity. A substantial number of small businesses have no coherent inventory control program to speak of, other than a "never-run-out" policy.

One business school study found that about 40 percent of all small businesses never take any count of inventory. That neglect not only invites bloated and unproductive inventories but is an open invitation to theft. It also robs the owner-manager of enormously useful information about customer buying behavior.

Every dollar of excess inventory is a dollar not available for productive use. In fact, it is more than a dollar, since the overall cost of holding inventories can be 20 to 25 percent of the dollar value of the inventories. Inventory carrying costs may include financing costs, storage and warehousing, depreciation, spoilage and obsolescence, and handling charges. So, a reduction in inventory from $90,000 to $60,000 could not only yield $30,000 in cash but might also produce additional profit of $6,000 to $7,500.

A small business has difficulty enough finding adequate

resources to survive and succeed; to misallocate what it has invites unnecessary risk and dissipates productive opportunities. Making the most with the least is a daily requirement in the small business world.

Maintaining a relatively efficient inventory control system for a small business is no more demanding of your time than an accounts receivable system. The object is to decrease the basic stock of inventory, increase its turnover rate, and thereby decrease the annual investment in inventory.

The pressures for an unnecessarily large inventory, especially in a retail operation, are considerable. Both consumers and suppliers, wittingly or not, bear down on the small business to carry ample stocks of goods. And the owner-manager is understandably loathe to understock and run out of any items customers might want. "Stockouts" happen in nearly all businesses from time to time, but they can be embarrassing or worse.

The trick, of course, is to find the ideal balance of inventory for each of the goods that must be held in stock. Above that level the firm is overstocked; below it, the firm incurs a danger of stockout before reorders arrive. Larger firms employ computers and esoteric mathematical formulas to try to determine the optimum. "Finding the balance" may sound like the proverbial advice of the baseball manager to a pitcher who has gotten into a jam: "Don't give him anything good, but don't walk him." While you may never find the ideal, you will probably not go too far wrong with some careful and educated guesswork, some practical experience, and subsequent analysis.

Three calculations are in order. For any item, there is a *maximum stock level, a minimum stock level,* and a *reorder point* between those two levels that allows sufficient time for new deliveries to inventory following the reorders.

To take a simple example: If you are a retailer and stock Wonder Widgets, you might make the following calculations:

1. Maximum Stock: 84 Wonder Widgets
2. Minimum Stock: 12 Wonder Widgets
3. Reorder Point: 36 Wonder Widgets (based on a
                     five day reorder/delivery time)

Thus, never more than 84, never less than 12, reorder at 36.

A good operations-oriented accountant can be of great help in establishing an inventory record-keeping and control system appropriate to the peculiar needs of your business. In addition, you can consult library texts and Small Business Administration or trade association handbooks germane to your type of business, or ask others in your general business area what has worked for them.

There are several control systems you can use to keep track of your inventory. "Perpetual" inventory systems are precise and keep you up-to-date. You maintain a card or list for each item stocked and meticulously post all daily additions to, and withdrawals from, inventory. Reorder points are automatically triggered when they are reached.

For many smaller businesses, though, a perpetual system may be unduly cumbersome. Instead, you might take periodic physical countings of inventory to determine reorder levels. Periodic or monthly counts will also establish variances with the prior month's levels and determine the relationship between sales and those variances. That is an essential aspect of theft prevention. Further, you can make occasional spot or surprise checks of inventory to determine that accurate postings are being made to the perpetual inventory records or to help make sure, on a sample basis, that there is no substantial theft from your inventory.

To assure a reasonably rapid inventory turnover rate you must know which goods sell rapidly and which are slow movers. "Specials of the day" and "50 percent off" sales are designed to move out the laggards and make space for the winners. Moderately simple inventory records will provide the sales data you need. They can be breakdowns of seasonal fluctuations and ongoing sales trends; or of sales by product line, size, color, year of item, and brand; or of sales in various territories.

Managing Your Money Tip

Accounting for purchases and sales of inventory is easy with Managing Your Money. Accounting for the inventory itself is not quite so easy — but it's possible. Essentially, you'll account for the cash transactions in your Money Accounts, and track the level of inventory itself by setting up a Portfolio.

First, let's look at setting up Managing Your Money for purchases of inventory.

1. Select Budget Categories from the Money submenu. Press F5, and establish Cost of Goods Sold as an expense-type budget category. Press F6 and be sure to classify it as "Cost of Goods Sold" under Tax Category if you're a sole proprietor that will file Schedule C with your Form 1040. Then press F10 to save your work.

2. Press F5, and establish Gross receipts as an income-type budget category. If you're a sole proprietor that will file Schedule C with your Form 1040, press F6 and be sure to classify it as "Gross receipts" under Tax Category.

Now you're ready to book purchases and sales of inventory.

If you're purchasing inventory, select Spend Money from the Money submenu. Complete the screen as appropriate, designating the party you're buying your inventory from as the Payee. Use Cost of Goods Sold as the category.

When you sell inventory, select Receive Money from the Money submenu and receive the value of the sold inventory. The party you're buying your inventory from should be listed as the Payor. Use Gross Receipts as the category.

Buying inventory on credit?

First, you'll have to have set up Managing Your Money to handle Accounts Payable. To do so, select Optional Features from the File submenu. Then press "M" (or select "Money options"). Select "Yes" for Accounts Payable and Accounts Receivable. Press F10 to save your selections.

When you buy the inventory on credit, spend money as you normally would under Managing Your Money, but be sure to select "Payable" as the method you're paying by. No money will be deducted from the Money Account. Instead, an account payable will be posted for the Money Account you selected. Until you pay it, the Payable will show up on your Net Worth statement as a liability. To pay the invoice, go to Payables in the Money submenu, mark the Payable you intend to pay, select the means you wish to pay by, and press F10. The amount you paid will then be deducted from the Money Account, and your Payables will no longer reflect the amount of the Payable.

If you sell inventory on credit, you'll "receive" money as you normally would, except you'll receive it "by" a "Receivable." When you designate the transaction as a receivable, Managing Your Money will do two things. First, it will create an invoice number field. Second, it will create an entry under Receivables in the Money submenu. If you go there, you'll be able to print the invoice by pressing F6. When you are actually paid, mark the Receivable, and press F10. The amount you received will be added to the Money Account, and your Receivables will no longer reflect the amount paid to you.

Tracking Inventory

Here's where it gets tricky. You'll want to set up a Portfolio account for your inventory. This way, transactions involving your inventory account won't corrupt your books, while you'll be able to track your inventory level, and the value of your inventory will be reflected in the Net Worth Report balance sheet.

Establish a portfolio, with an initial cash balance equal to the amount that you paid the supplier. To do this, first select Portfolios from the Portfolio submenu, and press F5. Fill in the information that Managing Your Money asks for. Don't fill in an initial cash balance, though. When you're done, press F10.

When you buy inventory, select Buy Assets from the Portfolio submenu. Fill in the information that Managing Your Money asks for. Use whatever symbol you like ("INV" for inventory?). Be sure to list the number of units purchased and the cost per unit.

When you're done, your Inventory Portfolio Account will display a cash balance of $0.00 and an asset value equal to what you paid for the inventory. If you select Your Net Worth from the Net Worth submenu and look at your Net Worth statement, it will show the same bottom line as before. You'll have the same amount of assets. But if you highlight Assets and press F10, you'll see that the Money Account that you paid the inventory supplier from decreased by the amount that you paid for the inventory. And you'll see that the "Marketable Securities" line increased by the amount of the inventory that you bought. (If you want this line to read "Inventory", highlight "Marketable Securities," press F2, and edit the line to your satisfaction.)

When you sell inventory, just sell it as you would a share of stock. Select Sell Assets from the Portfolio submenu and press F10. Fill in the information that Managing Your Money asks for. Enter zero ("0") as the sale price.

If you're selling all of the inventory units, just press F10. But if you're only selling some of your inventory, hit the <enter> key until you come to the cell indicating the number of units that you sold, enter that number and press F7. Then hit <esc> and press "U" to select Update Prices from the Portfolio submenu. Enter the original price you paid per inventory unit as the "Latest Price." Then press F6.

When you're done, your Inventory Portfolio Account will display a cash balance of $0.00 and an asset value equal to what you paid for the remaining inventory. If you select Your Net Worth from the Net Worth submenu and look at your Net Worth statement, your net worth will be increased by the difference between what you sold the inventory for, and what it cost you. The "Marketable Securities" line (of "Inventory" line, if you edited it) will reflect the value of your remaining inventory.

Things You Can Do

When you order more of an item, buy it for your portfolio, but append OO to the symbol, as in QUILT-OO. As you scroll down your inventory, you'll immediately see which items are OO—on order. As they arrive, go back and change the symbol to eliminate the OO. (If you use the prefix AA, instead—About to Arrive?—all the items you have on order will be grouped together alphabetically, and they'll appear first. A ZZ-prefix would put them all last.)

If you're small but have, nonetheless, two or more locations (your Grosse Point store eight months of the year, your Palm Beach store in the winter), set up a separate portfolio for each. You'll be able to look at them separately or in the aggregate.

Theft

It is better than even money that your business will be the object of injurious theft. Give it any name—dishonesty, fraud, embezzlement, or promiscuous borrowing—it amounts directly or indirectly to theft of your business's available cash.

The American Management Association estimates that up to 20 percent of the businesses that fail each year are victims of fatal crime losses. Serious theft can befall a business from any source, be it a professional robber, a customer, a supplier, or an employee.

For example, you should consider that, *statistically*, each and every employee has the potential for dishonesty and fraud, and the more temptations you provide, the stronger are the possibilities of actual theft. Good working conditions and relations of trust don't themselves make trustworthy employees of every last member of the staff. No matter what you know of each employee personally, you should remember that illusions of an adoring and faithful staff have cracked apart many an unsuspecting business. There is trust. And there is naive trust.

The intention here is not to draft a complete theft-prevention program for each and every business. That would be impossible in any case, for the pressure points and vulnerabilities to theft vary with the kind and size of businesses. But there must first exist in your mind a sensitivity to the potential for theft in your particular business. It comes in many forms and sizes.

Four lawyers were partners and absentee owners of a sizable steak restaurant in New York City. They could not understand why the food costs in relation to sales were so high. One of them discovered the root cause late one evening when he came upon three kitchen hands sliding half a steer out the back window, where a truck was waiting to carry it off. Employees like that are sometimes referred to as "midnight salesmen."

The possibilities for fraud are endless. Take a look at Checklist 20 for some examples.

A Theft Control Program

What's to be done? The need is to develop a considered and responsive theft control program. Spend several hours with your accountant, that operations-savvy we discussed earlier. Analyze the pressure points, the vulnerabilities of your partic-

CHECKLIST 20 Theft: Some of the Many Possibilities

1. Shoplifting is undetected.
2. Inventory is removed by either an outsider or insider.
3. Cash is stolen from the inside; cash registers are manipulated, for example.
4. Suppliers deliver less than the business is charged.
5. A sales manager splits unearned commissions with supplier salespersons on nonexistent sales; fictitious sales are represented by a salesperson, who then removes the merchandise to a secret warehouse where he hopes to sell the goods—another midnight salesman.
6. An employee in charge of credit does not collect certain receivables, writes off the bad debts, and then takes a kickback from the debtors.
7. A corrupt purchasing manager can mulct the company in dozens of ways, from straight kickbacks to documentation manipulation.
8. The petty cash supply system is abused—$100 of fuzzily vouchered documents today, $400 tomorrow, $50 the next day; the annual damage can be enormous.
9. "Payments" are issued to fictitious employees or suppliers or for the fictitious return of goods.
10. Employees ally with customers to cover nonpayment for goods sold.

ular business. What are the obvious dangers? Where are the other areas of vulnerability? Consult, as you might on the related matter of inventory control, library texts and trade publications and fellow businesspeople to determine what theft prevention devices and procedures are customarily utilized in your area of business.

You should consider at least the following as part of a practical theft prevention program.

1. *Install an appropriate security system*—alarms, mirrors, visible cameras, and the like.

2. *Limit access to inventory* and other valuables.

3. *Install inventory recording and control procedures.*

4. *Purchase a safe.* If it is small, secure it to the floor or wall.

5. *Devise a system for receiving goods.* You should know which items—maybe all—require detailed counting, measuring, or weighing before they are placed in inventory.

6. *Keep a close and skeptical eye on all cash operations.*

7. *Devise a step-by-step daily procedure for the handling and accounting of cash,* from its receipt to a proper counting, booking of it, its deposit in a bank, and eventual bank statement reconciliation.

8. *Separate or segregate duties of those with responsibility for the cash,* to the fullest extent possible. This includes employees who physically handle money, those who count it, the person who posts it in the books, those who deposit it at the bank, and whoever reconciles the monthly bank statements. Ideally, no employee should have responsibility for more than one of these functions.

9. *Devise a disbursements system,* from petty cash disbursements to check-writing controls, including rules and limits on what is presigned, who is authorized to write checks or spend petty cash, and in what amounts.

10. *Establish procedures for the purchasing function* that allow you to check the competitiveness of purchases.

11. *Use prenumbered and sequential checks, sales slips, requisition forms,* and so forth; keep track of the ones that are unused.

12. *Pay attention to the income statement.* A rise of several percentage points in the cost of goods sold is a signal that theft may be in process at one or more stages of operations.

I noted briefly in the last chapter the CPA's responsibility for helping detect fraud and theft. If the CPA has been charged with more than the minimum duty of preparing financial statements on the sole basis of the company's bookkeeping journals, he or she should have a clear responsibility for determining if the backup procedures and figures support the numbers in the journals. If the journals are kept inadequately, the accountant must determine exactly why this is the case. Full-blown audits are rarely necessary for this purpose. A relatively quick survey of the backup materials or intelligently selected spot checks should be adequate in most cases in a small business. An experienced CPA will have a special sensitivity to deceptive or inadequate backup figures and documentation and should provide you with early warnings of possible problems.

At bottom, theft control is cash management, and, whether or not you are actively involved in day-today administration, you have ultimate responsibility.

Other Ways to Squeeze Out the Cash

Consider the following:

1. *Eliminate prestige and nonproductive frills,* as mentioned in Chapter 3.

2. *Purchase used, not new, equipment.*

3. *Lease equipment instead of purchasing it.*

4. *Transfer idle cash balances in the checking account to an interest-yielding account.* One survey of small businesses found that for every $1 million of sales, the typical small firm keeps on hand an average of $30,000 of idle cash, which might be earning up to $3,000 a year.

5. *Take advantage of the checking account "float."* This refers to the delay between writing a check and the time the bank debits your checking balance. Banks themselves are notorious for requiring three to five days before your deposits are credited, and there is no reason not to take advantage of similar delays in your favor to reduce the amount of cash you keep in a bank account.

6. *Work closely with your accountant to find legitimate ways of deferring tax payments.*

7. *Tighten up on discount pricing;* apply it to key customers only. A moderately small Medford, Massachusetts, valves and

pipes manufacturer instigated such an effort and found to its surprise that it not only saved $15,000 a year, but also lost no business in the process.

8. *Consider, if you must borrow cash, ways of collateralizing your assets*—receivables, inventory, equipment, and real estate.

As owner-manager of a small business, you are a jack-of-all-trades. Very few small businesses can retain financially sophisticated employees to manage the cash they need to survive and grow. This finally is your own responsibility, and it is one of the few areas of small business that requires highest priority attention.

CHAPTER
9

THE PITFALLS OF EXPANSION: MANAGING GROWTH

Growth is highly desirable. And rapid growth is the stuff of business fortunes—*if* the owner-manager maintains steady control of the firm.

Everyone knows that too few sales are fatal. But very few owner-managers understand that too many sales, made too fast, also can kill a small business, nice and clean. Managing growth is another make-or-break condition of small business success.

This chapter is about the recurring perils of uncontrolled expansion. They have torpedoed untold numbers of highly promising ventures. For when rapid growth runs helter-skelter:

1. Profits are imperiled—and it has been said that a firm without profits is no more a business than a pickle is candy.
2. Even more serious, liquidity is threatened—and out-of-cash means out-of-business.
3. The proven strengths of the business are likely to be diluted as the firm moves in unwise and uncertain directions for which it isn't prepared.
4. Established administrative controls can collapse under the weight of new paper flows.
5. The staff is unable to assume the crush of new duties. As projects and tasks proliferate, new employees are belatedly hired in desperation, and the owner-manager's capacity to delegate, tested for the first time, may be found wanting.

When one or more of these phenomena occur, the firm is out of control—maybe too late for repair and recovery. It has grown "Too Far, Too Fast," in the pithy words of a *Wall Street Journal* headline.

Growth rates for many small firms are highly volatile. The fledgling firm's base sales are relatively small, and any appreciable increase represents a significant multiple of that base. That volatile growth—33 percent, 50 percent, even 100 percent in a year—is almost surely preceded or accompanied by other sudden and dramatic changes within the firm. Those changes are the sources of the characteristic pitfalls you must anticipate and avoid.

Many, many firms go under before their owner-managers adequately appreciate the dangers of overexpansion. James W. Duncan, Dun and Bradstreet's corporate economist and chief statistician, suggests that up to three of every four business failures are the direct or indirect result of overly ambitious and negligent growth. That seems high, but it underlines the need for knowledgeable and attentive management. Michael Tishman, professor at the Columbia School of Business, believes that less than 10 percent of owner-managers have the tools to guide a small business through substantial growth. By the end of this chapter, you should be among that 10 percent.

A Tale of Two Companies

Consider the situations of two companies. Which would you prefer to own?

Company A is three years old, has a quality product, and a decent potential market. But its owner-manager has not truly connected the product to the market. There has been little sales growth in the last 18 months, and profits are negligible. The company's record is marginal at best. The firm has potential, however, and therefore hope. This potential can be mastered if only the owner-manager establishes and implements a calculated and creative market plan. Company Able is a problem company.

Company B is also three years old. It has excellent products and proven markets. In fact, its owner-manager expanded both the product line and sales network dramatically, and revenues have tripled in the past 18 months. Much of this growth was bought at considerable expense. New sales personnel were hired, and expansion of distribution proved more costly than foreseen. Advertising and other promotional expenses were large. Other operating costs have also risen appreciably, and there were extra costs in materials and direct labor to produce the new goods. But moderate profits have been booked in six of the last nine months.

Also booked on the balance sheet, however, are large capital expenditures for the new plant and equipment needed to produce added output. Inventories, of course, have risen enormously. Easy credit terms were part of the expansion plans, and accounts receivable have rocketed. Many already have been identified as bad debts and written off (although these write-offs were deceptively called "extraordinary expenses" and not recorded on the profit and loss statement). All of these items, as we have seen in Chapter 8, are cash-consumers of the first order. Large interest payments, and now some principal, are overdue on a bank loan undertaken to finance a part of the expansion.

In fact, the additional cash expenditures related to the sales increases have exceeded the additional cash produced by receipts from those sales. The company, you see, has virtually no cash and is unable to secure even emergency cash transfusions. Friends, relatives, banks, and suppliers have all issued polite but resolute "no's." Tax payments of various sorts are two-to-six months delinquent, and the company has not paid the staff in two weeks. Accounts payable are piling up, and company checks have bounced. A key supplier refuses further deliveries. Nothing, now, will hold in place. The company is in effect bankrupt. The owner-manager terminates operations. Company Bankrupt is out of the business game, probably for good unless a buyer can be found. A buyer would pay little.

No matter, any more, that a good portion of Company Bankrupt's splendid sales growth would otherwise have proven short-lived. Some customers were buying only at the reduced prices and for easy credit terms. The quality of Bankrupt's goods also deteriorated in the rush to meet new orders. In the last six months there was a surge of customer complaints and new repair service work. Word-of-mouth reports were spreading.

And no matter, now that Company Bankrupt's doors are shut, that growing paper work had run amuck. Unlucky the poor persons who must sort out and clean up all the orders over the last six, even 12 months. For administrative chaos had deluged the unhappy company, and it is now seemingly impossible to tell which orders were received when and what action, if any, has been taken. Where is the correspondence? What deliveries were made? Or partially filled? Or disputed by the customer? What payments have been made against which orders? In full? In part? Nearly hopeless to determine. There will be a maze of contract disputes ahead.

The owner-manager of Company Bankrupt was so intoxicated with the continuing sales gush that he just never grasped that Miss Grundy was nearly drowning in paper work. The old procedures for administering the business were inadequate to handle the new volume and complexity of the new work. The whole business was awash in disorder and plain out of control.

Company Able at least has respected that most elemental rule for the small business: Never Run Out of Cash. It still can parlay a nice future. Company Bankrupt has played out its future. It has none. Company Able, problem-ridden and profit-poor as it is, at least is under control and has options. It can yet grow with profit. Company Bankrupt, by contrast, is a model of the uncontrolled and undirected expansion that is the recurring cause of thousands and thousands of small business collapses each year.

Growth Is the Servant of Profits

We hear so frequently of the spectacular sales growth that supported the success of highly publicized glamour-businesses. We rarely hear of the equally impressive growth that sabotaged the orderly, step-by-step development of many other promising enterprises.

There is a strain in our American culture that makes megagrowth particularly alluring and dazzling and blinds us to its perils. The big, new sales figures carry an intoxicating hubris. They call to mind Napoleon's headiness as he sleepwalked to his doom in Russia: "I felt I had been carried up into the midst of the air and could hear the earth turning below me."

Bigger, we think, is Better. Growth is unwittingly pursued for its own sake. It is lots of fun. It requires little discipline to grow, and all systems are go.

A failed California magazine publisher still recounts, four years after her demise, her subscription and newsstand triumphs; never mind that her losses were large and she had lost control of her cash flow. If you disregard the profit motive entirely, hefty sales can surely deliver emotional rewards, and they rationalize splendidly the failure to build a firm through sustained liquidity to growing profits.

I have mentioned the old chestnut about the merchant who loses money on every sale he makes but says he will make it all up in volume. If ever the phrase, "the bottom line," pointed to good business practice, it is here. The profits of the bottom line must dominate the quest for top-line sales. Survival precedes success.

The issue, of course, is *not* "to grow or not to grow." The obvious goal of a small business, either at start-up or following a big push, is rising profit propelled by impressive sales growth, always assuming cash liquidity.

Significant growth is a severe test of an owner-manager's skill to control and direct his firm and to do it based on an appropriate sensitivity to the specific pitfalls and vulnerabilities of rapid growth.

Let's take up the specific hazards of expansion.

The Paradox of Progress and Poverty

The most serious risk of explosive growth is financial instability. In the wake of new sales records, owner-managers are astounded to find low profits and, frequently, losses. Even more telling, growth can easily devour the company's cash.

The burgeoning firm experiences an acute liquidity crisis in the midst of apparent riches.

Growth is not synonymous with accelerating profits. It can sometimes destroy them. And the rapidly growing company is particularly vulnerable to the cash crises we discussed in Chapter 8. Neither growth nor profits must ever be confused with ready cash.

Escalating Costs Imperil Profits

Sales increases can be both the cause and the result of frightening cost increases. These new costs often increase as fast or faster than the new sales themselves. This usually comes as a major and belated surprise to owner-managers. They figure that once their sales equal the sum of "fixed" and "variable" expenses—the break-even point—additional sales are tantamount to additional profit, less whatever "variable" expenses are required to produce the additional sales. By fixed expenses, the accountant means those expenses that are thought to remain relatively stable whatever the level of sales. Variable expenses refer to those expenses that change depending on the amount of sales. Owner-managers assume that since all their supposed fixed expenses are already absorbed by existing sales, new sales, less additional costs of materials or goods, go directly to the bottom line.

Well, first of all, variable expenses can increase enormously with rising sales. If a firm's cost of materials or goods sold is 50 percent and sales rise $100,000 in one year, then additional costs already equal $50,000.

Poised on expansion, many owner-managers think that is more or less the end of it. But much revenue expansion is virtually bought, the result of major marketing, advertising, and promotion expenditures. Increased sales may in part be the direct response to one or more traditional sales gimmicks. Free samples are distributed massively. The company extends easy credit terms to old and new customers alike. The company may hire its first full-time salesperson, or sign up new sales representatives. Commissions may increase precipitously. Expenses for a beefed-up distribution system may be high—and higher than anticipated. Depending on the specific business, other variable expenses will rise as well. The company may incur increased warehousing and materials-handling costs, for example.

Further, it is a major fallacy to assume, as do many accountants who should know better, that "fixed" costs are truly fixed. Owner-managers will discover belatedly that their break-even analysis model for increased profit is soon inoperative, because those fixed costs rise suddenly and discontinuously in proportion to new sales.

Fixed costs have an almost predictable way of rising in a stair-step fashion, rather than in an even curve. A new bookkeeper may add another $2,000 a month in expenses. A new marketing manager will add another $3,000 or so. The company may undertake major debt financing to fund the expansion program. A new "fixed" cost on its monthly income statement is the payment of interest. Professional fees frequently rise. The work of the outside CPA increases. Lawyers' fees may be incurred. Requirements for new production or office space may result in new monthly rental charges. Even utility fees for electricity and the telephones may climb.

After two, three, or four months of escalating costs and expenses, owner-managers are no longer inclined to attribute them to the whims of this or that one-time happening. They recognize that the costs are high and recurring. In many companies, the new costs are seen to have risen almost as rapidly as, or perhaps more rapidly than, the new sales themselves. Profits have increased only slightly or perhaps have declined as rising costs increased disproportionately to sales growth.

Fast Track Losses

Each year, *Inc.* magazine highlights its "Top 100 Companies." These companies are the fastest growing public firms in the country. Typically, their annual sales were $50,000 or less just four or five years before. They have grown, usually, to between $10 million and $50 million in annual sales. *Inc.* lists only publicly held companies whose performance is on the public record, and by the time the companies are listed in *Inc.*'s Top 100, their explosive growth has propelled them well beyond the "small" business stage. Nonetheless, there is an observation of relevance here. Usually, about one in three companies on the *Inc.* 100 list is losing money.

In the May 1986 issue, there was the following: "Thirty percent of this year's *Inc.* 100, with their exploding sales, showed losses. In contrast, only 6.8 percent of the Fortune 500 last year failed to report a profit even though total revenues of Fortune 500 companies actually slumped by 1 percent over the period 1981-1984."

No doubt some of those losses were strategically planned, with a longer range goal of sustained market share and profitability. But when losses, even "planned losses," stretch out month after month and quarter after quarter, the situation is both risky and scary, especially if cash reserves are marginal and insufficient to cushion an unplanned emergency or downswing in sales. Negative earnings are no problem just as long, and no longer, as they stay on plan. But that can be a high-wire act, and a good number of these *Inc.* 100 companies eventually either file for bankruptcy, fall by the wayside, or are acquired and reorganized.

If it is any measure of the underlying soundness of the *Inc.* 100, in 1985-1986 they gained in market value by only 11 percent. The Dow Jones Industrials appreciated 31 percent and American Exchange companies, 13 percent in that period, and the average market value appreciation of NASDAQ Industrials (an average compiled for industrial companies in the over-the-counter market) was 15 percent.

Dazzling growth among the *Inc.* 100 was not only often profitless growth but in the aggregate it didn't result in substantial or even comparative appreciation of market value.

Rapid Growth Can Devour Your Cash

The pressures on scarce cash reserves can be even more acute than those on profits in the high-growth company. *New expenses may be less than new sales, but major new expenditures may exceed sales receipts.* In fact, the moderately or marginally profitable high-growth company may suddenly find itself in a woeful cash position. Growth can be a voracious devourer of cash.

First, there are those cash flow drains related to all the additional new operating costs. As we saw in the previous chapter, many of these expenditures may be made several weeks or even months before the customers pay for related sales, contributing to an unexpectedly early cash crunch.

Second, the company may have paid out substantial monies for capital investment in a new plant and equipment to generate the anticipated sales growth. These capital costs will not affect the income statement, but they will reduce the company's cash supply.

Further, the fast-growing company will frequently find its new balance sheet glutted with nonliquid assets. The inventory may soar in anticipation of additional sales. Easier credit terms and less rigorous credit investigations on new customers result in swollen accounts receivable, some of which will probably be written off. Growing pressure on the firm's slight administrative capabilities results in slacker enforcement of the receivables. Delays of just two weeks in collection of 30-day receivables mean that receivables are up by 50 percent after a month.

The Problem of Disappointing Sales Growth

The ambitious owner-manager's growth plan may risk double jeopardy. We have seen that the firm's expenditures frequently jump both in anticipation and in consequence of the company's growth. But what of the sales side?

Suppose that great leap of sales never materializes? Sales rise not 50 percent, but 20 percent. It was worth the risk, perhaps, and 20 percent growth is seemingly better than static sales. But what of all those capital expenditures and the monies paid out for the sales drive? And the new salesperson, the increased inventories, or the expenses undertaken to expand production? Misfirings are perfectly normal; they are part of the fabric of business life. But the question is, can the firm withstand the gap between expenditures and cash receipts? Is there still a cash reserve and can the firm scrounge some new cash to hold out until it has adjusted to its lower actual sales? Can it pare back its expenses?

What of the situation where the sales growth materializes and holds at new highs for month after month, followed by all those other steep rises in variable and new "fixed" expenses? The firm's profits are up and the cash flow has withstood the perils of rapid expansion. But will the sales hold? What if the economy relapses, and the firm's product is vulnerable? Sales decline 25 percent within three months. Perhaps a tough competitor intrudes or the company's technological advantage disappears. Or, the business eases its price reductions and toughens its credit terms. Perhaps the major sales promotion effort comes to an end, or a major customer severs ties. Sales cannot hold, and there is a new cost and expense structure. These costs, which escalated with such ease, never de-escalate except with painful effort. Cost-cutting is usually painful. Can the firm react decisively and quickly? Will it ruthlessly cut expenses? If not, the firm may soon run out of cash.

Squandering Competitive Strengths

Chapter 3 discusses the requirements of "keeping it simple" and shows why small business success dictates concentration of owner-managers' and their firms' precious skills and resources: talent, experience, and time; product quality and service; administrative control; severely limited capital. The small firm must focus on just a few, concrete, realizable business objectives, and it must master them. It is best off targeting its efforts where the firm is best qualified, where its strengths are centered, where its competitive advantage provides the best chances of success.

These basic strengths and advantages can be undone by rapid growth. Again and again, expanding firms move unwarily into areas beyond their core knowledge and strengths. They move off their home turf and begin playing someone else's game. They dissipate basic management and product muscle and squander scarce management time on peripheral and problem-consuming areas beyond their basic experience.

Premature Expansion

A recurring pitfall of business expansion is that it may be premature. Before expanding, the firm must substantially master the existing business, especially in the few critical areas vital to its success.

Product and service quality must be perfected. Customers must see these as consistently good and reliable.

Frequently a business will expand well before it has dominated its internal affairs. Its costs are still high and wasteful and jump about erratically from month to month. A solid team has not yet been developed. One or two key positions may be hard to fill. Routines—record keeping, day-to-day operations, production systems, and so on—have not been imposed and standardized. These inadequacies result in diluted profits and recurring crises. The expanding business invites more and worse of the same unless it first controls and consolidates what it already does.

Building on Your Proven Strengths

Another pitfall to avoid in expansion is moving from a position of strength to a position of weakness. Experienced entrepreneurs are unanimous: Don't abandon or squander your vital strengths, your major competitive advantages. Avoid growth patterns that are unrelated to what you know and have performed well enough. There has to be a fairly clear identity that drives a company. When the business strays too far from that it begins to develop serious problems.

The firm must usually develop from that foundation, step by step from proven strengths. How closely does the expansion fit earlier business activities? How will the tie-in be perceived by the customers?

It is pretty easy to rationalize this supposed fit. Fifteen to 20 years ago, dozens of the country's large corporations believed that if you can manage one line of business, you can manage any line. They engaged in an orgy of acquisitions. But they still tried to justify the new lines. They usually said there was "synergism," that the corporation's Group A and new acquisition B, seemingly unrelated, would complement each other's business. Two plus two equaled five, went the argument. And nearly all these conglomerates have sold off most of those vanity acquisitions. Even these huge businesses, with their massive financial strength and unlimited staffs, didn't seem to be able to manage what they didn't know and had never worked in.

What are a particular small firm's critical strengths? If you are a retail store, and your location is vital, is the location of a new branch store equally good? Why? Or is it just OK but pretty exciting nonetheless, because everyone says you could do a lot of new business on the other side of town? Is it important that rents are 75) percent higher on that side of town? How much extra business must you do to offset the higher rent? Is the typical customer in the new area apt to be attracted to your product? How do you know? And if you alter your product mix, do you really know about and can you control the new products?

A small women's clothing retailer built its success on clothing designed for "25- to 40-year-old women who want reasonably fashionable clothes at a competitive price." The business prospered and grew wonderfully on this simple, definable sense of mission. Then, the owner-manager determined to base a new spurt of expansion on tailoring fashion to "local tastes" wherever her firm's retail stores were located. The move was a near disaster. The company lost its sense of its particular, successful market niche and the special style of clothing adapted to serve it. It did not develop a touch for "local taste." whatever that vague standard might have been. Fortunately, the owner-manager was able to retrench in time to her original market niche. By providing a constant fashion theme, identifiable with her store's name and reputation, she put her company back on the track of steady, directed growth.

Typical of misdirected, ill-conceived growth is a small, barebones discount drug and consumer-goods store. Its vital competitive edge in its community was its low prices. It squandered that advantage immediately when it refurbished the premises, adding rugs, beauticians, trendy decoration, and an expanded product line of luxury goods. The business has lost its identity; it has frittered away its special appeal. It will probably go under before long. Only the largest and financially strongest of big businesses can play the all-things-for-all-people game. The little fellow must hue to a narrow path.

The owner-manager of a small printing company believed his critical competitive strengths were low prices, speed of delivery, and the quality of his printing. In order to further reduce his customer prices, he doubled his production facilities to lower his unit costs of production. He did reduce his prices, and he advertised this extensively. Business initially picked up. The problem was that for a variety of easily foreseeable technical and administrative reasons the quality of the work was materially compromised, and the firm lost its reputation for meeting delivery dates. It never recovered. It had veered too far from a foundation of proven strength. Low prices alone were insufficient inducements to buy a poor product. Quality of product and reliability of delivery were essential to its success; the business had squandered two of its three key competitive strengths.

Similarly, a Florida fast-food restaurant company, with three nearly identical outlets, had made its mark on the basis of a consistently good but limited menu and a highly effective cost-control program, based on maximum turnover and minimum waste of food supplies. The owner-manager came to believe, though, that he was not only in competition with other fast-food outlets but with traditional restaurants as well. He significantly expanded his menu. In the process, he doubled his supply inventories, thereby causing new waste and costs. He raised his average prices considerably and upgraded service moderately. The business was then positioned in a never-never land of lost identity and across-the-board mediocrity. Sales were erratic, and costs rose precipitously. It was a sure formula for decline.

Product quality and service are frequent victims of helter-skelter expansion. An owner-manager of specialty stainless fittings for the piping industry recalls his own firm's expansion. His company was noted for its high-quality custom work, and for reasons he cannot describe precisely, he risked a brief and nearly ruinous attempt at mass production. "It was like asking an ace southpaw to pitch right-handed in a World Series game. We were trying to compete by using our weaknesses, not our strengths."

Unforeseen Difficulties of Multientity Management

Another area of constant trouble for the rapidly growing company is management of a multientity business. For example, a restaurateur opens two new restaurants, one shortly after the other. A tools manufacturer develops a major new product line and builds a new factory. The firm is now operating two divisions, and, except for common overhead expenses, there might just as well be two separate companies. A public relations firm opens a branch in a city 200 miles away.

Venture capitalists know something about this. They know multientity management is difficult, especially if the owner-manager has no previous experience in operating such a business. They doubt the odds. They want to see a proven track record of success at multientity management before investing.

There is no inherent reason owner-managers shouldn't venture into multientity management just because they haven't been there before. But the point is, as always, that it should be done with careful calculation and sensitivity to the common dangers. Will the former business be neglected, or is it really on rail and requires only circumspect supervision? Has the owner-manager thoroughly trained and delegated wisely to those who will have direct responsibility for the older activities? Or is the owner-manager incapable of effective delegation and will undertake the responsibilities of managing both the expanded and the established activities of the firm? Will sufficient attention be devoted to either of the activities? Will there be enough time to see customers and to retain a sufficient hands-on grip on the business? Will anyone else take up the slack? Is the present team of management up to the wider responsibilities?

Take some cases.

An established restaurant develops a catering business. A newspaper article mentions its interesting off-premise locations. The phones are ringing. The number of catered parties triple. The owner-manager is a natural extrovert, and he loves it—all the people, all the parties. He is on the phone half the day; he attends the parties. He does not attend the restaurant. The kitchen declines. Employee morale is terrible. Employee theft is rampant. Food costs are up, but the owner-manager is insensitive to that and the related pricing implications. Service suffers. The restaurant loses money.

The owner-manager delivers the new catering orders adequately but does a poor job of administering related employee, food, and beverage costs. Sales are all that count for him. They are, in fact, deceptively high, because the owner-manager set unrealistically low prices without knowing his true costs, which are much higher than he had supposed. The catering business rises from $90,000 one year to $250,000 the next. Its profits are only $20,000. The company barely breaks even.

The owner-manager either did not calculate the related needs and consequences of growth, or he is in way over his head. In any event, the company's profits would have been higher had he done no catering business at all. He doesn't know that. He basks in the supposed glory of his catering sales growth and his friends give him hearty congratulations.

There is no reason whatsoever, though, that this company's expansion into catering could not have been calculated to produce orderly growth and controlled management of both the restaurant and catering divisions. Additional development of competent and trained employees was probably the key requirement, but the owner-manager was simultaneously reluctant, first, to acknowledge that the restaurant was floundering in a management vacuum and, second, to delegate adequate authority where needed. Entirely missing was a carefully considered analysis of the company's needs, its strengths, and limitations, as it ventured toward new catering sales growth. Both divisions suffered badly.

Moving into multientity management is difficult because it invokes so many of the basic requirements of small business success discussed in this book. It requires that you know what makes your business sing and how you must continue to allocate your scarce resources if you are to maintain your market and other business advantages. You must know your firm inside out and plan its growth on the basis of calculated needs and anticipated pitfalls. You must appreciate your own and your firm's shortcomings and understand how they must be compensated in a period of growth. You must prepare or develop a staff for the new requirements of growth. You must understand the requirements of delegating some of your authority and duties to the rest of the staff.

It is difficult enough to maintain product quality and differentiation in the course of incremental growth. But when the growth proceeds through new products and new facilities, the task is harder. Not at all impossible, just harder. It calls for more foresight and anticipation, and more management control and direction. The requirement is calculated growth from a base of strength to related strength.

Otherwise, it is, in the words of a disillusioned owner-manager, "like adding to the number of balls a juggler has in the air—eventually they become too many to handle."

Administrative Chaos

When the company takes off, clerical and operating tasks proliferate almost overnight. Old administrative procedures for handling them are inadequate. But owner-managers frequently don't recognize the new needs. Or they are incapable of adjusting and refuse to relinquish direct control over each and every nook and cranny of the business. They are incapable of delegating responsibilities to an existing, or possibly upgraded, staff. The firm is unable to cope with the daily increase of paper work. The company can't seem to keep track of anything.

Typically, a salesperson may object that the "product is just fine" but everything else "just stinks." Deliveries are chronically late. There is a backlog of orders and no one seems to know the status of each one. Customers are issued sloppy and incorrect billing. Customer complaints increase.

The company's old accounting system may no longer produce the timely and useful information for which it was originally designed. Gordon Black, owner-manager of a rapidly growing research company in Rochester, New York, remembers the syndrome. His firm's annual sales already exceeded $1.5 million, and he was increasingly bringing home new six-figure contracts with some of the local giants such as Eastman Kodak and Gannett Co. The firm's prosperity was illusionary. "We were totally swamped with work, but we had outgrown every one of our internal control systems. I had no idea how much our current jobs were costing, and nobody else did either. We were underpricing our bids by about 20 percent." And incurring losses of about $40,000 a month.

Control systems relating, for example, to cash, purchasing, payments, customer billings, and receivables collections rapidly deteriorate. They are overloaded and obsolete. Some bills are paid twice, and some customers are never billed. Lax controls over cash are exploited. Employee theft increases. Some suppliers underdeliver their goods, knowing the errors will not be detected. The company experiences growing difficulty in collecting accounts receivable when they are due. Personnel fail to acknowledge customer orders responsively, and future contract disputes are hatched.

Employee training and supervision suffer. All is busy, busy, busy. The firm rushes from one new order to the next, from one brush fire to the next crisis. The owner-manager has seriously neglected the administrative requirements of rapid growth. He is unlikely to make the same mistake twice—if he is still in business.

Managing Growth

Because rapid growth is so difficult to manage, because it is so frequently mismanaged, most owner-managers who have experienced the explosive growth trap counsel a very watchful eye. A *Harvard Business Review* survey of the growth problem concluded: "Most firms do better with conservative growth rates." *Most* firms do better growing incrementally, one step at a time. Not *all* firms. *Most* firms. Some firms, of course, must plunge ahead for fear of losing a major one-shot opportunity, or, "missing your niche," in the words of business consultant Robert W. Philip. He points out that a firm may "need to move as fast as it can to exclude competition."

The point is, however, that rapid expansion is perilous, and owner-managers must *manage* growth. They must control and direct it, lest it control and direct the company itself.

By all means, grow—and take calculated risks in the process. Grow and grow some more. just don't let it kill you. Manage that growth.

Anticipate the Pitfalls

What does it mean to manage growth? It means first an acute sensitivity to the various pitfalls of expansion I have discussed above. Those are the problem areas that have demoralized or destroyed so many thousands and thousands of fast growth firms.

Anticipate the dangers. And keep a close eye out for any actual evidence that the firm may be veering out of control. That requires an intimate understanding of the specific needs and behavior of the firm.

You must carefully consider *before* the business takes off how much growth is anticipated and where that growth is apt to affect the firm. How soon will the growth occur? For how long? What are the critical areas within the firm that will most likely be affected? Consider these factors:

1. What impact will the growth have on the costs?

2. Is the present staff up to the burdens of additional responsibility, of growing complexity?

3. Will the increased paper flow necessitate more sophisticated accounting and administrative procedures?

4. Where will the firm be likely to suffer? Will the expansion damage an established product line or the company's main business? Can deliveries continue on schedule? Will customer service suffer? Will product quality be imperiled? How, why, and when?

5. Where is the firm feeling the pinch already? Where are its relative weaknesses? Will they be aggravated by the pressures of expansion? Can the firm withstand the consequences of growth without significant adjustments? Which adjustments should be implemented in the short-term? Which later?

6. And what does all this mean for the cash requirements, both short- and long-term?

To manage growth requires that you consider such questions and many more before as well as after, the growth is underway.

Planning for Growth

Successful management of growth also requires that you *plan* growth, at least to the extent of keeping these factors right before you and anticipating and planning changes in the firm appropriate to new circumstances, new needs, and pitfalls of the growth.

If you are not directly building on an established, solid foundation of achievement and expanding into areas where you know well enough what the business is about and what it is doing, there must be good reasons. What are the risks and how do you suppose you will, or can, cope with them?

Are you dissipating your own and the firm's strengths, or is the firm in fact exploiting an innovative opportunity for which it is reasonably prepared? If the firm is moving into virgin territory, are there any crippling surprises that might *possibly* beset it? Have you talked with other experienced businesspeople about your own particular expansion? And if and when the firm encounters problems along with the expansion, will the firm's established business activities be jeopardized through management neglect? Can the expansion be carried through in separate stages, so that the firm can cut its losses on a solid showing of failure? And if it is an all-or-nothing project, are there contingencies for failure?

The Need to Delegate

Prior to takeoff, you should carefully consider your own role in the expanding company. The character and needs of a company evolve as it matures and expands. Initially, you *are* the business. In the start-up and survival stage, your energy, spontaneity, intuitive hunches, and the immediacy of your knowledge and control of the entire operation are probably responsible for its survival and success.

It is no sign of weakness, though, that the management needs of a growing company may quickly outpace the capacity of one owner-manager. A basically one-person show will no longer suffice. You have to relinquish some responsibilities. You must decide which ones to delegate and which to retain. You must share control and oversee the imposition of new organization structures. You must not be afraid to seek help as the firm moves to new waters.

You may need to hire new employees to ease the burdens of growth. The need may be for a new bookkeeper or additional clerical employees. Perhaps you should hire a comptroller to manage the cash and internal controls. Here is the comment of one perspicacious owner-manager: "I realized that I did not have the mind-set of even an average comptroller. I knew that if I wanted to reap the benefits of our excellent growth, I would have to solve the control problem and instill law and order before our success was destroyed by the company wobbling out of control." You may need to relieve yourself of increased daily work tasks by hiring one or more functional managers, for sales or production, for example.

Adapting the Accounting System to New Needs

With or without added personnel, the company would be wise to institute more ample or new information, accounting, and internal control procedures. That will allow the firm to accommodate a likely explosion of paper work and related information and assure that it can be readily collected, organized, and used. The business may, for example, automate those operations. So much the better that that be done in advance of a predictable explosion of growth. Installation of data processing or a bevy of new administrative procedures in the midst of a paper crisis will usually create new and worse crises.

It is likely that more precise records and procedures governing costs and cost control will be essential to an owner-manager who has determined to manage his firm's growth. The owner-manager will probably also require assistance from his

CPA in devising new and responsive procedures for controlling inventory. Customer billing and accounts receivable record-keeping and operating procedures should be reviewed in advance. If growth surges as expected, can the firm continue to cope with these seemingly routine matters? Or will one or more of them become smothering problem areas?

Guarding the Cash

Above all, your highest priority and responsibility must be to anticipate the cash needs, before the onset of expected growth and well down the road. You simply have to face this one squarely. A "who-can-tell?" attitude won't do, even if it may be partly correct. You must make a best-effort stab at systematically understanding how and where the growth will affect the business and how that may exhaust the firm's cash. Consider, in turn, estimated sales, associated expenditures, and cash needs.

1. *Sales*. Sales projections, based on growth expectations, must be ventured and constantly reviewed and adjusted. Scrutinize these revenues. Ask questions about the sales:

   a. What are the implicit assumptions on which the growth is expected? How realistic do those assumptions appear in cold daylight?

   b. How soon is the growth expected?

   c. Is the growth based entirely on a sales or marketing campaign? Will sales drop as soon as the campaign is over?

   d. Is the growth based on product advantage? An innovation? Technological superiority? How long will those advantages last? What then?

   e. When will these sales be realized in hard cash—when will customers pay you?

   f. To what extent are easy credit terms a part of a promotional campaign? Have you discounted in advance a certain amount of bad debts or taken into account probable contractual dispute problems that will forestall actual payments?

2. *Expenditures.* Next, estimate the increased or new expenditures associated with revenue increases. Capital costs, if any, must be estimated. This shouldn't be difficult, since they will normally be expended relatively early. What other expenditures are involved? What ongoing expenditures are likely to increase, now that you think about it? What new ones will be incurred?

3. *Cash Needs.* Check Chapter 8 again, for the discussion of cash flow analysis and cash management requirements. They are particularly germane to the rapidly expanding business. The firm must budget for whatever cash needs can be foreseen in the months ahead. What is the magnitude of those cash needs? Will sales receipts really be sufficient to meet them? And what about the "bad luck" factor and the inevitable contingencies? For example, sales may never take off as planned, but the firm will have incurred relatively huge expenses, such as expanded inventory and debt financing, in anticipation of a surge. Or the economy may flatten out, and the firm's products will be among the nonessentials that first suffer in a downswing. Or extraordinary expenses may arise—a tax assessment from the past or an unanticipated but major repair or capital replacement, for example.

Is the company's cash sufficient for the periodic crises that often besiege growing companies? Can you fall back on your personal wealth if and when necessary? Are there other ready sources of cash when needed?

In short, if a realistic cash analysis, constantly reviewed and updated, shows the possibility of a liquidity crisis, you must engage in advance in some first-rate cash management. You can consider ways of preserving and producing more cash from the firm's working capital (again, take a look at Chapter 8, if necessary). Or you can develop contingency plans for reducing expenses drastically in time of need. You may, for example, determine that a large number of older accounts contribute no profit, while causing a disproportionate amount of expenses, and simply cease doing business with those customers. Sales will fall; but profits and cash will increase. You can develop plans to shrink the product base and cut associated costs quickly.

The owner-manager of the Rochester market research firm mentioned earlier took swift action to stem hemorrhaging that resulted from bloated costs. He renegotiated prices on some major contracts and instituted an immediate cost-reduction program especially in the personnel area, where he laid off 11 people and cut salaries across-the-board. At last report, the company appeared on the way to recovery.

And finally, if necessary, you must plan to acquire additional funds from outside sources before it is too late. Otherwise, you are unnecessarily rolling the dice.

This is the kind of management that is required to guide the business beyond the pitfalls of expansion. Owner-managers who direct and control growth, eyes wide open, are seldom heard bemoaning their "bad luck," or reciting the associated litanies of "but for this or that…" that issue erroneously, if understandably, from the ruined business. And few, beside themselves, know just how difficult that achievement was and the first-rate management that was responsible for it.

CHAPTER
10

UNDERSTANDING THE
BUSINESS INSIDE OUT

Many owner-managers, I observed in Chapter 7, devote more effort to actively analyzing their stock portfolios than to determining the health of their own businesses. They seem to believe that they already know as much as they possibly can about their own firms and that a determined search for further information and insight will be unproductive. As a result, their understanding of their companies is often dangerously shallow.

It is nearly impossible to maximize profits without a deep and comprehensive understanding of the business.

Understanding the business requires:

1. Obtaining hard, reliable information;
2. Developing a sense of the significance and uses of that information;
3. Finding the latent problems and resolving them resourcefully before they seriously damage the company;
4. Finding or creating opportunities to improve the business.

This chapter is about those requirements and what it takes to build that understanding and use it as part of a dynamic decision-making process.

The Purposes of Understanding the Business

There are two key reasons why in-depth understanding of the company is a make-or-break condition of small business success:

1. It is the foundation of management direction and control of the business.
2. It is a necessary condition for improving the business and realizing hidden profit potential.

Control and Direction

Unless you really know what's happening in all areas of the business—where the company is, how it got there, and where it is heading—you will be out of touch with the needs of the business and therefore thoroughly unable to attend to them.

In the words of the great 19th-century railroad pioneer, Charles Francis Adams, Jr., the ill-informed owner-manager "wallows and flounders about in a mire of uncertainties and surprises, bewildered at his situation, and equally unable to say how he got there and how he proposed to get out of it." In short, what is lacking is control and direction of the firm. Purposeful activity is impossible. Seat-of-the-pants management is the result.

Aiming for Potential Profits

Without a comprehensive, hands-on knowledge of the business, you cannot really envision the business as it might be, and not just as it is. Problems and opportunities go undetected and unheeded, and possibilities for improving the business are forfeited. You will wrongly suppose that whatever is, is right and that the way you are currently running the business is the only way it can be run.

Even if the company's profit levels seem acceptable, there will be a gap between the *actual* profits and the *potential* profits. If only the difference could be measured, the unrealized profits would be seen in the same light as stolen profits.

Curiosity, Questions, and an Open Mind

Successful business venturers seem to have developed an insatiable curiosity for new information, insights, and fresh ways of perceiving the business. Coupled with this is a disdain for the superficial and for easy answers.

They look at all aspects of a situation with an open mind to facts, ideas, and the opinions of others. They use their analytical and creative intelligence to pose question after question to challenge all the operating assumptions of the business and assault the status quo.

These questing owner-managers are forever asking, "What's missing? What don't I understand? What don't I see that would facilitate damage control? What are some new or more efficient ways we can run the business?" They don't stop with the "What's going on?" question, but proceed to "What ought to be?" "What could be?" and "How do we get there?"

They wonder endlessly about the factors limiting the effectiveness of the business and how they can reshape those constraints or adapt to or sidestep them.

It may be ignorance of certain key matters that is a constraint. Or, in the words of Mark Twain's Pudd'nhead Wilson, it may be "not what you don't know what gets you into trouble; it's what you know for sure that ain't so." An underlying root problem, *not* the surface symptoms the owner-manager is grappling with, may be a key constraint.

The process of understanding is active, probing, and continuous. It represents a deep commitment to exploration and forceful evaluation. It is analytic and diagnostic. It is also creative in its search for new efficiencies and innovative arrangements to enhance the profits of the firm.

The Rewards

The more you understand the complexity and possibilities inherent in the business the greater are your opportunities for improving the performance and profits.

Inevitably, you must make decisions and take actions based on incomplete and ambiguous information. And the outcomes of such decisions and activities will be uncertain. There are no "right" answers in advance.

But the effort to fully understand your business will reduce the margins of fuzziness. It will enhance your clarity and vision and capacity to recognize palpable nonsense or menacing chaos.

Assessing the probabilities with greater marginal certainty and distinguishing what is possible and maybe "right" from what is most likely impossible or wrong can significantly tilt the chances for a business's survival and success.

Reading the Numbers

A very good place to start is a thorough reading and interpretation of the firm's financials and other numerical data. Although you can't live behind your desk and manage by the numbers alone, you can't manage *without* the numbers, either.

Numbers talk. Determining what they signify, what exactly they are saying, though, is your responsibility. Reading the numbers is not the accountant's or bookkeeper's or anyone else's primary responsibility.

"The worst thing," notes a banker who specializes in loans to small businesses, "is when the business owner doesn't understand the numbers himself. If I ask a few questions and, right off the bat, he hesitates, that's a clue that there's a problem—a serious problem. And that makes me…hesitant [to make the loan]."

The numbers point to magnitudes, to new phenomena, to trends, and to areas of concern. They say, in effect, "Here are some items or areas of interest: Take a deeper look and see what their significance is. Dig further. Determine if there is a problem and if it requires some kind of action." If you ignore or misinterpret these signals, you may be missing some areas of vital concern.

Don't think, "Well, I'm just not a numbers person. Never had a head for numbers." It isn't a question of being good at numbers but rather of being vitally curious to know what the numbers are saying about the business and where they indicate you should be paying attention.

Bill Veeck, the legendary baseball club owner, wrote: "I like to poke around the financial statements, in the early morning hours at the park, looking for opportunities for fun and profit." Poking around is a good description of the process. And it really can be fun, because it is a process of discovery.

The Income Statement

Let's start here, in an attempt to see how you can systematically read the financials and get an indicative lay of the land.

Income statements start, top to bottom, with the gross sales, the cost of goods or materials sold, and the gross profits. There is then an itemized listing of all the company's operating expenses, grouped in useful categories, followed by the "bottom line," or net profits.

Each one of these numbers can be usefully examined. After some experience, you will be able to read the numbers relatively quickly because you will retain past numbers in your head and recognize patterns more quickly.

Managing Your Money Tip

The two key reports to monitor here is cash flow and profit and loss. To monitor cash flow, select Forecasting from the Money submenu. Managing Your Money will take your budgeted income and expenses from your Budget Categories and project your end-of-month cash position into the future. (For more information, see the instructions on page 183).

To track profit and loss (that is, income and expense), select Budget Categories from the Money submenu. Highlighting the field opposite F7, and then pressing F7, will allow you to look at the current month, tax categories, annual totals, and status (is the category included in net profit and cash forecasting?).

To generate a detailed report, press F4. You can select annual totals, budget vs. annual, etc. If you select "comprehensive," you'll get a month-by-month, budget vs. actual breakdown of every expense and income category that you've included.

Start with the revenues or sales. Checklist 21 shows some

CHECKLIST 21 Analyzing the Sales

---

1. *Compare current sales with expected or budgeted sales.*
   a. Are they higher, lower, or the same?
   b. If there is a telling variance, what does it mean, and what further information do you need to explain it?
2. *Compare current sales with prior sales.*
   a. What changes have taken place since the last month, the last three months, a year ago?
   b. When did the changes begin?
   c. Is there a trend?
   d. Are the changes predictable or acceptable?
   e. What are the causes of the changes?
   f. If there are no real changes, is that significant?
3. *Break down the sales, if useful.* Go into the backup papers or develop information which shows:
   a. *Products*
      (i)   Which products are selling well and which are the laggards?
      (ii) Ask why.
      (iii) Ask if you should continue to carry the laggards.
      (iv) What is the ratio of customer inquiries to actual sales orders? Any trends here?
   b. *Customers*
      (i)   Who or what category or subgroups made most of the purchases? Did 20 percent buy 80 percent of the goods? If so, should more attention be paid to key customers and to cultivating new key customers?
      (ii) When do most of the sales take place: Time of day? Which days? Why? Are there more customers at those times, or are the same number spending more? How can you apply this information to the pricing, advertising, staffing requirements, or product selection? To other areas?
      (iii) Where are the sales made: Which stores, which regions, for example?
      (iv) Through what sales channels were they made: direct, mail-order, or sales reps, for example?
      (v)   Which salespeople sold how much? Is this entirely a function of their sales skills? Are other factors at work?
      (vi) What were the average amounts of each sale? Any changes or trends at work here? Why?

CHECKLIST 21 Analyzing the Sales *(Continued)*

---

4. *Relate the sales to other data.* For example:
   a. Sales per square feet of retail space;
   b. Sales in relation to employees, or some subgroup of employees;
   c. Other ratios.
5. *Compare these ratios to industrywide averages.*

---

illustrative questions you can ask to get a feel for the significance of the numbers. Items (4) and (5) refer to certain ratios and suggest that the results be compared with those of other businesses in your field. Some of the more useful or frequently used ratios will be discussed later in this chapter.

Regarding the industrywide comparisons, suffice it for now to note that this kind of information is readily available. The Small Business Administration (S.B.A.) has dozens of publications that compile industry data, as do the hundreds of trade associations that represent different kinds of small businesses.

Next, move on to the cost of goods sold. The cost of goods sold, as I mentioned earlier, is usually expressed as a percentage, indicating the ratio of the direct cost of the goods sold by retailers in a given period to the total sales in that period. In manufacturing companies, the term used is the "cost of materials (and direct labor) sold."

When a company sells more than one similar type of goods or services, it is usually essential to break them down into subgroups. For example, a restaurant manager needs to have separate figures for food and beverages sold. And if that restaurant has a catering business, the catering cost of goods should be separated from those of the restaurant business. The object is to avoid combining apples and pears.

The knowledgeable owner-manager has an excellent idea what the cost of goods sold ratios should be, knows what the industry average is, and understands to what extent that average applies to his or her own business. The owner also knows the "pure" costs before any waste, theft and the like occur, and after calculating a tolerable margin of error, sets a standard. A few percentage points above that standard means something is happening. Perhaps purchasing costs have risen, or there is waste or spoilage or obsolescence. Even a modest rise is worrisome evidence of unacceptable operations inefficiencies or employee dishonesty. It could be that suppliers are delivering less than they are charging for. There are many possible explanations, and the owner-manager goes to work to narrow the likely causes and institute timely remedial action. Even a 2 percent rise in the aggregate cost of goods will cause a loss of substantial profits over a year—$20,000, for example, if annual sales are $1,000,000.

The net profits. Most owner-managers jump down to the figure for net profit for that month and, perhaps, for the "year-to-date." They want to know, obviously, how it all came out and if they are "winning" or "losing." They also will compare this figure with their expectations and with prior periods, to determine if the profits are moving in any meaningful direction.

But unless you are content with some vague notion of "acceptable" profits, the net profit is a very difficult number to evaluate. First, whatever the profit actually is, it says nothing of the extent that the upward potential for profit has been realized or squandered. Second, profits are simply the outcome of the sales, the cost of goods sold, and the monthly expenses. Profits are a function of dozens of variables and the extent to which all these factors have been well managed.

There are, however, some tentatively useful tools for analyzing profit levels, and in each case, you must relate the profits to some other number. At best, these ratios are indicative of the quality of the firm's profits.

They can be very misleading if you use them primarily to justify your firm's performance.

The test, or ratio, most widely used is the "Return on Sales" (R.O.S.). If sales are $500,000 annually, and the net profit is $50,000, the R.O.S. is 10 percent.

It is useful to compare one period's R.O.S. with other past periods. Beyond this, the R.O.S. is, on its face, a relatively meaningless number. Four percent in some fields, such as grocery stores, signifies superstar performance. In these businesses, profit margins are deliberately thin and the goal is high volume and large aggregate profits. In riskier businesses, a 20 percent R.O.S. is a dud and can signify gross mismanagement.

As a starter, it is important to know what the industry norm is for the particular business. Equally important is understanding that R.O.S. is highly dependent on sales levels and that a 5 percent R.O.S. in a startup company may represent a far better management job than a 15 percent R.O.S. after a few years of sales growth. Once a business's sales have passed the break-even point, those sales may conceal some grossly inefficient costs and expenses. Profits appear to be good, both absolutely and on a R.O.S. basis. But the firm's actual profits may be only a fraction of obtainable potential profits.

Another measure of profit performance is the "Return on Investment" (R.O.I.). This ratio is simply the annual net profits divided by the equity investment in the company. If net profits are $40,000 and the investment is $500,000, the R.O.I. is 8 percent.

In small businesses, the R.O.I. is primarily useful in comparing the return from the business with alternative investments. If a virtually riskless investment in AAA bonds produces a yield of, say, 10 percent and the small business's profits do not take into account a reasonable salary for the owner-manager, then that 8 percent R.O.I. looks, on its face, disappointing.

It is altogether possible to have a high R.O.I. and a low R.O.S., and vice versa. The only really reliable way to judge profits is to sense how closely they approximate the company's potential for profits—and that isn't directly found in the numbers.

The operating expenses. You can study each item of expenses in much the same way you consider sales and other items.

Take the "payroll," for example:

1. Is it up or down? Is there a trend?
2. Why? Where are the changes taking place?
3. Is the number of employees increasing?
4. What is the breakdown between "executive," "clerical," and "manual," for example (or other relevant categories of employees)? Evaluate the magnitudes of these sub-categories. Compare them with those of prior months.
5. Look at the overtime, the absenteeism, and sick leave. What percentage of the payroll or working days do they represent? Any changes? Anything significant here?
6. Calculate the payroll as a percent of total sales and total expenses. How do these figures compare with the industry norm? How do you explain any significant variance? Is there an underlying inefficiency at work: overpayment, too many employees, too little production per employee, for example?

When you "poke around" and pursue the cues, you will find a surprising amount of useful information.

A restaurant manager, for example, notices that "Restaurant Supplies" has risen significantly over the last three months. But "Restaurant Supplies" covers a variety of purchases, and the effective cause of the increase isn't apparent. Only after examining the related backup materials, invoices and all, does the owner-manager find that 95 percent of the increase is attributable to the purchase of new glassware. Further investigation shows that a new supplier's glasses are considerably thinner and more fragile than the glassware formerly purchased and are easily damaged or broken on the way to or inside the dishwasher. The outcome? The owner-manager locates some sturdier glassware of the same design. "Restaurant Supplies" are down in the ensuing months, and the *annual* savings are substantial.

Cost-Cutting Analysis

Most small businesses, I repeat, have very little tolerance for wasteful or unproductive expenses. And so, each time you review the income statements (in fact, each time you write a check) ask yourself some basic questions about the necessity or relative productivity of each particular expense item and the amount of that expense.

The fundamental question is whether a particular expense is justifiable at any level or that particular level. Now, anything is "justifiable" on a one-dimensional basis. Of course there are "reasons" for carrying any expense. Some of those reasons may be good ones and others bad. Some may be good ones until it is asked if there aren't *better* ways to spend the same money in other areas of the business or if the same results couldn't be achieved with half the present expenditures. For example, one employee could do what two are now doing, or an employee working 20 hours a week could achieve the same results as in the present 40-hour week.

Checklist 22 contains questions that may help to locate relatively unproductive expenses.

The Balance Sheet

Monthly analysis of the balance sheet can be just as useful as examination of the income statement. The balance sheet is the key to insights into liquidity and control of the working assets.

There is no substitute for an actual cash flow analysis over an extended period. But the monthly balance sheet will provide a quick read on the current cash situation and the company's capacity to pay its debts.

Managing Your Money Tip

Managing Your Money keeps excellent track of your balance sheet. Your Managing Your Money net worth statement (which is what your balance sheet is) will be as up-to-date as your last transaction. Every item in every Money Account that you establish will be reflected in your net worth statement. The only thing you have to add is

CHECKLIST 22 Cutting the Costs

---

1. If you *had* to reduce each expense item by 10 percent, what would you cut and what would you lose of any real value?
2. If you *had* to reduce total expenses 10 percent but could cut them any way you wanted, what would the priority reductions be? Would anything really productive be lost?
3. Are all the expenses either necessary or relatively productive in relation to any alternative expenditures that could be made?
4. If you started all over again, which expenses would you eliminate, in whole or part? Why not now? Are the reasons truly good ones?
5. If this or that item were reduced by 5 percent a month, what would be the annual increase in the company's profits? If you made five similar reductions, what would the aggregate effect be? (It is wonderfully astonishing how a number of small monthly, savings on unnecessary expenses add up in a year. Don't forfeit this additional profit simply because the savings on a reduction of a particular expense item are only a few hundred dollars a month and don't seem worth the effort.)
6. Have all the purchasing operations been reviewed recently? Are you getting good value? Are the prices you pay competitive? When did you last check? Do you know why some suppliers have raised prices in the last month? Have other suppliers also raised their prices?
7. Are you taking discounts for which you are eligible?

---

the names and values of your property and similar assets (for example, equipment owned by the company).

To account for property, select Your Net Worth from the Net Worth submenu. Highlight Assets, press F10 and then F5. Enter a description of the net worth item (such as "Business equipment"). If you're describing a class of items (such as "business equipment"), select "aggregate" as the type. If you're describing a type of item (such as "typewriter"), select "individual" as the type. When you're done, press F10. If you added a class of items, press F10 again, and repeat these steps for each item in this category, remembering to select "individual" as the type for each individual asset.

To print a net worth report, Select Your Net Worth from the Net Worth submenu. Press F4, and select the style of report (bank-style, corporate, etc.). Then press F10, and select whether you want to display the report on your screen, or print a copy on your printer. Then press F10 again.

Here are some particular things to examine:

1. *Cash-on-hand.* Is it rising or falling? Is there a trend? If falling, why—declining sales? New or increased operating or capital expenditures? An increase in the other working assets?

2. *Working, nonliquid assets* (such as accounts receivable and inventory). Have they increased? Which specific ones? Are they too large and require pruning to free up additional cash (see Chapter 8)?

3. *Current liabilities.* Are they rising or falling, absolutely and relative to the cash?

There are many balance sheet ratios that can be helpful when you use them to compare changes or trends over a period of several months or compare them with acceptable norms.

Four of the more useful ratios are:

1. *The Current Ratio.* This compares the firm's current assets to current liabilities. For example:

$$\frac{\$50,000 \text{ (current assets)}}{\$20,000 \text{ (current liabilities)}} 5 \ 2.5$$

This is a very healthy ratio. Conservative bankers hope to see a positive ratio of about 2.0, which is a rather unusual accomplishment in the startup company. A ratio of 1.5 is generally adequate, assuming there is considerable cash in relation to other current assets. A negative ratio is a sign of trouble: You may not generate the cash to meet your current obligations.

2. *The Acid Test*, or *Quick-Asset Ratio*. Here, the company's cash, plus other current assets that can be quickly converted into cash, are divided by current liabilities. For example:

$$\frac{\$12,000 \text{ (quick assets)}}{\$20,000 \text{ (current liabilities)}} \; 5 \; 0.6$$

Bankers hope to find a positive ratio of at least 1.0. If the preceding examples represent the same company, it is apparent that an unhealthy amount of working assets is absorbed by the nonliquid assets. Depending on the volume of sales the following month, there may be a looming cash crunch. The owner-manager should look deeper, locate the problem, and take some action to spring loose some more cash.

3. *Accounts Receivable to Sales Ratio*. This ratio is primarily useful to compare one month's performance with that of past months. The lower the ratio, of course, the better. What constitutes acceptability here depends on the extent that you sell on credit and the levels of efficiency achieved by similar businesses in your field. If, however, your receivables average 40 to 45 days old or more, you should work hard to reduce them to as close to 30 days as possible, assuming 30 days is the term of payment required of customers.

4. *The Inventory Turnover Ratio*. It is calculated this way:

$$\frac{\$500,000 \text{ (annual sales)}}{\$50,000*} \; 5 \; 10$$

The objective is a high turnover of your inventory (see Chapter 8). Again, an acceptable ratio depends on what kind of business you are in. Compare this ratio with past performance. Compare it, too, with other similar businesses to determine your relative efficiency.

---

* Either the average monthly inventory or the inventory at the end of a particular month.

Hands-on, Mind-on Understanding

The numbers are necessary and they are useful. They provide a kind of map of the business environment. They indicate where you are and where you may be going. They suggest areas of attention and concern.

But statistics, someone said, are like a bikini. What they reveal is suggestive; what they conceal is vital.

An owner-manager can sit behind a desk for 60 hours a week, reading reports, scanning the financials, attending to all the hustle and bustle, and may not really know much about the company, certainly not where it counts. Beyond that desk, out there on the floor, in the work areas and the market, are the staff, the customers, the products, the competitors, and the suppliers. Those are the realities behind the numbers. Beyond the desk and the written reports are the customers' perceptions, the quality control problems, the customer complaints, and product rejects. Out there are the employees' interests and concerns and their sense of what's to be done and how to do it. Beyond the desk are all the company's vital needs.

The reality beyond the desk and the numbers is wonderfully messy, disorderly, and seemingly chaotic and mysterious. Without the curiosity, skepticism, and probing instinct that pushes you beyond your desk to sniff around, ask questions, listen, observe, and ask more questions, you will be bound to a flat, one-dimensional, and very incomplete perception of your business.

Do you recall the Caliph of *The Arabian Nights?* Despairing of the reliability of reports from his viziers, eunuchs, and other official reporters, he sat in the marketplace disguised as a beggar to learn personally, directly, firsthand, what was really going on.

Hands-on management means getting "into" things, getting a personal taste and feel of situations. It allows you to sense the intangibles, the unspoken, and the unquantifiable.

The owner-manager who is skeptical of secondhand, processed, abstracted information seeks unfiltered reality and goes to the sources. The owner-manager who is uncomfortable with hearsay, speculation, and "obvious" but unsupported assertions of fact cuts through the thick brambles hiding the matters reported and investigates the situation firsthand.

As Yogi Berra said, "You can observe a lot just by watching." And listening. Checklist 23 gives some ways to increase your hands-on understanding.

CHECKLIST 23 Hands-on Management

---

1. *Make daily inspection tours* of the business: Check the appearance of the premises and the presentation of the products.
2. *Make contacts with the customers* (see Chapters 4 and 5):
   a. Observe them as they shop.
   b. Talk with them, ask questions.
   c. Field some of their telephone calls to find out what's on their minds.
   d. Read customer complaints.
   e. Check accounts receivable to see if there are patterns of customer problems.
3. *Try and use all the products:* Open, taste, weigh, clean, assemble, or do whatever else customers do with them.
4. *Spend time with the employees* (see Chapter 6):
   a. Get to know them.
   b. Ask about their work.
   c. Elicit suggestions, ideas.
   d. Observe their work and how they treat customers and products.
   e. Monitor work delegations and develop independent, direct sources of information.
   f. Communicate and enforce your operating values and standards.
5. *Investigate firsthand the efficiency of the operations:*
   a. The service: the installation, repair, provision of spare parts;
   b. The actual time between orders and delivery;
   c. Customer complaint and refund procedures;
   d. The manufacturing or product preparation areas;
   e. The administrative procedures: the payroll records, the inventory control systems, suppliers' invoices, payment procedures, and the billing procedures.

Hands-on management also requires a built-in baloney detector to develop hard, verifiable facts. Otherwise, you are headed for some ill-informed and misguided management decisions. Again, you have to pierce through superficial appearances and easy answers and go to the source for direct information.

Harold Geneen of ITT once wrote a memo to his executives, in which he said, "The highest art of professional management requires the literal ability to 'smell' a 'real fact' from all the others and moreover to have the temerity, intellectual curiosity, guts and/or plain impoliteness, if necessary, to be *sure* what you do have is indeed what we call an 'unshakable' fact....No matter what you think, try 'shaking it' to be sure."

Make an effort to pierce through incomplete or distorted information. You should consider whether the information you are getting is:

1. Based on hearsay;
2. Based on speculation, impression, or opinion;
3. Based on hidden or questionable assumptions;
4. Self-serving, or intended to show a "can-do" spirit;
5. Wishful thinking;
6. Deliberately deceptive;
7. Shaped to flatter or please you with selective good news;
8. Incomplete, inconsistent, contradictory, or illogical.

When people give you information, ask for their sources, how comfortable they feel about the information, what the basis of their confidence is, and so on. If you feel in your gut a lingering discomfort, continue to investigate and probe, looking for unprejudiced, direct sources of verifiable information.

When you hear the old, "They say," ask, "Who says, and why, and based on what?" When an employee gives you assurances that something important is completed as instructed, go to the source and see if, in fact, the job has been done satisfactorily. If information just doesn't seem "right," dig further.

The information that emerges may not always be expected or pleasing. It is said that a frequent cure for admiring a particular situation is to go and see it firsthand. And the search for one kind of information can turn up something entirely different and equally useful.

As an example of the second category, a consultant at a restaurant/bar asked a waitress what the three most common customer complaints were. The first thing she said was that no one had ever asked her such a question before and that the owner-manager was out of touch. One of the common complaints of the customers, she said, was that the by-the-glass servings of wine were "small, cheap." Now it happened that the house policy was to serve five ounces of wine per glass, which is very liberal. And, when a test was made, it proved that invariably the customer was getting six ounces of wine—a minor Guinness record, it would have seemed.

The underlying problem was that new glassware had been stocked, and the design of the wine glasses created a subtle visual break near the top of the glasses. Unless the wine was poured at or above that line, it looked as if the customer had been shortchanged. Nothing less than seven ounces in those glasses would do the job in the customers' eyes. Yet at six ounces, the house was barely breaking even. New glasses were of course required, both to satisfy customers and reduce excessive, not "cheap," pourings.

At the same restaurant, a close look at guest checks showed that very few desserts were sold. Why? Was it poor quality? Were customers being overfed? Were the desserts not appropriate to the setting or the other foods? Well, a series of questions to a particular waitress finally revealed that none of the waitresses were allowed to taste the desserts. Not only was there no basis for enthusiastic promotion, but if the truth were known, the waitresses held a small grudge against the house and were just not going to sell the desserts. That problem, too, was solved at the root by a policy change.

Understanding the Business to Improve It

Ambitious, questioning owner-managers are not content to sit back on the status quo simply because they make a profit. They focus on the likely gap between actual and potential performance and profits. They assume there is room for improvement and actively search for latent or hidden problems and opportunities.

A CPA tells of an owner-manager who learned of the assistance provided to small businesses by the Executive Service Corps, an organization of retired businessmen. The CPA asked him where he wanted help, which areas of his business needed improvement. The owner-manager drew a blank. The question had never occurred to him. Not that the firm didn't have significant problems. It did. And one of the main problems was management's lack of knowledge or curiosity about what and where the problems were.

Finding Problems and Opportunities

The Chinese use the same character for "crisis" and "opportunity." When confronted effectively, each results in a better situation than existed before. Good owner-managers actively go after better situations. They hunt—and pull—little weeds before they grow and strangle the company. They probe relentlessly for opportunities to do new things or do old things better. "A wise man," as the saying goes, "will make more opportunities than he finds."

Effective owner-managers make it their business to see information and things "in 95 different ways," in the words of David Mahoney, former CEO of Norton Simon. On the other hand, as a small business consultant points out, "It's not that the [owner-managers] can't solve problems; it's that they don't see them." Perception precedes analysis, as well as solutions or decisions. Open-minded exploration precedes policy and action. How we see a situation largely determines what we think and do about it.

When you understand that, you can make an active, conscious effort to detach yourself from prepatterned thoughts and attitudes. You can see things from a different perspective.

It is as if our business world is a 360-degree landscape, but we habitually look out only one window and take in only 60 degrees of the view. When you resolve to explore the business for fresh information, visions, and sights, you will shift your attention and frame of reference to other windows on the business landscape and begin to take in the remaining 300 degrees.

The Processes of Creative Exploration

I have noted in earlier chapters a pronounced tendency of the activist entrepreneur to "get on with things." Yet there is a lot of evidence that innovative, creative people spend more time than other people in exploring and formulating problems. Gary Steiner of the University of Chicago writes, "Creativity is characterized by a willingness to seek and accept relevant information from any and all sources, to suspend judgment, defer commitment, remain aloof in the pressure to take a stand."

To see the business freshly, to break out of habitual ways of doing things, the innovative owner-manager must challenge old ideas and operating assumptions about how things are and ought to be. In that way, the firm can be liberated from inappropriate, outdated, or limiting ideas and assumptions.

Look for new interpretations and new patterns and connections in existing data. You will then be able to generate new ideas and alternatives for leading the business effectively. Albert Einstein once said there was nothing really new in his theory of relativity, that he had simply taken information that had been in the public domain for 30 years and combined it in a slightly novel way.

Owner-managers who consistently seek to improve their businesses are wary of the first interpretation, explanation, or solution that comes to mind or is proposed. They would no more accept those first ideas than they would buy the first house shown them by a real estate broker.

They defer conclusions and even analysis and evaluation until after they have looked at things in a number of different ways.

They have learned that the best way to encourage fresh, potentially useful perceptions is to suspend judgment of new ideas so they can go with the flow of these ideas. Rather than kill a new idea, they try to extract whatever part of it might later point to a new direction or be combined with other new ideas and converted to practical use.

Paradoxically, we tend to stick to the comfortable and habitual ways of doing things until they become very painful. One way of maintaining the status quo and resisting new ideas is to kill them with thoughts such as, "Yes, but…"; "There's no time to develop it"; "It's not logical"; "It's impractical"; "It can't work"; "So-and-so won't like it"; "The weakness here is…" Creative businesspeople stay with new ideas no matter how silly or absurd they seem.

"Either/Or" Killers

Creative managers also know that an excellent way of prematurely closing exploration of a situation is to frame an issue in an "either/or" fashion, so that it requires a "yes" or "no" answer. If, for example, the issue is, "Shall we spend another $10,000 this year on advertising?" a "yes or no" answer forecloses a number of possible interpretations of the effectiveness of that expenditure or consideration of alternative investments. It may be that a particular $5,000 portion of the advertising is highly productive, the rest a waste, and the ineffective $5,000 should be invested in a public relations campaign or another type of promotional activity. Perhaps the entire $10,000 could be invested more productively in new designs or packages for the company's products or in redesigning and brightening the premises of the firm, if it's a retail business. Or perhaps the money would be better spent improving the incentive compensation of the sales force. In fact, unless the issue of advertising is considered as a part of an entire package of questions regarding sales growth, an early "yes or no" decision will probably be very ineffective.

Improving Your Creativity

In the last 10 to 15 years, there have been a number of excellent books on ways to improve your capacity for day-to-day creativity that are highly relevant to the small business world. They emphasize problem-solving and opportunity-finding skills.

If you are not content with the status quo but doubt your "creativity," you would do well to read any of Edward de Bono's books on creative thinking skills, such as *Lateral Thinking* and *Practical Thinking.* Another useful book *Getting to Yes,* by Roger Fisher and William Ury, spells out creative negotiating techniques and the problem-solving processes behind them.

Two books specifically targeted for the businessperson are Russell L. Ackoff's *The Art of Problem Solving* and Michael Ray's and Rochelle Myers' *Creativity in Business,* based on a course they teach at the Stanford Business School.

Questions, Questions, Questions

It may be, though, that the best way to generate fresh perspectives on your business and discover latent opportunities for improving performance and profits lies nearer at hand. Questions and more questions are your stock-in-trade.

Rudyard Kipling wrote:

I keep six honest serving-men
(They taught me all I know)
Their names are What and Why and When
and How and Where and Who.

Asking the right questions is your entry to new business truths and activities. But this isn't easy, and it frequently invites ridicule or recrimination. The "right" questions often seem "dumb," "silly," or "innocent." Or they are provocative and disturb the peace. Asking the "right" questions takes practice and persistence. But the payoff can be truly wonderful in terms of incremental and major structural improvements in the business—improvements that yield increased profits.

What follows are a number of questions you might want to ask in a variety of circumstances. Sustained questioning can be a powerful tool in loosening preconceptions and rigidities that prevent a small business from reaching its potential.

"What's Important" Questions

These are questions to help you focus on the "heart-of-the-matter" issues that not only are conditions of your firm's success but that, once grasped, will save you hours of valuable time.

1. Where are we, where do we want to go, and how do we get there?

2. What's really important here?

3. How can we do a better job of finding areas of improvement and implementing appropriate changes?

4. Where are the major trouble points?

5. What's the underlying problem as distinguished from the surface symptoms?

6. What's the vital question? What's the preeminent concern?

7. What are the central components of this situation?

8. What hasn't been asked, what's missing, what is vital but unclear so far?

9. What would a valuable, knowledgeable business consultant, or a trusted, wise friend ask? Or do?

Challenging the Accepted

The tendency, noted earlier, is to assume that what is, is right. We lose sight of more productive options unless we can crack through the stubborn defenses of the status quo.

1. Is this the best way?
2. Is this the only way?
3. Why are we doing it this way?
4. What are the underlying assumptions here? Why does everyone accept them? Has anyone ever asked? Tested them? Are there other equally valid assumptions? What is the directly opposite assumption?
5. Is this the way it would be done by:
   a. An experienced owner-manager?
   b. A marketing pro?
   c. A production expert?
   d. An engineer?
   e. A representative customer?
   f. A great salesperson?
   g. A CPA?
   h. An efficiency expert?
6. What changes does the staff want and why?
7. What changes do customers want and why? Why are we reluctant to undertake them? Are there truly sufficient reasons?
8. Would another way possibly yield better results?
9. What if we did…?
10. If this situation were actually done differently or improved, how would it then look?
11. If we absolutely had to improve this (for example, sales, costs, product, operations, efficiencies), what would it look like?
12. How would we go about realizing it? What would have to be done to achieve it?

Always, examine the response to a "why" question and ask:

1. Is that sufficient? What's missing?
2. What is the other side of the argument?
3. What are the alternatives?

There are always "reasons" for doing almost anything. But the question is, how do you weigh the "pros" against the "cons," and, in turn, how do you weigh them against alternative explanations or courses of action?

For example, if you ask an employee to explain a request to purchase some new equipment for $2,000, and the answer is, "It will help us do the work faster," ask, "True, but what are the negatives? Let's discuss alternative uses for that $2,000 and see if it can't be invested even more productively than in the new equipment you recommend." It could be that doing the work *better* and not faster is the real issue. There may be a bevy of alternative considerations that must be factored into a decision.

"Three-Things" Questions: Probing for Constructive Changes

Forcing yourself to generate options to the status quo is a way to liberate yourself from inadvertent blindness to attractive opportunities for improving the business.

1. List three critical areas of the business where improvements might be made.
2. List three problems in the business.
3. List three problems or opportunities in each of these areas:
   a. Costs and expenses
   b. Staff productivity
   c. Product quality
   d. Cash availability
   e. Declining or static sales
   f. The owner-manager's time
   g. Customer knowledge or acceptance of the product
4. List three things that the following might ask or recommend to improve the business or any area of the business:

    a. A marketing pro

    b. A customer

    c. An employee

    d. Others

5. List three favorable and three unfavorable adjectives customers use to describe the products, the service.

6. List three things that could be eliminated, or three things that could be added to make this situation or these things better.

7. List three ways of interpreting this situation.

8. List three questions about this situation that haven't been asked and that might open the door to improved results.

More Probing for Changes—"What If..."

Ask yourself "What if..." about each item in the following list.

1. We cut the staff in half?

2. We added to the staff?

3. We opened a new outlet/branch in...?

4. We redesigned the premises? The product?

5. We had a meeting with all the staff and gave awards for the three best suggestions?

6. We put live models in the showcase window?

7. We eliminated the middleman?

8. We closed on weekends? Opened on weekends?

9. We wanted to achieve this—what would we have to do?

10. We started out all over again, what would we do that we're not doing now, or not do that we're doing now? Why not implement those ideas now?

11. This were bigger, smaller, more, less, faster, slower—what would it look like, what would the results be, how would we achieve it, and at what cost?

12. We did this, what would happen? What wouldn't happen? What don't we know?

Finding Useful Connections

Often, seemingly random phenomena are related in important ways that, once understood, yield more productive policies and activities. When key cause and effect relationships are perceived in the area of sales volume, for example, you are far less likely to waste time and money on futile courses of action.

1. Does product reliability, for example, relate to customers' acceptance of the product?

2. Do these phenomena relate to declining sales?

3. Do cash shortages relate to inflated costs, or to declining sales, or to inadequate staff productivity?

4. Does my use of time relate to a staff problem?

Converting Ideas into Realities

Ideas in a vacuum may appear highly unrealistic until you force yourself to think about what would have to happen to convert them into actual results. Also, it sometimes helps to visualize some improvements in the business and then work backwards to the specific actions that are necessary to bring about these improvements. Here are some questions designed to provoke this process.

1. If I *had* to change this for the better, where would I start? What would I look for?

2. How do I *know* this can't be done? Why do I *assume* it can't be done?

3. What would this idea look like if it were converted into a reality? What results could we expect?

4. How do we go about making it real, practical, useful?

5. What are the preconditions to making it happen?

6. What has to be developed?

7. What are the problems, obstacles, constraints, and risks?

8. How can we remove, modify, or avoid these constraints?

9. What are the costs? How do they compare with expected benefits?

Identifying and Applying the Business's Strengths

Focusing on your firm's strengths and weaknesses is a good way of finding additional ways to improve the firm's performance. Below are two sets of questions to move your attention to those factors and help you apply them constructively.

1. What are we doing best?

2. What are we doing well?

3. What works well?

4. Who works well?

5. What methods work well?

6. What motivates the staff well?

7. What products sell well?

8. What resources/assets produce the best results?

9. Why? Can we extrapolate any lessons and apply them to other areas of the business? Or redouble the successful efforts?

Weaknesses and Liabilities

1. What are the relative weaknesses of the firm? Of the management? Of the staff?

2. Which can't be helped? Are we sure of that?

3. Which could be improved with more time and effort? Why haven't we devoted more attention?

4. Which seem to require more talent or money than we have? Are we sure of that?

5. What's not going as well as expected? Why?

6. What are the constraints to better performance here? If these constraints weren't there, what would the situation look like? What would the results be?

7. If we *had* to remove just one or two of these constraints, which would it be and how would we do it?

8. What have other businesses done in similar circumstances?

9. Where is the chaos? The potential chaos? What should be done now?

10. What are we neglecting? What do I fear might happen if we continue to neglect it/them? How can we come to grips with it/them?

11. What might work better? How? Why do we leave it that way? Is that a truly good reason?

12. How can we convert some so-called liabilities into assets? Are there analogies in our business to sales of "reject clothing"? Or to the canned salmon that didn't sell because customers thought it wasn't pink enough (sales turned around the moment it was advertised as "the only *pale* salmon")? Or to the supermarket that takes relatively worthless end pieces of beef, puts them on a stick with tomatoes, onions, and peppers, calls them shish kebobs, and charges a whopping markup?

Effective Decisions

Most of your daily business problems and issues can be decided quickly, on-the-spot. Either they are relatively easy to decide, or any decision is better than none. The consequences of many decisions are not particularly far-reaching.

Some questions, though, are sufficiently complex and important to require the degree of analytic and explorative understanding described earlier in this chapter. They make the same demands for:

1. Fact-finding and relentless pursuit of hidden, constricting assumptions and missing information;

2. An open-minded, judgment-free search for alternative diagnoses, explanations, and options.

It's not just that the "wrong" decisions in such cases can have costly and misguided long-range consequences. The "right" answers to the wrong problems can also have equally injurious consequences.

If anything important is at stake in making a decision, give it time, wrestle with it, develop a personal interest in seeing it through. President Eisenhower used to tell his staff, "Now boys, let's not make our mistakes in a hurry." The amount of time spent grappling with a major problem or decision is relatively small compared with the time devoted to the daily hustle and bustle. The payoff can be splendid.

Checklist 24 contains suggestions to consider when an important and seemingly baffling problem or issue arises.

Items (1) and (6) on the list are matters we have not discussed. How you frame a problem largely governs how you will proceed in answering it. It determines what you assume, what you look for, and what you see.

It is best to start with a relatively expansive definition of the issue. "Why are sales declining?" for example. That will help you isolate any hidden assumptions that might limit you to a predetermined conclusion. If the same issue were defined as "Which prices shall we lower?" you would be precluded from discovering a multitude of other possible underlying causes of declining sales. It may be that the company's costs are bloated and prices are necessarily high. There may be any number of reasons for declining sales that are totally unrelated to either prices or costs.

For example, salespeople at a small Ohio auto parts manufacturer were producing disappointing results. The owner-manager assumed the problem was inadequate "job enrichment." He therefore gave the salespeople more products to sell, hoping to stimulate their interest in the company's business.

A year later, sales were still sluggish. The owner-manager one day observed that the sales staff was young and inexperi-

CHECKLIST 24 Solving Problems and Making Decisions

---

1. State the problem/issue. Try it several ways. A problem well defined is a problem half-solved.
2. Get the facts: What's the story?
3. Determine what's known, unknown, and fuzzy. What information is still needed?
4. Tentatively analyze or come to a "sense" of what the situation is all about and where it is pointing.
5. Simultaneously, expose and examine the assumptions that are governing the interpretation of the situation. Are they really valid? Are there other equally valid or better working assumptions?
6. Try restating the problem/issue now.
7. Develop several options and alternative solutions.
8. Now examine and analyze those options, individually and comparatively. Look at:
    a. Achievability
    b. Feasibility
    c. Costs/benefits
    d. Risks/rewards
    e. Preconditions of success
    f. Your own concerns and worries
9. Decide. Rationally analyze, yes, but go with your intuitive feel, your hunches: "It works," or "It just doesn't work."

---

enced. The problem then was correctly defined as an overload of products and related training and technical knowledge, not too few products. The salespeople had not been able to absorb all the necessary information well enough to sell the products convincingly. The solution flowed quite naturally: Substantially reduce the range of products assigned to each salesperson. Sales soon increased.

One further observation. No effective decision is complete without an associated action plan. We will discuss this more fully in the next chapter. The point now is to realize that *what* you decide is inextricably bound to *how* you carry it out.

If the ends and means are not integrally aligned, it's not a good decision. Purposeful activity, I have suggested, is the hallmark of effective management. Those activities that flow from a decision must be feasible. They must be calculated to achieve the desired results. And they must be doable within the boundaries of acceptable costs, risks, and side effects.

A necessary precondition for aligning goals and activities is the same as that for running a successful small business: You must understand your business inside out.

CHAPTER
11

PLANNING FOR ACTION AND RESULTS

This chapter is about planning for the future, those not so distant tomorrows that are shaped by what we want and do today.

Owner-managers who focus only on immediate and concrete tasks often regard planning for the future as remote and visionary. But business planning most definitely does imply vision, and it is quite certain that where there is no vision, businesses as well as people perish.

Effective planning for a small business is action oriented and results oriented. It involves converting challenging but realistic and concrete goals into productive activities. The purpose is improved performance and higher profits.

What follows in this chapter is a discussion of the reasons planning is so important to the future of any business and the specific elements that make up the planning process.

Practical Business Planning

Let's first note what effective planning for the small business is *not* and try to get rid of implications of irrelevance.

Planning does *not* require those bulky and speculative documents, replete with history, biographies of key employees, fantastic profit projections, and put-downs of the competition, that are designed to impress outside investors. Nor does it require those lengthy and laborious exercises, with their frequently irrelevant analyses, prepared by subunits of *Fortune 500* companies.

We are not concerned with fancy projections and detailed blueprints for the next five years, nor with their opposites—those three-sentence statements of noble but fuzzy intentions, followed by plug-in-the-numbers projections of present trends. Those plans are deservedly filed away forever. They are useless dust-gatherers.

What we *are* concerned with are the practical, operating requirements of the small business. That means assessing where your business is, what its needs are, where you realistically choose to steer it, and how you propose to get there. Abraham Lincoln said it best: "If we could first know where we are and whither we are tending, we could better judge what to do and how to do it."

There is nothing more or less involved in small business planning than conscious, coordinated decisions about where and how to apply the business's limited resources for maximum results.

Benefits of Effective Planning

Unless a firm is to be forever imprisoned in reacting to daily hustle and bustle and consequent fire fighting, planning is a necessary and supremely practical activity. The real payoffs for the small business are not in the day-to-day tasks and diversions, but in the realization of longer term opportunities. Those can be achieved by carefully conceived, productive allocations of the firm's resources and doable action programs.

The business plan helps you to focus on the firm's key factors of success and its preeminent priorities. It helps you track the really important objectives that must be achieved to assure the firm's success and deal with particular situations as they arise in light of those priorities. Most important, it is a plan for *action*.

The specific benefits of business planning include the following:

1. *The process itself is a powerful discipline* that forces you to step back, detach yourself from the daily battles, and take an overview of the entire business. It concentrates your mind on the essentials for survival and success. It pushes you to address the vital, specific needs of the company irk-the coming months, not just the next day.

2. *It is a game plan* for marrying activities and specific and challenging objectives so that those needs will be met.

3. *It summons staff contributions* and allows you, in turn,

to immerse the staff in the company's values and goals and your own expectations for their work results.

4. *It is a personal commitment* to what you alone must decide, initiate, and contribute to the firm's success.

The prospects for survival and success are greatly increased by knowing what you want to do to improve the profits, how you propose to go about it, and what specifically has to be done to achieve it. "In the long run, men hit only what they aim at," observed Henry David Thoreau.

Many owner-managers, though, don't know what such planning entails or why and how the effort yields disproportionate rewards. They believe that the future is too volatile and uncertain to direct and control. That is not a good reason not to avoid planning. Among other things, business planning reduces the imponderables and helps to prepare for surprises and deal with them early, before they become menacing. The business plan is not a straitjacket, and heads don't roll if specific objectives are not met. Far from inhibiting opportunistic changes in direction, development and frequent review and revision of the plan will liberate you from rigid perceptions and commitments to the past.

Elements of an Effective Business Plan

As you develop your plan, keep the following general points in mind.

1. *Put It in Writing.* The discipline itself justifies a written plan. If parts are incomplete or fuzzy in your mind, you will have difficulty writing them down. Or they will look fuzzy on paper. Getting it all down on paper tends to reveal where the plan is vague or undeveloped. If it's not in writing, it is too easy to skate over the process, and you will likely have a laundry list of good intentions, but no hard, feasible action commitments.

You tend to develop a kind of dialogue with your written words. For example, a written plan exposes inconsistencies.

You may note, for example, that you have described your product's strength as its "durability." Yet the product is distributed in fancy specialty shops, advertised in upscale media, and touted for its chicness and appearance.

Or, the plan may call for hiring for the first time a director of a particular product line. It may also assume that the employee in question probably won't produce break-even returns for eight months. This will drain the company of $16,000 in cash that is budgeted for some new equipment. Either the company will have to forgo the investment for equipment or the owner-manager will have to take a personal salary reduction. Those kinds of relationships are much better seen in the black-and-white of a written plan.

2. *Make It Short.* Probably six to ten pages is adequate. Focus on what you realistically want to have happen to improve the business and on what has to be done to realize those improvements.

3. *Limit the Plan to One Year.* Six months ought to be the minimum. You should take a hard look at the plan every two or three months and revise it as necessary to adjust for actual events and results. But if you do revise the plan, make sure that variances between planned and actual experience are caused by errors or changes in the underlying assumptions or by factors outside your control. If the variances are the result of insufficient effort to achieve the projected targets, you should be very wary about changing the plan without quietly acknowledging that it is not the plan that is wanting and that the purpose of management is to achieve desired, feasible results.

4. *Get the Staff to Participate.* In many cases, they know best what the realistic needs of the company are and what has to be done to meet them. The staff's open agreement with the plan is also a key to its success; that consensus will provide the basis for the cooperative assumption of action responsibilities. Without the participation and cooperation of the staff, you risk quiet sabotage of your business plan.

The exact organization or format of the plan is something you will have to decide. It isn't the form, but the understanding, challenge, and feasibility that count.

In preparing the plan, it will become clear that it does not evolve in a nice sequential fashion. All the parts interact. For example, you may develop or place the cash flow at the end but it in fact affects other areas—limiting plans to expand the product range or the staffing for the year, for example.

An effective, comprehensive plan for the small business should include certain specific components. Checklist 25 outlines those elements. Let's now discuss them separately.

I. Overview

"We review the whole damn thing from scratch once a year," says one owner-manager. And that is what is required.

This is the best time to cover the whole landscape and organize all your thoughts and assumptions regarding the company's prospects and profits. It is the best time to make a really intensive, comprehensive review of the company to arrive at the understanding of the business suggested in the previous chapter. Knowing what's going on is a daily, ongoing process, but a systematic examination once or twice a year is especially productive.

Preparation of the Overview shouldn't mean you have to start from zero. If you have given ongoing consideration to the issues and requirements raised throughout this book, the Overview, is simply a fresh and coherent summary of your specific thoughts and evaluations.

Section A (General), for example, encapsulates your best sense of the business's mission and the critical factors of success, as discussed in Chapter 3.

The Functional Review under Section B will mainly incorporate your key findings and assumptions regarding the matters discussed in Chapters 4 to 9.

Checklist 25 Elements of a Business Plan for Small Firms

I. *Overview*
   A. *General*
      1. The company's mission
      2. Its critical factors of success
   B. *Functional Review*
      1. *The market plan.* Analysis, assumptions, and needs regarding:
         (a) Customers
         (b) Products and services
         (c) Assessment of competition
         (d) Prices
         (e) Promotion and selling
      2. *Production and delivery operations*
      3. *Staff:*
         (a) Review of personnel
         (b) Review of compensation
         (c) Staffing needs
         (d) The owner-manager's supervision and organization of the staff
      4. *Financial status:*
         (a) Cash situation and needs
         (b) Costs and expenses
         (c) Working assets
      5. *Administration:*
         (a) Day-to-day operations and procedures
         (b) Adequacy of accounting system
         (c) Internal controls
      6. *The business environment:*
         (a) The economy
         (b) Demographic changes and trends
         (c) Government regulations, taxes and the like
      7. *Contributions of the owner-manager*
   C. *Summary and Conclusions.* List the priority needs, problems, and opportunities.
II. *Concrete, Priority Business Objectives*
   A. First tier
   B. Second tier

Checklist 25 Elements of a Business Plan for Small Firms (*Continued*)

III. *Action Plans*
IV. *Budgets* (and backup as relevant)
   A. Cash flow
   B. Income and expenses
   C. Other

Hopefully, those considerations and the Summary and Conclusions under Section C will be enriched by a comprehensive, hands-on understanding of the business, as discussed in Chapter 10.

By no means should you attempt to include in the plan *all* your analyses and ideas on such matters. The dominant considerations that relate to the next 6 to 12 months of business are the ones to focus on.

II. Where Should the Company Go—Concrete, Priority Objectives

This section of the plan flows straight from the Overview.

Here, you state the operating conclusions of this Overview in terms of where you want the company to move in the next 6 to 12 months. That should be based on the company's needs, risks, problems, and opportunities. These goals are expressed as specific objectives.

The objectives are not just a laundry list of desirable improvements, though. A small business is particularly constricted by the disparity between what it would like to accomplish, on the one hand, and what it must or realistically can achieve on the other. There are not enough employees, talent, money, or time to undertake more than a few key priorities, if you intend to do them well and really bring them home on target. It is on these make-a-difference undertakings that the firm's resources should be concentrated.

A business without goals and objectives will look like a

sandlot basketball game without a hoop. The trick is to first determine which are really the priorities—"where the money is." You can outline the top three objectives under "First Tier Priorities" and follow with, say, three or four more in a list of "Second Tier Priorities." The purpose of this approach is to keep your mind and energies, and the firm's resources, focused on the truly important activities that cannot be sacrificed or suspended in the rush of day-to-day events.

Second, you have to express the priorities as concrete, specific objectives. That way, you will avoid any tendency to wishful thinking and well-intentioned vagueness. When the objectives are well defined and stated in quantitative terms where appropriate, you will know what the end results should look like if achieved and whether subsequent action is successful, a near-miss, or a failure.

Each of these goals, expressed in specific terms, may be followed by a brief description of the approach or strategy that will be followed, as a frame for a specific action plan.

Some concrete priority objectives might be stated like this.

1. *Reduce costs by about $45,000 to $50,000* in the next 12 months:
   a. Reduce cost of goods sold by 3 to 5 percent—about $28,000.
   b. Reduce bookkeeper's work to three days a week; don't replace Jones when he leaves in March—about $20,000.
2. *Improve speed of deliveries 40 to 50 percent* through modernizing production facilities by September 1:
   a. Purchase ABC equipment at auctions for no more than $20,000.
   b. Contract electrician and other labor to install equipment and effect necessary structural modifications at work site for no more than $4,000.
   c. Finance this by:
      (i) Reducing inventory by 15 percent and the average receivables by 10 days (new cash available—about $9,000);

      (ii) Securing loan for $15,000; if no loan, try to lease the equipment; if necessary, invest profits.

3. *Improve customer service* in three areas where it is weakest:

    a. Hold weekly meetings with waiters/waitresses and bartenders to improve knowledgeable, friendly, and timely table service. I will devote at least two hours a day on floor to monitor and act on problems as they arise.

    b. Improve cleanliness and appearance of premises: Replace Joe; issue detailed instructions to floor managers; most important, monitor personally on daily basis.

    c. Reduce waiting time for food service: Add one extra kitchen employee and one extra waiter at peak times—Friday and Saturday nights, and Saturday and Sunday afternoons.

    d. Estimated cost will be $1,000 a month.

    e. Estimated effect on sales will be to improve sales over long-term, by amounts unknown. But it must be done—present situation is damaging to word-of-mouth reputation.

III. Action Plans

For each of the priority objectives, a detailed action plan must be devised, or the plan will be a futile paper exercise. The point is to lay out exactly what is necessary and sufficient to achieve the objectives.

The decisive elements here are fairly simple:

1. *Who* does *what;*

2. By *when* (progress benchmarks are often useful);

3. What *resources* are needed and when;

4. What are the possible *obstacles,* which of these are controllable, and how will they first be recognized; tentative *contingency* options;

5. What are the *reporting* and *monitoring* responsibilities;

6. What are the procedures for *revision* and *correction,* as appropriate.

IV. Budgets

This part of the plan is probably the scariest for all but old hands and some who have had disciplined experience in a well-run big corporation. Samuel Goldwyn, the movie mogul, is alleged to have said "Forecasts are dangerous, particularly those about the future."

But look at it this way. A budget is nothing more or less than a quantified list of assumptions or expectations. And the more time you have spent reading and playing with the possibilities of the numbers, the easier it becomes.

First among these budgets is the cash flow. It is a very good idea to include this for all but mature, or cash rich, businesses (see Chapter 8). The cash estimates not only signal if and when there will be a cash crunch, but also set a frame on your activities within the year. The projections for the second six months are the toughest. But your best calculated estimates will probably be both adequate and useful, provided they incorporate major assumptions regarding expenditures related to expansion, capital investment, or large financial liabilities coming due, and anticipated changes in the sales and operating costs.

An income and expenses budget is also a useful tool. These figures will have been estimated already in preparing the cash flow (recall the critical difference between cash and profit as discussed in Chapter 8). This will allow you to check actual results against the budget and to assess variances as they develop.

Remember, you can always revise the budgets, either upward, if targets are being exceeded and it is desirable to restore challenging objectives and incentives, or downward, if events overtake your plans and the assumptions behind them prove unrealistic, incorrect, or uncontrollable.

Both these budgets are particularly useful in revealing significant departures from the plan and warning that follow-up action is required—soon.

Give the plan a go. If you are feeling strong inner resistance, ask yourself, "Why?" Consider whether the immediate, felt resistance really expresses underlying resistance. Be honest about this. Remind yourself that you are "planning" already, whether you know it or not. What you do with your time and how you allocate the firm's resources each day represent a statement about the future and what is important, even if your decisions are not articulated or deliberate. The point is that a conscious, systematic planning process, if you give it a chance, yields rich rewards beyond the time and effort required.

Managing Your Money Tip

You can review your business' budget in Managing Your Money. Select Budget Categories from the Money sub-menu. Highlighting the field opposite F7, and then pressing F7, will allow you to look at the current month, tax categories, annual totals, and status (is the category included in net profit and cash forecasting?).

To generate a detailed report, press F4. You can select annual totals, budget vs. annual, etc. If you select "comprehensive," you'll get a month-by-month, budget vs. actual breakdown of every expense and income category that you've included.

EPILOGUE

TAKE YOUR CHOICE

Breaking the Business	Making the Business
1. Your strengths will cancel out any limitations, and your hard work will attest to the firm's success. Avoid the observations and suggestions of outsiders—what do they know?	1. Be objective and assess your and your firm's strengths and weaknesses. Then, compensate for or nullify the weaknesses.
2. Everything is equally important, so do everything equally well and spread the firm's resources sufficiently thin to please everyone. Give priority to the needs of the moment.	2. Keep it simple and focused. Develop priorities and concentrate on what is truly important to the success of the firm.
3.–4. Start with the products and make sure they reflect your own values and tastes. Build a better mousetrap or a me-too product and the public will beat a path to your doorstep— good products sell themselves.	3. Provide excellent and distinctive goods and services that meet the wants and needs of select groups of customers. 4. Determine how to reach out and sell to your customers.
5. Since you are responsible for everything, do it all yourself— no one else will do it as well, after all.	5. Build, manage, and motivate a team to do what you can't do yourself.

Breaking the Business	Making the Business
6. Don't bother with the accounting records and financial controls. Others in the business can do that, and they will tell you what the financial data means. Save money on an accountant—anyone can produce the data needed by the tax authorities.	6. Keep the accounting records and controls you must use to understand and manage the business. Hire a first-rate accountant.
7. Ignore the working capital and invite fraud. As long as there are profits, you will have all the cash you ever need.	7. Manage your assets so you never run out of cash; don't confuse sales and profits with spendable cash.
8. Concentrate on spectacular sales growth—that is the point of a business and only rapid growth will generate the profits and cash you need to survive and succeed.	8. Avoid the recurring and often fatal pitfalls of rapid growth. Manage and control that growth.
9. A good manager is so close to the business he can run it from his desk. There is no point wasting valuable time in careful analysis or search for new information, problems, and opportunities. If you are working hard, any conceivable opportunities for improving the business will be obvious.	9. Understand the business inside out. There is no company whose profits cannot be improved. Search for ways to improve the business.
10. Don't plan—it's impractical. Don't set goals. Take care of the day-today operations and the future will take care of itself.	10. Plan ahead. Set challenging but realistic goals and fashion action plans to achieve them.

Breaking the Business	Making the Business
Conclusion	*Conclusion*
Small business is ultimately a roll of the dice and a prayer. Good Luck!	Small business is ultimately about effective management: the understanding, direction, and control of the firm by one person—you. When you manage the business effectively, you don't need good luck. Success is the natural result!

SUGGESTIONS FOR FURTHER READING

A moderately well-stocked public library is likely to carry books on almost any aspect of small business, from credit control to running a mail-order business. What follows is a short list of books of more general interest or direct application to important matters discussed in this book.

If you are considering starting a business or are still in the pre-start-up stage, these three are useful:

Jeffry A. Timmons, Leonard E. Smollen, Alexander L.M. Dingee, *New Venture Creation: A Guide to Small Business Development*. Homewood, Il.: Irwin, 1985.

Clifford M. Baumback, *How to Organize and Operate a Small Business*. Englewood Cliffs, N.J.: Prentice-Hall, 1985.

Donald M. Dible, *Up Your Own Organization*. Reston, Va.: Reston, 1986.

At various times in the course of organizing or running your firm, you will want to consult a comprehensive nuts-and-bolts reference. William A. Cohen's *The Entrepreneur and Small Business Problem Solver: An Encyclopedic Reference and Guide* (New York: Wiley, 1983), is precisely that: An encyclopedia of handy information. The Baumback book, already cited, is a similarly oriented "how-to" reference text.

Deaver Brown's *The Entrepreneur's Guide* (New York: Ballantine, 1981), is an owner-manager's record of his own business venture. The lessons learned are valuable. Robert Townsend's *Up the Organization* (New York: Fawcett, 1978), is also the work of a practicing manager. It is a pithy, idiosyncratic work that extols the virtues of no-frills, results-oriented firms.

Anything written by Peter F. Drucker is worth reading, even though his focus is management of larger concerns. Two of Drucker's books in particular relate to a special small business need for priorities and concentrated allocations of scarce resources: *Managing For Results* (New York: Harper & Row, 1986) and *The Effective Executive* (New York: Harper & Row, 1985).

Similarly, Thomas J. Peters' and Robert H. Waterman, Jr.'s *In Search of Excellence: Lesson's from America's Best Run Companies* (New York: Harper & Row, 1982), underlines the importance of developing clear priorities and doing them well.

In Chapter 3, there is reference to an important need to manage your time. Here are two books on this.

Stephanie Winston, *The Organized Executive*. New York: Warner Books, 1985.

R. Alec Mackenzie, *The Time Trap: How to Get More Done in Less Time*. New York: McGraw-Hill, 1975.

Peter Drucker's *Innovation and Entrepreneurship. Practice and Principles* (New York: Harper & Row, 1986), while aimed at the larger concerns, is an excellent treatment of the ways an entrepreneur contributes something of new value to the marketplace.

Here are two books which deal with small business marketing considerations.

Elizabeth Deran, *Low-Cost Marketing Strategies: Field-Tested Techniques for Firms with Limited Budgets*. New York: Praeger, 1987.

Robert T. Davis, F. Gordon Smith, *Marketing in Emerging Companies,* Reading, Mass.: Addison-Wesley, 1984.

In Chapter 7, I mentioned two books on accounting written for the businessperson and not a numbers expert.

Benjamin Graham and Charles McGolrick, *The Interpretation of Financial Statements.* New York: Harper & Row, 1987.

Joel J. Lemer, *Theory and Problems of Bookkeeping and Accounting* (Schaum's Outline Series). New York: McGraw-Hill, 1978.

Almost any bookstore, and certainly any library, will have more than one related book.

Before you automate the firm's record keeping, it is worth consulting a book or two dealing with small business needs. One is Jack Bender's *A Layman's Guide to Installing a Small Business Computer* (Princeton, N.J.: Petrocelli, 1979).

In Chapter 10, I referred to several books designed to expand your practical creativity and problem-solving skills.

Edward de Bono's *Lateral Thinking* (New York: Harper & Row, 1970) and *Practical Thinking* (New York: Penguin Books, 1981) are good starters.

Roger Fisher and William Ury, *Getting to Yes: Negotiating Agreement Without Giving In.* Boston: Houghton Mifflin, 1981.

Russell L. Ackoff, *The Art of Problem Solving.* New York: Wiley, 1987.

Michael Ray and Rochelle Myers, *Creativity in Business.* New York: Doubleday, 1986.

The monthly magazine *Inc.* is a must. It is specifically devoted to small businesses and each issue is filled with case studies and practical recommendations on managing the various parts of a small firm.

The bimonthly *Harvard Business Review* is well worth a look. Each issue contains a feature on "Growing Concerns." In addition, each issue is likely to contain three to four articles of relevance to a small business owner. These articles are of high caliber and considerable practical value.

APPENDIX

C

ABRIDGED
MANAGING YOUR
MONEY MANUAL

FROM CHAPTER 1: GETTING STARTED

QUICK START

Welcome! To get going fast, just follow the steps below. But then be sure to read, or at least skim, the rest of this chapter.

You've paid a lot of money for Managing Your Money and will be using it extensively, we hope, for years. It's important to get off to a good start. Please don't dive in until you can find a couple of uninterrupted hours to lay a good foundation. In that time, you should be able to master the basics, get the program running on your system, and take an informal tour of its myriad capabilities.

One more thing. Before you even start, send in your registration card. With toasters, it's silly to send in a warranty card. With software, it's silly not to. Please—do it before you forget.

> HINT: Hard Disk Only: Managing Your Money requires a hard disk.

QUICK START INSTRUCTIONS

1. Insert Disk 1 in Drive A (or B).

2. Type a:install (or b:install).

3. Follow the prompts to install, and then run Managing Your Money.

   If you have any trouble with this, come back to the manual and read the more leisurely getting-started instructions later in this chapter. Initially, you'll need about 3MB of free space on your hard disk for the program and your data.

4. Your first time into Managing Your Money, we offer to take you straight to Hello, New User, our tutorial. We hope you'll accept. But you can also select the Quick Start option (F6) and visit the tutorial later.

   We next show you some of our program settings and let you change them if you want (F6). This is where you can specify what printer you have and whether F10 or Enter is your Action Key. You can change any of this later using Program Setup on the FILE menu. When you're through, be sure to save your changes.

5.   Choose New Data Set on the FILE menu to create a data set called "Herb92" (if you're Herb and it's 1992). Use it for your data; keep the set of data Managing Your Money comes with—which you'll see goes by the name "Original"—as a blank slate. Doing this is not required. But it takes just a minute (and about 260K on your hard disk), and will save you a little trouble should you later want to set up new sets of data for your spouse or your business.

Please ... once the program is up on the screen and you've had a chance to look around, come back here and read the rest of this chapter.

A BRIEF TOUR

There's an awful lot here, which is why it's important to have an overview and to decide which sections of the program you'll want to start using first. Any one of our sections is a simple, powerful program all by itself, easily mastered and put to use in an afternoon. But don't expect to start using them all the same afternoon! Take your time! Here's what each does:

FILE is a catchall for housekeeping chores: customizing the program to your system, choosing screen colors, turning off our beeps if they annoy you, switching date formats if you're Canadian, setting up passwords if you want them, setting up separate sets of data for your business or a family member—and much more. Some of this is important, and it's all described here, in this chapter of the manual.

DESK contains ten pop-ups you can summon from anywhere in the program. Three of them are just small conveniences—a five-memory Calculator (Ctrl-N, as in "Number cruncher" — hold down the Ctrl key and press the N key), a graphic Date Display (Ctrl-D), and a Quick Key List of our shortcuts (Ctrl-K). But the other seven are complete programs:

•   Five of them—a Time Summary and the four tributaries that flow into it—help you organize your time and work. With them, you'll never forget a birthday or CD maturity again. You can keep your daily schedule here—with notes attached to each appointment— or even keep lists of ongoing projects, prioritized by importance and sorted by which employee or family member is responsible for each. The Time Summary (Ctrl-T) pulls together information from Phone Calls (Ctrl-P), Appointments (Ctrl-A), Reminders (Ctrl-R) and To-Do's (Ctrl-O). The Time Summary also lets you know when your insurance policies, driver's license and passport are about to expire (it gets this information from INSURE, described below).

- With the Card File (Ctrl-C), you can store vital statistics on friends, clients, patients, associates, fellow alumni—whomever. It prints phone lists and address labels, in case it's your job to get those fellow alumni to show up for the reunion. And it retrieves selectively, in case you want a list of only those alumni you've coded "Big Givers." It dials phone numbers, addresses letters —in concert with our built-in word processor, it even generates your very own personalized form letters.

- A Word Processor (Ctrl-W), popularly known as MYM-Write, that lets you write letters or speeches or anything else without having to leave the program, and lets you edit the reports we print for you, in case there's some touching up you'd like to do. (MYM-Write's "iceberg mode," accessible in many places with the F2-View/Edit key, lets you attach notes of almost any length to specific data entries.)

For details on how these seven features work, please see Chapter 2 of this manual: DESK.

MONEY is, for most of us, the heart of the program. If you write a check to the doctor here, your checkbook balance automatically knows, your budget automatically knows, your cash flow projection automatically knows, Schedule A of your taxes automatically knows, and so does your Net Worth. MONEY helps you budget, forecasts your available cash, and generates reports. It tracks loans and credit cards and, if you want it to, accounts payable and receivable. It prints checks and invoices and can even send electronic payment instructions.

TAX is an estimator that handles Schedules A, B, C, D, E, F, SE, Form 1040, a variety of worksheets, and the Alternative Minimum Tax. All you have to do to see a schedule is press its letter. A second later, it's there. We've made it easy to accommodate changes in the tax code—and to switch between tax years and regulations at the touch of a key. And we've provided a W-4 calculator to help you figure out how many income tax withholding allowances to claim.

Tax doesn't print your actual return; our companion program, TaxCut, does that. But it's a powerful tool for planning.

INSURE tells you how long you are likely to live, given your background and habits (we claim no special accuracy here), helps you calculate how much life insurance you need, and tells you what it might cost. It also helps you record and organize all your insurance policies—not just life— in one place. And it provides a Vital Records section that prompts you for virtually everything you and your spouse may wish to keep track of— from your blood types to the location of your safety deposit box key.

It even prints a comprehensive report, complete with a letter of instructions to your spouse or executor.

ANALYZE is more than a dozen programs in one. Though you won't use it the most, in some ways this is the most important part of Managing Your Money. It will help you decide—in English—whether to refinance your mortgage, how to save for your kids' education and other goals, and how to plan for retirement. It has a powerful rental property module, another to help you decide whether to buy or lease your next home (or car), and one to help you figure out how much home you can afford. *ANALYZE* has all the features of an ordinary business calculator (sections on present and future value, annuities, bond maturities and such)—but with everything in English (and HELP), so you're sure it's answering the question you meant to ask. There's even a screen for deciding whether to make a new contribution to your retirement plan and another to help you estimate what your Social Security benefits will be when you do retire.

Over a period of years, the decisions this chapter helps you with affect huge amounts of money. Our hope is to help you make these decisions just a little bit smarter—and feel more confident about them.

PORTFOLIO knows the difference between taxable, tax-deferred (IRA/ Keogh/401K) and hypothetical portfolios, and can handle many of each, as well as brokerage accounts with check-writing privileges (CMA's). You may use it for your stocks, bonds, mutual funds and options; someone else may use it to catalog and code stamps, coins and antiques. It's powerful and flexible. It can even compare the performance of your assets with that of the market as a whole, both individually or in the aggregate. Our optional communications package, Managing the Market, will call Dow

Jones and update your prices automatically.

NET WORTH takes what it knows about you from the other parts of the program, lets you add as much or as little detail as you want (a complete household inventory, for example), and prints your balance sheet. It also keeps a historical record of your progress and tracks your "debt/equity" ratio.

Its Asset Allocator can help you decide how best to deploy your assets among various classes — stocks, bonds, real estate and gold, for example — to achieve your investment objectives with the least possible risk. Designed by one of the leaders in the field of asset allocation, we believe our asset allocation model is at least as sophisticated as its leading stand-alone competition. And it's built right into MYM.

THE COMMUNICATIONS OPTION

An optional sister program, Managing the Market, allows you to "call Dow Jones" direct from within Managing Your Money and update your portfolio prices automatically over the phone (and to access all the other Dow Jones/News Retrieval Services).

THE TAX OPTION

A second sister, TaxCut, imports much of your data from Managing Your Money and prints an IRS-acceptable tax return.

THE ELECTRONIC PAYMENT OPTION

Managing Your Money includes a built-in link to CheckFree, a service that allows you to pay your bills electronically with your existing checking account.

STEP #1: INSTALLING THE PROGRAM

Okay, let's get going. The disks in your package contain all the Managing Your Money files in compressed form. We call them the "master disks." To install them on your hard disk, simply insert Disk 1 in Drive A and type A:INSTALL <Enter>. (It's OK, but unnecessary, to switch to the A> prompt first. And it's OK to use Drive B, instead, and type B:INSTALL.)

Once you do, we will guide you through a brief series of questions, with help for each at the bottom of the screen, and prompt you to insert the other disks as needed.

When you're all done, put the master disks someplace safe.

To run the program, just type MYM. The first time you do, we'll offer to take you straight to Hello, New User, our tutorial. Even if you're a computer pro, I urge you to take the few minutes required to breeze through it. You're bound to discover at least a few things about the program, and a few navigational shortcuts, you might miss otherwise.

> HINT: If You Got MYM for Christmas—Lie. If it's right near the end of the year and you don't plan to record transactions with Managing Your Money for real until the new year begins, you may want to lie to us about the date when you first start the program. Tell us it's January 1992, even if it's December 1991. That will spare your having to run through our Close Out Past Year procedure a few days from now.

WHAT INSTALL DOES; WHERE WE PUT THINGS

What we're doing is decompressing the files on our master disks and copying them onto a directory of your hard disk.

We put all the program files in the main \mym8 directory (or whatever you tell us to call it). These are files that any set of data can share. We put all the data files (except for those that can be shared) into a subdirectory of the \mym8 directory called \mym8\original. These are the original data files we start you off with. If you use our "New Data Set" command on the FILE menu to make up new sets of data files—for your spouse, say, or your business—we will put them into new subdirectories we create called \mym8\spouse and \mym8\business (or whatever name you give). To switch between separate sets of data, you just use FILE's "Open Data Set" command and choose the one you want.

CAN'T SEE THE SCREEN?

On certain monochrome monitors—laptop and notebook computers, for the most part—you may not be able to make out the screen. If so, try installing by typing A:INSTALL -M instead.

NOTHING HAPPENS WHEN YOU TYPE "MYM"?

We've put MYM in its own directory—called \mym8, unless you instructed us to call it something else. To run the program, you must first change into that directory. Type CD \MYM8 first and then type MYM.

ONE OF OUR FLOPPIES DEFECTIVE?

It's highly unlikely you will have a problem. But if your computer should give you an error message that it can't "read" one of the disks that came with the program, try removing it from the disk drive and tapping its edge gently against your desk, as if trying to slice the desk with the disk. Now insert the disk and try again. If your computer still can't read it— but is reading other disks OK—you'll need to send it to us for replacement.

NOT ENOUGH ROOM ON YOUR HARD DISK?

Initially, you will need about 3MB for Managing Your Money's program and data files—more as your data grows.

FILES YOU CAN DELETE TO SAVE SPACE ON YOUR HARD DISK

This is not a good idea. There are really only two files you can get away with deleting from the \mym8 directory of your hard disk if space is tight: INSTALL.EXE and, if you do not plan to use CheckFree, CFMYM.EXE. You can later install new copies by running Install with the floppies that came in your package. But what if those disks aren't handy when you decide you need them? Or what if you forget you can do this? Theoretically, you could delete even more, such as our large HELP.HLP file, and copy it to a separate floppy. But if you ever pressed

F1 for help—and we hope you'll press it often!—the program would hang until you inserted the floppy with HELP.HLP. Not recommended!

SEPARATE SETS OF DATA

HINT: Pre-Version 7 customized-setup hard disk users: As part of the install-upgrade routine, we will put one of your sets of data in the \mym8\data subdirectory and create separate subdirectories for the rest. If you upgrade from Version 7, we'll create a Version 8 data subdirectory with the same name as your Version 7 subdirectory.

When we install Managing Your Money on a hard disk, we put its program files in a main Managing Your Money directory called c:\mym8 (unless you direct us to call it something else) and its data files in a subdirectory called \mym8\original. All you have to do to set up a new set of data is select New Data Set from the FILE menu and follow our instructions. We'll create a subdirectory for that data—c:\ mym 8\ grandma—and other subdirectories for as many more sets of data as you care to create.

Once created, you can switch from one to another simply by choosing Open Data Set from the FILE menu and selecting the one you want. Do some work there, then choose Open Data Set again, if you like, and switch back. Eventually, you'll have several subdirectories, including one for each prior year. But Open Data Set gives you easy access to them all.

You may assign separate passwords to each set of data, just in case you'd rather not have him looking at hers or them looking at yours. But note: MYM normally starts with the set of data you were last using. If you and your daughter, Felicia, each have separate passwords, and you were the last one to use the program, when your daughter starts it up, it won't budge if she can't supply your password. The solution is to have her type mym felicia to start the program and load her data (assuming her data set is called "felicia").

WARNING! Just be careful, when you're leaving the program and we offer to backup your data to floppies, to insert the correct backup disk. You don't want to backup grandma's data files over your own.

COLOR YOUR DATA

I suggest you use a different color scheme for each active data set so you don't inadvertently pay your mother's bills from your personal data set. I use black and white—like an old movie—for all prior years' data sets.

HOW NEW DATA SET WORKS

When you select New Data Set from the FILE menu, we ask you for the name you want to give your new set of data. We then create a subdirectory of \mym8 by that name and copy the current set of data files to it. (So before you create a new set, if you have more than one, be sure to load the one you want to copy.) Typically, you'll want us to copy the almost-empty "ORIGINAL" data set MYM came with, so you or a family member can start fresh.

When we're done, you'll be at the title screen of your new set of data. If it wasn't copied from a virgin ORIGINAL set, the first thing you'll probably want to do is go through and delete all the Money Accounts, and so on, that don't apply—clean the slate, as it were.

This can be a bit of a chore if you've got loads of data throughout the program, which is why in Getting Started we suggested you leave our ORIGINAL set of data files empty. If you followed that suggestion, just open your ORIGINAL data set before you create a new one. (Or else use your original, master disks to load a fresh set of database files onto this new subdirectory—being very careful not to copy them over your own, real database files by mistake. Just insert Disk 1 in Drive A and, from DOS, type a:install and follow our prompts to install only the data files, copying these empty ones into the new subdirectory where you want empty ones.)

> Hint: When you start up the program, we load whichever data set you were using last. To start it with another data set, type the name of the data set after the name of the program: mym dataset.

TO SWITCH BETWEEN SETS OF DATA

Just select Open Data Set from the FILE menu. The name of the currently loaded data set appears at the bottom center of the Menu Bar screen.

TO DELETE A SET OF DATA

You normally wouldn't want to do this, of course. But if, say, you had used New Data Set to create a new data set called GRANNY and then decided, nah, you didn't want to do this after all, here's what you'd do. Just go into DOS and change into the \mym8 subdirectory. Type del granny and, when DOS asks if you're sure, say Yes. The contents of the GRANNY subdirectory will be gone. Now type rd granny to remove the granny subdirectory itself. That's it. Just be careful not to delete the wrong subdirectory by mistake!

FANCY SETUPS

You actually have three choices when you use New Data Set to create a new data set:

1. By far the best choice (if you ask me) is to give us a simple name, like JACK92, and leave it at that. We'll create a \jack92 sub directory under your \mym8 directory and put your new set of data there.

2. You can type a drive letter before the name if you have more than one hard disk in your system. If you enter D:JACK (no slashes or spaces), we will create a \mym8\jack directory\subdirectory on your Drive D (assuming you have a Drive D), and put the data there. (If you used a different directory name when you originally installed the program—say you had us install it on a directory called "\mym8v8"—we'd automatically use that name instead—\mym8v8\jack.) But why make life complicated unless you have a really good reason? And if you do have us stick your data on Drive D, note that you will have to type "D:JACK" each time you want Open Data Set to load it. Only the data subdirectories directly under your c:\mym8 directory (or wherever you installed the pro-

gram) are displayed by Open Data Set; any other you want to use must be entered manually.

3. You can enter just "A:" or "B:" as the name—nothing more. In that case, we'll copy the data set onto the floppy in Drive A or B (and onto a second, if it won't all fit). Whenever you select this data set with Open Data Set we'll look to Drive A for your data. (And look there, also, the next time you use Managing Your Money, if that's the data set you were using last, because we always start with the same data set you were using last.)

STARTING A NEW YEAR, CLOSING OUT AN OLD ONE

Every time you enter Managing Your Money, we make you tell us the date. The first time you enter a 1993 date (if you began using the program in 1992), a screen will appear asking you whether you really mean 1993. If so, a new selection appears on the FILE menu: Close Out Past Year—"COPY." Under COPY is another menu. The last item there is also called Close Out Past Year, and here we really mean it.

Don't choose it! At least not for a while. As we'll advise you, Managing Your Money is able to keep track of two years at once, so at least for the first month or two, until you're sure all your prior year's data has been entered and reconciled, it will be easier just to live with both sets of data. Some of you, in fact, may wish to wait until the end of the current year before closing out the prior one, to make it really easy to look up old transactions. ("Honey, how much did we pay the plumber when the pipes burst last year?")

Eventually, you may find your budget.dbs file growing too large to fit on a floppy backup disk. Otherwise, you can pretty well wait as late into the year as you want to choose Close Out Past Year. (But you must choose it eventually: we can't start recording next year's transactions until you've dispatched last year's. We can't keep three years in mind at once.)

Whenever you do choose to run through COPY, just follow the instructions that will appear. What we'll do, simply, is copy all the past year's stuff into a new subdirectory of your hard disk. (You should then copy it onto a floppy, so you have a backup someplace safe.) At the same time, we'll delete all those prior year transactions from your current set of data.

Of course, we only delete past transactions. We don't delete any of the other work you've done.

USING A PREVIOUS YEAR'S DATA

After you've gone through Close Out Previous Year, it's very easy to look at or print reports from—or even change—a previous year's data. Just use Open Data Set on the FILE menu to select that data set when you start the program.

Of course, once we've closed out a year, changes you make to its data naturally won't affect your current balances. They're no longer connected.

Say you visited your old 1991 data and recorded an extra $1,000 in income you had forgotten. Fine. But the bank balance in your current, 1992, data set naturally won't reflect the extra $1,000. So if your bank balance really is off by $1,000, go into your current data and record a receipt of $1,000 from a payor named "To Balance," or else go to the account balance directly, by selecting this Money Account, and adjust it.

But this is not likely to be a problem if you reconciled your bank statement before you went ahead with Close Out Past Year. A $1,000 discrepancy is kind of hard to miss.

PRINTING

SETTING UP YOUR PRINTER

Select Program Setup from the FILE menu, then Printer, and read the instructions on the screen (and F1 for HELP). Mainly, press F6 to select your printer from our list.

Note that "GENERIC" is not an obscure printer brand but, rather, the "lowest common denominator" that should accommodate just about any parallel printer. (If you don't know whether your printer is serial or parallel, rest assured it's almost certainly parallel—so be sure to leave the "baud rate" and "parity" fields blank, also.) GENERIC won't do underlined printing or bold face or any of that, but at least it will print something until you have time to consult your printer manual for the proper setup strings it needs.

We don't support Postscript printers directly, but most Postscript printers can be set to emulate something else on our list—usually a LaserJet.

While you're on the Printer Setup screen, you can also press F7 to enter custom printer setup strings from your printer manual, or F8 to test your printer.

If you've made changes to the printer setup, turn off your printer and then turn it back on, so it can reset itself before you attempt to test the changes.

F4—THE UNIVERSAL PRINT KEY

On screens from which a report or document may be printed, F4 will normally be displayed. Typically, you will press it two or three times on the way to producing your report—first to summon one or more screens on which you can define the kind of report you want, then to start the actual printing. (Some of those screens may say to press the Action Key, but F4 will usually work, too.)

PRINTING SCREENS AND GRAPHS

Whenever you'd like to print out the contents of a screen where F4 is not offered, just press your computer's Print Screen key. (On some keyboards, you need to hold down the Shift key when pressing PrtSc; on the Tandy 1000, it's Alt-P.)

Microsoft Windows takes over the Print Screen key. If you're running Managing Your Money full-screen in Windows, the Print Screen key will save the screen to the clipboard. You'll need to load text screens into another program, such as Windows' Notepad, to print them (retrieve them from the clipboard file, which is probably DEFAULT.CLP in your Windows directory). You'll have to load graph screens into Windows' Paintbrush to print them.

PRINTING REPORTS

Managing Your Money prints scores of them, including many you can customize to suit your own needs. Reports may also be printed to disk (see below) and then edited with any standard word processing program—or with our own. Until you've amassed a few months' data, they're not much to look at. It may even be hard to picture how they'll look or how useful they will be. But as your data builds, I think you'll be impressed by their power and flexibility.

At the end of the year, you'll be able to print in minutes a complete report of the year's transactions. In fact, print four:

- A report organized and subtotaled alphabetically by payee

- Another organized chronologically

- A third organized by check number

- And, best of all, a fourth organized and sub-totaled by budget and tax category, ready to hand your accountant—or for your own tax preparation.

    I make a set of reports like this three or four times a year with the Report Generator (on the MONEY menu). The last set, printed at year's end, I keep permanently. **With these four reports, it should never take you more than a few seconds to find anything.** (As for those who say there's no place in the computer age for paper—well, I disagree. Sometimes, as in this case, a printed report can be very handy.)

PRINTING CHECKS

See "Step #10: Printing Checks."

PRINTER PROBLEMS

Don't panic! Before you call Tech Support or your printer manufacturer, please see the "Neat Printer Trick" below).

PRINTING TO DISK

We give you a choice. You can print reports to your printer—which is to say, on paper. You can print them to the screen. Or you can print them to a disk.

If you choose "disk," we ask for a filename, preceded by the letter of the disk drive you want us to aim for. For example, "b:budget.doc" would send whatever you're printing to the floppy disk in Drive B and stick it into a file called "budget.doc." Careful: If such a file already existed, it would stick it there anyway, overwriting the previous contents.

Once the report is in its own file, you can manipulate it with your word processor or by pressing Ctrl-W and loading it into ours. Include it in a proposal; insert a little poem in the middle; improve our format; add, delete or rearrange things. But note: This is a one-way street. You can send copies of Managing Your Money reports to files all day long; but there's no way to take your newly word-processed version (with the poem in the middle) and stick it back into Managing Your Money. We don't do poems.

> HINT: The ".doc" Extension Is Handy. You may want to give your reports a ".doc" extension. Because when you ask our word processor to show you a list of the files in your data directory, its first instinct, as you'll see, is to display all your ".doc" files.

> NOTE: Avoid Invalid Filenames

If you're new to DOS, you may not realize that filenames must follow certain rules. For example, they can't have spaces. If you try "92 CASH" instead of, say, 92CASH, we'll burp and ask you to try again. Also, never use ".dbs" or any of the other extensions we use in labeling files!

PRINTING TO SCREEN

Note that when you choose this option, you may scroll back and forth through the report and—if it's wider than 80 columns—left and right. Just use the Arrow keys.

NEAT PRINTER TRICK

If you print to "disk" but to a file named, simply, LPT1, your report won't print to disk after all—it will print to the printer connected to your computer's first printer port. If your printer is connected to port #2, use LPT2 as the filename.

This has limited practical application, because all the special formatting— compressed or emphasized printing—will be lost. But it does serve two functions:

- If you have two printers connected to your computer, it's a way to switch from one to the other without having to visit Program Setup and change the printer port selection there.

- If you're having trouble printing, this is one of the tests Tech Su port uses to determine whether it's a problem with Managing Your Money (if nothing prints out to LPT1 or LPT2, it may be!) or whether our reports are working fine, but you just haven't specified the right printer codes in Printer Setup (a lot more likely).

FROM CHAPTER 2: DESK

DESK

You need never use the DESK pulldown menu, because all ten of its offerings can be evoked at any time, from any place in the program (except
within MYM-Write or the Calculator), with Quick Keys:

Ctrl-T   Time Summary. See below: "Time Summary—Ctrl-T."

Ctrl-P   Phone Calls. See below: "Time Summary—Ctrl-T."

Ctrl-A   Appointments. See below: "Time Summary—Ctrl-T."

Ctrl-R   Reminders. See below: "Time Summary—Ctrl-T."

Ctrl-O   TO-DO List. See below: "Time Summary—Ctrl-T."

Ctrl-C   the Card File. See the section of this chapter that begins on
          page 310: "The Card File—Ctrl-C."

Ctrl-W   the Word Processor (MYM-Write). See the section of this
          chapter called: "MYM-Write—Ctrl-W."

Ctrl-D   a graphic Date Display. See "The Date Display—Ctrl-D."

Ctrl-N   a Numeric Calculator that works with the data entry fields
          onthe screen. Press F1 for HELP.

Ctrl-K   a display of all the Quick Keys.

TIME SUMMARY—CTRL-T

This section of the program is a powerful organizational tool all its own.
A quick glance at the Time Summary tells you "what's on for today"—
what you need to do, where you need to be, whom you need to see or call
or sing Happy Birthday to. (I drive everyone nuts with my singing, like
clockwork.) It reminds you of upcoming deadlines and keeps lists of ongoing projects, prioritized by importance and tagged by which colleague,
employee or family member is responsible for each one.

The Time Summary gets all this information from Phone Calls, Appointments, Reminders and the TO-DO List. Since these parts of Managing Your Money are so tightly integrated with the Time Summary,
we'll discuss them all here.

(Time Summary also pulls birthdays and anniversaries from the Card File, and key dates from INSURE.)

The Time Summary summarizes today's reminders. (To see them for some other day, press Ctrl-F, enter that date, and press F6.) Although the screen itself has room to display just a dozen or so, you can quickly move through the entire list with the Arrow keys and PgDn, PgUp, Ctrl-PgDn and Ctrl-PgUp. Or print a report—F4.

SIX KINDS OF REMINDERS

The Time Summary keeps track of six separate types of reminders (as you'll see, we couldn't resist starting you off with a few samples).

1. **Appointments** are displayed first: 5:15 pm—accountant. Press Ctrl-A to visit the screen where you add new appointments and edit existing ones. F5 on that screen pops up the screen for adding a new appointment; F2 lets you change one; F7 copies one, to make it easy to enter multiple appointments where the only difference is the time and date.

Appointments are persistent. We leave them on the Time Summary screen until you point and press F8 to deactivate one. When you do, it remains on your Appointments screen, only the status changes to "Completed." You thus have a permanent log, though you can always weed it out, deleting unneeded entries with F3 on the Appointments screen.

> HINT: Loads of Room for Messages, Memos, Notes... The "Message" field on this screen appears to be quite small—but as with all Message, Memo, Notes, Comment and Detail fields in Managing Your Money, pressing F2 opens it up to provide almost unlimited room to write. In the case of an appointment, you could jot down travel directions and/or an agenda of the items you hope to cover. And if new items occur to you as the appointment nears, just come back and add them.

2. **Phone Calls** are second. Press Ctrl-P to add one. And note the power of this screen!

    • You can simply press F5 to add a call you want us to remind you to make. (Or, if your secretary has access to your computer while you're out, he or she can enter your messages, all set for you to deal with at the touch of a key when you return.)

- You can press F7, when adding a call, to have us pull the phone number from the Card File. To call each member of your softball team, press F7-Select Caller, speed scroll to the shortstop, and press the Action Key. We'll enter the first number we see listed for that person. (If you want one of the other numbers, just arrow to it before pressing the Action Key.)

- You can dial phone numbers if you have a modem (F6).

- You can sort your calls any of five ways (F9).

- That's important, because in addition to using Phone Calls to remind you of calls-to-be-made, you can also use it as a historical log of calls you already have made. Want to see—or print—a record of all your conversations with a particular client? Sort by name and there they are.

So one way to use Phone Calls is **prospectively**, to remind yourself to call each of your teammates on such-and-such a day, or remind yourself to call someone two weeks from now. ("When we last talked on April 12, Harry, you asked me to call back in a couple of weeks. Here I am.")

But an even more important way to use it may be retrospectively, to keep a permanent log of important calls you've made, with notes attached to each. After a call's been completed, you'd press F8 on the Time Summary to "deactivate" it, so we stop bugging you about it. But then it sits in Phone Calls permanently, or until you delete it. (Every so often, you might want to print the hard copy reports you'll need and then use F3 on Phone Calls to delete the oldest ones.)

And, of course, you can combine these two kinds of uses. Picture it. It's Sunday and you're doing your bills in MONEY. The one from Book of the Month Club reminds you you meant to call BookSearch to see if it can locate a copy of Freddy the Pig Goes to College, for your nephew. (Don't laugh. I loved that book.) But they're closed Sunday, so you press Ctrl-P and F5 to add a new call, F7 to get their number from your Card File, and the Action Key to record your work. Press ESCape and you're back paying your bills ... but tomorrow, Monday, you're reminded on to make the call. When you do, you press F2 to append a brief note: "Sally says should take about 3 weeks and cost $35 if they find Freddy/College.

Asks me to check back in about three weeks." But now, just before you leave, you use F7 on the Phone Calls screen to copy that call—with a date three weeks hence. Three weeks go by, we remind you to make the call, and when you do, and Sally says it's only been a week, you politely tell her, no, your last call was April 12th at 2:45 PM.

Obviously, not everyone is this organized, and not everyone will leave Managing our Money running all day, as I do. But the tool is here if and when you want it. And it can be most handy for tracking conversations with clients, patients, employees, suppliers, contractors—you name it. If you save copies of your letters, why not a record of important calls?

Phone Calls are persistent. We leave them on the Time Summary screen until you point and press F8 to deactivate one. When you do, it remains on your Appointments screen, only the status changes to "Completed." You thus have a permanent log, though you can always weed it out, deleting unneeded entries with F3.

3.   **Reminders** are displayed next. We tell you the date of whatever it is you're trying to remember and how many days off it is. Press Ctrl-R to visit the screen where you add new ones and edit existing ones. F5 on that screen pops up the screen for adding a new reminder; the Action Key confirms what you've done and adds it to your list. F2 works the same as in Appointments.

> SHORTCUT: if it's a one-time reminder, just leave the Type field blank. We'll fill it in for you.

Reminders may be one-time (March 6: my CD matures), annual (January 30: Johnny's birthday; May 1: plant the tomatoes), quarterly (for estimated tax payments), semi-annual (for bond payments), monthly (pay the rent), weekly (leave key for the maid), biweekly (gardener comes every 2nd Tuesday—chain the dog), half-monthly (fertilize the forsythia), daily (soak your contact lenses), biweekly (you pay the kids their allowance every two weeks)

> NOTE: PORTFOLIO generates certain financial reminders automatically. Those show up on the Financial Reminders screen under the PORTFOLIO menu—see page 397: "Your Financial Reminders."

When you add a Reminder, you also get to specify the number of days in advance of the actual event—Warning Days, as we call them—you'd like the Reminder to begin showing up.

SHORTCUT: leave Warning Days blank if you don't need any warning. No need to type a zero.

Want us to start reminding you of Christmas 364 days in advance? Just enter Christmas as an annual reminder with 364 "warning days," and you'll always know how many shopping days are left. (Unlike appointments, which all show up the same number of days early, you get to set warning days for each reminder individually.)

One-time reminders are persistent. We leave them on the Time Summary screen until you point and press F8 to deactivate one. When you do, we delete it just as though you had deleted it with F3 on the Reminders screen.

Periodic reminders are ephemeral. They vanish from the Time Summary when their time has past—and are automatically updated on the Reminders screen in preparation for their next appearance. (F8 on the Time Summary screen lets you banish them early, so you don't have to keep seeing one if you've already taken care of it.)

4.   **TO-DOs** are displayed fourth. These are projects rather than events. Press Ctrl-O to visit the screen where you add new ones and edit existing ones and then F1-Help for hints on how best to do so. You'll see that you can assign your projects levels of priority and then rank them in order of importance. You can also assign responsibility to members of your staff, committee or family—and sort them that way too, so you can pull up a list of all Bill's projects before Bill comes in for his weekly meeting.

REPORT HINT: Selective Printing. Because you can print TO-DOs selectively—only those projects assigned to Jennifer, for example—and because you can add detail to each project as it progresses, you could in effect print out a year's report (or longer) of every project Jennifer has been assigned, along with your notes on how she's handled them.

TO-DO items are persistent. We leave them on the Time Summary screen until you point and press F8 to deactivate one. When you do, it remains on your TO-DO screen, only the status changes to "Completed." They don't disappear from your TO-DO list unless you delete them—F3. (If you need to extend a project deadline, just press F2 on the TO-DO screen to edit it.) Otherwise, they hang around forever with their completion dates—testaments to your progress and achievement, in case you want to print a copy for the boss.

5.   **Key dates** from INSURE are next. These are expiration dates for insurance policies entered in the Insurance Policy Organizer and for passport and driver's license expirations entered in the Vital Records log.

Key dates are persistent. We leave them on the Time Summary screen until you point and press F8 to deactivate one. Listen: it's usually pretty important to renew an insurance policy or driver's license—we don't want you to forget!

6.   Birthdays and Anniversaries entered in the Card File (Ctrl-C) are imported and displayed on the Time Summary. What's more, if you point to a birthday or reminder and press F2, you'll see we've automatically appended the first address and phone number from that person's card, in case you want to send a card or make a call.

CAUTION: Don't Append Detail to Birthdays and Anniversaries. It's unwise to append notes to these imported birthday and anniversary reminders, because the next time we import them from Card File, we'll "overwrite" the current ones—including your notes. Thus, you may prefer to enter certain birthdays and anniversaries on the Reminders screen, as annual reminders, instead (or in addition). You can then append all the notes you like without fear of losing them. For example, you could keep a running list of the gifts you've given this person over the years. I switched to this method after accidentally giving Allison Kraus the same book of poems, Garbage Delight, on three consecutive birthdays. The first time, she was too polite to say anything. But when she turned eight, and I gave her her third copy, she rolled her eyes and pointed to the other two.

Birthdays and Anniversaries, like periodic reminders, are ephemeral. They vanish from the Time Summary when their time has past—and are automatically updated on the Reminders screen in preparation for next year.

ADDING/VIEWING DETAIL—F2

The displays you see in the Time Summary show just the first line of your Appointments, Reminders and TO-DO entries. But you can attach a great deal of detail. Just point to any item on today's Time Summary screen and press F2. (Press it twice if you're on the Appointments, Phone Calls, Reminders or TO-DO List screens.) Your appointment might just say "accountant," but beneath that you can list all the issues you and she need to discuss.

Once you've attached detail to an item, an asterisk will be displayed to its right, reminding you it's there. Press F2 again to see or change it.

It's as simple as that, though in fact you'll have most of the power of our word processor at your command when you're adding or editing detail—except the ability to change margins—so at your convenience, you should learn how that works. It's described in this chapter beginning on page 321: "MYM-Write—Ctrl-W."

DEACTIVATING—F8

When you press F8 while pointing to an item on the Time Summary screen, we "deactivate" it. It vanishes from the Time Summary screen.

- If it's a periodic reminder, we send it into hibernation until it becomes timely again.

- If it's a one-time item, like an appointment or phone call or one-time reminder or TO-DO project, we return it to the list from which it came, for you to preserve in a historical log, if you like, or delete with F3.

- Note: *periodic reminders are automatically sent into hibernation after their due dates,* even if you haven't deactivated them with F8.

To avoid having one vanish before you've tended to it, enter it with a later date. Say you expect rent from your tenant on the 1st of each month. You might wish to enter that as a monthly reminder for the 25th of next month—but with 27 warning days. That way, you'll start noticing the rent is due a few days before it really is—but keep noticing it's due for 25 days more. If sometime during those 25 days it's paid (let's hope!), just position the cursor on this reminder and press F3 to make it disappear ("deactivate" it) until next month. (To avoid confusion, the reminder itself might read: "Mrs. Gilhooley's rent due the 1st.")

If you wanted, you could go a step further and use F2 to keep a running diary of your relations with Mrs. Gilhooley. Position the cursor on her monthly reminder and, at any time, add some notes. "12/3—complained no hot water; 12/16—paid Dec. rent with check #756; 12/25—threw loud party, neighbors complained." Or you could do this on Mrs. Gilhooley's card in the Card File.

PRINTING—F4

F4 is our universal "print" key. On the Time Summary screen, tell us the dates you'd like to include, tell us whether or not to include any notes you may have appended ("detail"), tell us whether to begin each day on a new page, and press F4 again. Just keep answering the questions and pressing F4.

If Enter is your Action Key, it will be displayed for printing where we think that's the action you're most likely to want to take, and it's fine to use it. But F4 will work, too. Either one.)

On each of the other screens—Phone Calls, Appointments, Reminders, TO-DO List—we offer reports as well. Just press F4 (and keep pressing it!) to see them.

COPYING—F7

You've just been to the dentist and—gosh I hate to tell you this—he's scheduled you for four successive appointments. Rather than have to enter all the stuff four times (including the name of his hygienist, his address, and directions for getting to his office, which you somehow always manage to forget), just enter it once, point to that new entry, and press F7. Everything will be the same, and in a couple of keystrokes you can change the date and/or time. Then press the Action Key to add it to your list. Repeat twice and you're done.

If you've assigned the same TO-DO project to each of your 14 employees, use F7 on the TO-DO screen to copy the first entry 13 times, changing only the "WHO" to whom it's assigned.

The same Copy capability is there on the Phone Calls and Reminders screens.

TIME SUMMARY OPTIONS

If you select Optional Features from the FILE menu, and then Time Summary Options, you can customize the Time Summary.

What items do you want us to display? Tell us which of these entries you want us to display in the Time Summary: Appointments, Phone Calls, Reminders, TO-DOs, Birthdays and Anniversaries, and Key Dates from INSURE. Chances are, you'll want them all.

Display them early? You can see any day's appointments just by entering that date on the Time Summary screen and pressing F6. But it may be easier simply to instruct us to start displaying your appointments a day or two ahead. Just tell us here how many "warning days" to use—and come back and change it any time you want. If you choose to begin displaying them two days early, as a rule, but have one crucial appointment that requires a lot of preparation, you might want to set that one up as a Reminder with lots of Warning Days, in addition or instead.

You can do the same thing with Birthdays and Anniversaries from the Card File, and with Key Dates from INSURE. Just tell us here how many warning days. I set birthdays 8 days ahead to give me time to send a card. Key dates probably require more lead time, lest you be left driving without a license or uninsured, or you dash off for a spur-of-the-moment tour of New Zealand's fjords, only to realize your passport's invalid.

Display them first time in each day? If you answer Yes, you'll never forget to check your Time Summary, because—like it or not—we'll show it to you the first time you use the program on any given day (but only if there's something to show you that day). If you don't like it, just come back and change Yes to No.

DON'T MONKEY WITH THE DATE!

There's only one way to gum things up. Please don't monkey with the date when starting the program. If you start it up with a date weeks or months in the future, and save your work, Managing Your Money will send many of your periodic reminders into hibernation, thinking their time has passed. Then, when you start the program with the correct date, we'll fail to remind you about Grandpa's birthday—it won't come around again for another whole year. This can be a hurtful thing, as any grandpa knows.

COMMONLY ASKED QUESTIONS

How do I delete imported birthdays early on the Time Summary? You can deactivate one with F8, but each time you re-import dates from the Card File, this one will reappear. To get rid of it (maybe you had a falling out with the birthday girl), you'd have to press Ctrl-C to summon the Card File and delete that date. Same thing on key dates from INSURE— delete them there.

How do I keep the reminders from popping up each day? Select Time Summary Options from the FILE menu.

What do you mean "-2 days or -17 days"? As the dates for Time Summary items approach, we count down the days—"2 days" to go, "tomorrow," "today!" But then, until you press F8, we keep counting down—"yesterday," "-2 days," "-3 days." The longer the item is overdue, the larger the negative number.

But remember: periodic reminders (and birthdays/anniversaries) automatically get sent into hibernation after their day has passed.

Why don't you sort TO-DOs alphabetically? We do. But when you ask us to sort your TO-DO projects by "who" is responsible for them, we assume you've used initials—J.F.K.—and so we sort alphabetically by the third initial (last name), not the first.

Why doesn't the date print next to each TO-DO item? When you print from the TO-DO screen, we don't repeat unnecessary information. If you sort by date and rank, we'll only print the date and rank each time they change. Your printout will look like this:

Due Date	Rank	Who	Project	Completed
6/30/1992	A	bld	Drop off dog to be groomed	
		jmd	Pick up kids after school	
		jmd	Deposit check at bank	
	B	bld	Pick up cleaning	
	C	bld	Buy theater tickets	

THE DATE DISPLAY—CTRL-D

Press Ctrl-D on Today's Reminder screen—or any other screen in the program (except MYM-Write)—and our graphic Date Display appears. If you want to see what date the first Monday in September falls on this year (or in the year 2001), just use the keys shown to move to that month and year. Use the Arrow keys to highlight a specific day. If you then press the Action Key, that date will drop into the date field your cursor was on when you pressed Ctrl-D (if you were, in fact, in a date field). Press ESCape instead of Enter if you don't want that date.

Alternatively, if you enter your birth date into a date field and press Ctrl-D, the Date Display will pop up showing you the calendar for the month and year of your birth. A good way to remind your spouse of your up-coming anniversary is to pop up the Date Display and absentmindedly leave the cursor on that month, day and year. "Honey," you can shout downstairs, "would you mind shutting off the computer? I think I'm gonna hit the hay." (Or you could just tape a large sign to the refrigerator door.)

THE CARD FILE—CTRL-C

This section keeps your list of clients, patients, relatives, employees, colleagues, classmates, friends, and anyone else, and lets you enter addresses, dates, phone numbers and other personal data.

- It can print:
  - a phone list
  - an address directory (with or without detail)
  - Rolodex cards
  - labels (one-up or three-abreast)
- It can dial phone numbers.
- It can auto-address letters and envelopes.
- It can retrieve selectively—only your contacts in Chicago; only your fellow alumni; only fellow alumni who are women who are not married and who are not lawyers who are, however, from Chicago.
- It can find your florist even if you've forgotten his name.
- In conjunction with our word processor, it can generate personalized form letters.

> HINT: F7 to rotate phone numbers. To rotate our display from Home Phone to Work to Other, just press F7. No need to jump down to the choice cell first—just keep pressing F7.

Take a look at the Sample card for Ronald Reagan and be sure to press F2 when you do. See all the information you can store?

Everything you need to know about the Card File is in its handful of HELP screens. Reading them as you encounter each new screen is the fastest way to learn it.

FINDING YOUR FLORIST

On the main Card File screen you will ordinarily want everyone listed alphabetically by last name. Type the first letter or two of that name and Speed Scroll whisks you there.

But don't miss the capability—F9—to sort also by First Name ("Harry ... Harry ... It's on the tip of my tongue!") or by Who ("The florist—you know: Mr. What's-his-name.") or even by Phone number, which is a quick way to group everyone you know in the 713 area code (Houston).

FED EX'S FIRST NAME

A number of users have wondered how to enter cards for "people" like Federal Express or Blue Cross or Sears—or any other business or organization. The problem: Managing Your Money insists on a first name.

The solution: Just use a period as the first name (or any other unobtrusive character). Or, if you like, use that space for some useful information you'd like visible on the main Card File screen, like your account number.

COPYING CARDS

You've just come back from Matsushita in Japan and you have 11 business cards in your pocket. It takes forever to enter the first one in the Card File, because you have to recheck the spelling of the address three times, the phone and fax numbers have extra international digits, you have to set up a new Special Code—J, for Japan—and you've appended some general notes about the company, as well as some specific ones about this guy.

Rather than do the same thing 10 more times, use F10 on the main Card File screen to copy that card and change only what's different.

THE POWER OF SPECIAL CODES

You may assign each card in your Card File up to nine different Special Codes. The advantage of special codes comes when you ask us to print a selective list. With auto-marking, as described below, you'll be able to limit printing to only cards that meet the criteria you want.

How to assign codes to a card: Just cursor down to the Special Codes field when you add or edit a card.

QuickEdit Codes: Or, if you already have a big Card File and suddenly decide you'd like to go down the entire list assigning the codes "f" for "friend" and "b" for "Business," select "QuickEdit" to the right of F8 on the main Card File screen and press F8.

Group-deleting codes: QuickEdit is also a handy place to group-delete codes. Say you initially used "L" to mean Los Angeles, but now you want to use it to mean "Lawyer." (You figure you can do that, because the Card File can already pick out folks from Los Angeles using area codes and zip codes.) Rather than hunt for each Los Angeles card individually to blank out that code (lest you later think that roller-blade champ from Redondo Beach is a lawyer), just use QuickEdit's F3-Delete function, being careful first to set it to "Specific" codes and then choosing the one you want to delete. You'd ordinarily not choose to delete "All" codes, unless you really want to start over assigning codes entirely from scratch.

Remembering what they stand for: To remember what F and B, and any other codes, stand for, we provide a two-page note pad. Press F8 when adding or editing a card to see it, and to assign meanings to the letters of the alphabet, and anything else you use as a code.

More than 52 possible codes: Your codes may be the 26 lower-case letters of the alphabet plus the 26 upper-case letters—plus any other key on the keyboard. Press F6 on the Special Codes screen to see the upper-case codes; press it again to return to the lower-case ones. Want to code all the people you tip at Christmas with a semi-colon? Fine. Everyone from the Boston area with a capital B and all your business associates with a small b? Dandy. Just remember that if you use the hyphen and the colon on the lowercase screen not to reuse them on the uppercase screen. (We only show letters of the alphabet on these screens, but you can jot down any others you want. A notation like "% = accountant," even if you squeezed it to the right of an alphabetical code, would remind you that you've used the % sign as a code for accountants.)

AUTO-MARKING

When you press F4 from the main Card File screen to print—whether it's to print on paper or simply to view on the screen—you get a screen called "Select Cards To Print." There you'll see your entire list of cards, with three choices for each—Home, Work and Other.

There are three ways on "Select Cards to Print" to specify what you want us to include:

•   You can just scroll down the list manually, marking each item individually. But that can be a lot of work.

- You can press F8 to have us mark absolutely everything. But what if you just want to include friends, not business associates? What if you want just a single mailing label for each card, not both Home and Work?

- Or—what's often best—you can press "F6-Auto-mark Cards," specify the characteristics of the cards you want, and then press the Action Key to have us mark them for you. With a big Card File, this can save you hours.

When you get to the Auto-Mark window, we let you customize the criteria we should use in marking your cards. Only items that satisfy ALL the criteria will be marked when you press the Action Key:

This Column Only? When you press F6 from the "Select Cards to Print" screen, we first ask whether you want us to include just "Home" data, just "Work," just "Other" or "All" three. Easy. Just tell us.

Only If Address Present? Next we ask whether we should include an item only if it has a phone number or an address. It's fine to select "Don't Care." But if you do, you're likely to get a lot of blank phone numbers ... which is fine, if you're trying to spot the gaps of co-workers whose home phone numbers you really ought to have for an emergency ... and a lot of address labels that have the persons name at the top, but no address below.

Limit to one mark per card? If you want to send everyone you know a solicitation for some charity, you'll probably only want to send them one. If you answer "Yes" here, we'll simply use the first address we find— Home if you've entered one, Work or Other if you've not.

Include only certain states or zip codes? Be sure to leave these fields blank unless you want us to mark only cards from Maine (ME), say, or from within some other geographic area. If you want a list of everyone you know in Cambridge, Mass., just enter **02138**. (No need also to enter MA for Massachusetts). Or, if you want to be sure not to miss friends or prospects on the periphery of Harvard Square, just enter the first four or even just the first three digits: 021. We'll select any of your records that have zip codes starting with those digits.

Special Codes? The final field on this window, for Special Codes, is the most powerful, and requires a little explanation:

Enter "B" here, and, when you press the Action Key, we'll automatically mark all the cards you've tagged "B" (for "brainy," say).

If T means tennis players and S means squash players and R means racquetball players and you want to include all three, just enter all three—TSR. *Any code not preceded by a plus or minus sign will be included.*

If you've also assigned the codes M and F for male and female, and lower case m's for married (f's for free?), you could enter B+F, meaning only brainy people who are also female. *Linking two or more codes with a plus sign means both (or all) have to be present.*

Or you could enter B+F-m, and we'd mark only brainy females who are not married. *A minus sign before a special code tells us not to include anyone with that code.* (T-SR would thus include any cards of Tennis players or Racquetball players, so long as they were not Squash players.)

OK, class. Final exam. Are you ready? What if you want this to be a tennis tournament for brainy unmarried women from Boston? That's right: B+T+F-m (and, in the Zip Code field, 021).

*   If you goof, just press F9 to erase what we've auto-marked and do it again.

*   But if you don't erase your previous marks, any additional marking you do will simply supplement the existing marks. So you could include all your tennis, squash and racquetball partners the first time—TSR—and then, when you remembered you'd forgotten to include your ping-pong buddies, you could auto-mark all the P's.

NOTE: Auto-marking is very literal. If you do use F6 to auto-mark—as you generally will want to—note that it respects all criteria you specified. Only cards meeting all of them will be marked by F6. A friend entered the word "all" in the zip code field (which allows letters as well as numbers in case you're Canadian or British) and then was stymied for hours because no cards got marked. But that was because not one of the many cards which met her other criteria was located in the "all" zip code.

Automarking: Useful Even If You Don't Print

You can use these selective features to discover, fast, who, if anyone, really does play all four sports you're interested in. Just auto-mark as described and then, if any cards meet your criteria, print that brief list to the screen.

> IMPORTANT: We don't automatically erase your marks. Perhaps the first thing you should do when you come to the "Select Cards to Print" screen is press F9, to erase any marks from last time. We purposely keep them in memory in case you're working on a project, like going through your whole list deciding whom to invite to a big party, and don't want to have to do it all in a single session. Quit Managing Your Money, go off for the week-end, and then pick up where you left off when you get back.

AUTO-DIAL A PHONE NUMBER

If you have a modem that's compatible with Managing Your Money, we'll make phone calls for you. Just point to one of your records and press F6. (If F6 is set to Auto-Write, press Ctrl-F, D first, to set it to Dial.) When we've finished dialing, pick up the phone and press the Spacebar (or any other key) while you wait for your party to answer. Simply picking up the phone will not activate voice connection.

You can also dial from the full-card screen. If you're not pointing at a phone number when you press F6, we'll ask which one you want.

> HINT: Turn everything off. Modems are touchy. I don't understand anything about how they work, but I do know that it's best to turn them off, briefly unplug them from the phone line, turn off your computer—that is, turn everything off to totally clear the slate—before starting up and trying out new switch settings or a new configuration.

If auto-dialing doesn't work, it means:

- Your modem isn't plugged in.

- You haven't told us what we need to know about it. Select Program Setup from the FILE menu and then Modem Setup to try again.

- Your modem isn't strictly Hayes compatible. (Sorry; the Card File doesn't work with all modems.)

- If your modem won't work with the Card File immediately, or after just a little tinkering, please don't let it become a "project"—for you or for MECA. It's not central to the function of a personal finance program, and the time you could wind up spending on this will more than wipe out any time you'd save having us dial those seven or eleven digits instead of you.

Dial M for MCI or Sprint

If you use a long distance carrier that requires dialing a local number and account number first, select Program Setup from the FILE menu, then Modem Setup, and enter them there. Then, here, place a capital M in front of any Card File phone number you'd like us to dial that way: 202-456-1414 if you're calling the White House.

AUTO-WRITE A LETTER

More of a time-saver is Auto-Write, which shares the F6 key with Auto-Dial. (Press Ctrl-F and then "A" if it's set to Dial.) Just point to one of your cards and press F6. (On the full-card view it's F7.) We'll summon MYM-Write and start you off with something like this:

April 1, 1992   Ms. Harriet Smiley
President
Smiley, Snicker & Frown
231 West 109th Terrace
Andersonville, IL 60698-2198

Dear Harriet:

Sincerely,

Ima Mimm Yuzer, Ph.D
.pa
Ms. Harriet Smiley
President
Smiley, Snicker & Frown
231 West 109th Terrace
Andersonville, IL 60698-2198

We put the address twice, separated by a ".pa" page advance command—once for the letter, a second time for the envelope or label. You can set the default to have us put the envelope first, or to not print envelopes. (To set this and other Auto-Write defaults, choose Optional Features from the FILE menu and then Card File. You can tell us how you like to close your letters and how to adjust certain margins. Next year, we hope to allow more customized margins.)

Which address? The address we choose—Home, Office or Other—is determined by the Phone column displayed on the main Card File screen (press F7 to rotate that column). If you choose Home or Other, we won't include the Company Name or Title, on the theory that it's a personal letter.

Salutation? We normally use the first name in the salutation ("Dear Harriet"). If you fill in the Salutation field on the card, we'll use what you put there, instead. One letter may thus begin, "Dear Ms. Lehmann-Haupt," while the next will begin, "Dear Joey Baby Doll!" We'll automatically know how you like to address each person. This also works in Mail Merges.

You may well want to make changes to what Auto-Write starts you off with. Still, it's a lot easier to delete a line, say, or to change "Dear Harriet" to "Dear Ms. Smiley," than to type all this boring stuff. With a single keystroke, all the boring stuff is typed for you!

PRINTING ENVELOPES

There's another way to print an envelope with the Card File which, depending on your printer and the way you work, you might prefer.

Press F4 and then Speed Scroll to the address you want. Mark it (press F9 first to erase existing marks if there are any) and press F4 again. (Note the horizontal bars we use on this screen to let you know which records have addresses, which have phone numbers, and which have both.)

Now choose "Labels" as your report type, press F4 again and experiment with the top and left margins until you learn what works for your printer setup. Once you do, the program will remember them (if you save before quitting). In my own case, the Top Margin is set at 20, the Left Margin is set at 60, and the number of Lines per Label is set at 25. These weird settings are because I use a laser printer (see below). I don't actually have 25-line addresses, but, as the error message reminded me when I was getting all this straight, the number of lines per label must be set at least 5 higher than the top margin.

Now just go ahead and print the envelope. **Hereafter, all you have to do is Speed Scroll to the item you want, mark it, and (presuming you've still got the report-type set to "Labels") press F4 four times. Out it prints.**

Printing More Than One

And while you're at it, don't miss the opportunity to print up to 9 copies of the same label or envelope. When you're marking the address(es) you want us to print, use a 9 (or some lower number) instead of the traditional "X." Whatever number you mark, that's how many we'll print.

Are there a few people you write to frequently? Why not make up a bunch of envelopes for each all at once? (Instruct us to pause after each envelope so you can feed in the next; or to print them continuously, if you have continuous-form envelopes or an envelope tray.)

Printing Them With a Laser

The reason my margin settings are so weird (see "Printing Envelopes," above), is that I use a Hewlett-Packard LaserJet Series II. If you have one, you know you have to feed the envelopes in lengthwise—the long way—and print sideways (called "landscape mode"). So the trick is to find a way to tell the printer that the address you're sending it should be printed sideways, on its ear.

At first glance, this might seem difficult, since the only printing choices we give you are Normal, Compressed, Emphasized, Quality and Daisywheel—not "sideways." But with a laser printer you don't need the Quality choice (because lasers print only in quality mode to begin with), so it's simply a matter of redefining that printing mode to mean "sideways." It will still say Quality on the screen, where you choose it, but you and your printer will know differently.

To get Managing Your Money to use the "Quality" designation to mean landscape mode (printing things on their side), as I have, select Program Setup from the FILE menu, then Printer and then (assuming it's already set up for the LaserJet) press F7. Set the "Quality" strings so they look like this (remember, these are the strings for the Hewlett-Packard LaserJet II—not necessarily for your printer):

Near Letter Quality On: 27 38 108 49 79

Near Letter Quality Off: 27 38 108 48 79

Then save your work.

Now whenever you choose to print something on your laser printer in "Quality" mode—assuming your printer uses the same codes mine does—we'll send the code that instructs it to print things sideways.

Once you've gone through the learning curve and gotten set up this way, printing an envelope from the Card File will be as fast and easy as speed scrolling to it, placing an X beside it (or a number from 2 to 9 if you want more than one), and pressing F4 four times (having first checked to be sure printing is directed to the printer, and in Quality mode).

COMMONLY ASKED QUESTIONS

Can I keep separate sets of cards? Yes. It's a little inconvenient, but there are two reasons you might want to. First, there's a limit to how many cards you'll be able to fit on a single backup disk, and you should always back up these valuable records to floppies, just in case. (I have 932 entries in my Card File right now, many of them heavily laden with notes, which take up 458K, or about a third of a high-density floppy.) Second, even if you have plenty of room, as you probably will, there may be some records in your file—or some comments in those records—you'd just as soon not share with family members who use the program.

So you might have a Card File for yourself (or even two); your spouse might keep one for everyone involved in his/her charity; your son might have one for all his high school classmates, so he can send them personalized campaign letters, become class president, get into Duke and bankrupt you with tuition payments.

If you keep your data on floppies, it's very simple to do this. Just put the file records.dbs, which is your Card File, on a floppy all to itself—and have a separate such disk for each different Card File (each clearly labeled, of course, and each with its own backup).

Whenever you press Ctrl-C, Managing Your Money will look for the records.dbs disk (it doesn't care whose, so long as it finds one) and, not finding one in your drive, will beep and ask for it. Insert whichever Card File you want to work with.

If you keep your data on a hard disk, as most of us do, just use New Data Set on the FILE menu to set up as many different sets of data as you want, and Open Data Set, from then on, whenever you want to switch from one to another.

New Data Set clones a new set of all the data files, not just records.dbs. If you have a lot of data, this could take up a lot of disk space. To create a new, empty data set, put your original Managing Your Money Disk 1 in your drive, type a:install (or b:install) and press Enter. Press F2, F2 to install specific files. Move the cursor down to the "Data files" area, use the Spacebar to mark all the data files, and press Enter. On the next screen we'll ask you where you want to install your program files; just tell us where your program files already are, even though you aren't reinstalling them. Then tell us which subdirectory of your program directory to create for your new data set (mym\ben, say). The next time you start Managing Your Money, you can load this new set with Open Files on the FILE menu.

Or, instead, you could create the new data set on a floppy disk. When you want to load it with Open Data Set, type a: or b: instead of a data set name to indicate which floppy drive the disk is in.

It's a good idea to use different colors for each data set so you don't inadvertently enter your house payment in a data set you've created just for a Card File.

MYM-WRITE—CTRL-W

All this and a word processor, too. We call it Write on the Money—though it's become, simply, MYM-Write for short—and it has two distinctly different uses, depending on how you summon it.

1. **Word Processor Mode**—to write or edit any kind of document. Wherever you are in the program, press Ctrl-W. Whatever you were doing is temporarily suspended and up comes MYM-Write.

    Say you were paying your bills but noticed someone had overbilled you. Then and there you could press Ctrl-W, compose and print an angry letter, then pick up where you left off.

In truth, a lot of you already have this convenient capability with programs like SideKick. Or you can pop up your real word processor with Windows or Software Carousel. But MYM-Write has a second use:

2.   **Iceberg Mode**—to attach detail to a line on the screen. In early versions of Managing Your Money, there were many places where you had only a single line, if that, for comments. Now, such lines are just the tip of the iceberg. With MYM-Write, you can attach notes of almost any length—and add to or edit them as often as you like.

HINT: Don't be alarmed! The first couple of times you jump into iceberg mode, it's disconcerting: The screen you're looking at is suddenly gone and there, in its place, is our word processor. But when you're done typing whatever you want to type, or looking at whatever you typed previously, just exit (by pressing the exit key shown at the bottom of the screen—ESCape, unless you've customized it) and you'll be back where you were.

Say you're on the Spend Money screen or Receive Money. You'll see room for a one-line Memo. But press F2 (from anywhere on the screen) and you're instantly in MYM-Write, with all the room you want to add, view or edit text. (With check memos, only the first line will actually print on your check; the rest is for your own records only.)

With MYM-Write, the memo line on your transactions or accounts receivable suddenly becomes as long as you need to make it. If you're using Managing Your Money to print invoices, you don't have to say "For Services Rendered"—you can itemize your bill in full detail and include a thank you note at the bottom.

Where once you were limited on the Portfolio Summary screen to entering just the name and number of your brokerage account, with MYM-Write you may dive beneath the surface and append the office manager's name along with your broker's name, her assistant's name, a rough sketch of the commission schedule they charge, and a history of all the prior account numbers the portfolio had been assigned, as the firm went through each successive revamping of its computer system ("to serve you better," but also to confuse you totally if you have several different accounts at the same brokerage house).

Similarly, the comment line on each of your assets becomes just the tip of whatever iceberg you care to attach. You could easily need this extra room for notes if you'd originally bought 300 shares of Nike at 15 and now, at 95, wanted to record the 10 different charities to which you'd given shares . . . or if you wanted to jot down a running log of your broker's advice and comments. (But Dave, you told me on May 8 you expected sales to pick up in the 3rd quarter. And then on the 23rd you said—and I think I'm quoting pretty accurately here—"I don't see how it can go any lower." On June 14 you said the indictments were just an S.E.C. bluff and on July 6 you told me—and again, I'm quoting—"This is the classic example of a Wall Street over-reaction. OK, we were a little early buying the stock," you said, "but if I were you, I'd buy more.") This won't make your stocks go up, but it could make you feel better.

Using MYM-Write to append detail, the line you have in IN-SURE to add comments about each of your insurance policies can be expanded to include the entire history of that policy as the years go on—claims, scheduled items you've added (furs, jewelry)—as well as your own shorthand interpretation of what the policy actually says.

In Loan Records you could keep track of when your variable-rate mortgage adjusts and when you're allowed to convert it to fixed-rate.

Notes on each of your Card File entries can become ongoing histories of your relationships: when you saw or talked to someone, what gifts you've exchanged over the years—a veritable electronic diary or photo album, if you will, for personal relationships, and a way, also, to keep track of business relationships.

If you have a modem, you'll be able to use the Card File (Ctrl-C) or Phone Calls (Ctrl-P) to dial someone up; but also, while you're waiting a few seconds for him or her to get on the line, to review the last few contacts you've had—and then to add a phrase or two summarizing this one after you've finished the call. It's true, this could quickly grow to consume huge amounts of disk space; but additional disk space is becoming more affordable at what may be an even more rapid pace.

In sum: You can press Ctrl-W on any screen to create a whole new document that's not attached to Managing Your Money in any way. In addition, on many screens—not all—you can summon MYM-Write with F2 to attach detail to the line you've highlighted with your cursor.

> NOTE: MYM-Write plays possum if you have the calculator (Ctrl-N) active on the screen. And, conversely, Ctrl-N is disabled while you're in MYM-Write.

FROM CHAPTER 3: MONEY
THE NUB OF IT

You certainly don't have to use Managing Your Money to print your checks, and not everyone does. But one way or another, you have to pay your bills. Doing it with Managing Your Money spares you a tremendous amount of drudgery. After the first time, you never have to write out the name of whomever you're paying ... or your 18-digit account number ... or the amount of the check in English ("One hundred eighty-seven and no/100") ... or the date. In fact, you don't even have to address envelopes. After the first time, all you need tell us is the amount.

> HINT: When you're setting up your accounts in Managing Your Money, it's helpful to have your last bank statement from each account you want to set up. Get your checkbook, too. Then you won't have to go hunting when it's time to enter bank balances, addresses and other information.

There are three advantages to this:

- It saves time.

- Our handwriting may be better than yours.

- Your data is "captured," and thus available for use in printing reports and graphs, budgeting, projecting your available cash, balancing your checkbook, estimating and preparing your taxes—and more.

Naturally, you'll still write some checks by hand; Managing Your Money makes it easy to record these, as well as your cash and credit card expenditures. But overall, once you get the hang of it, it should take you less time to be better organized; less time, not more, finally to be in control of your finances.

By recording your transactions in Managing Your Money, you can see at any time:

- Customized reports of all your income and expenditures, organized and subtotaled by budget category and/or by payee (select Report Generator from the MONEY pulldown menu)

- Your account balances (select Money Accounts from the MONEY pulldown)

- Your actual spending versus budget, both for this month and for the year-to-date (Budget Categories) and what's left to spend

- Your cash forecast for the months or years ahead (Forecasting)

- The status of your loans (Loan Records)

- Your tax status (select TAX from the Menu Bar)

- Your total available cash and credit (select Money Accounts from the MONEY pulldown; then F4 to print: your total available cash and credit are at the end of that report)

- Your up-to-the-minute net worth (select NET WORTH from the Menu Bar)

- And more.

PART I: WHERE DO I BEGIN?

For many users, MONEY is by far the most important part of the program. Here you can design budget categories that fit your finances; set up your checking, savings and credit card accounts (among others); spend, receive and transfer money; set up Quick transactions and Alert transactions; record loans you owe (or own); forecast your available cash; print checks, invoices and reports—even pay bills electronically without having to write checks at all.

If you like, you can dive right in. Just select Spend Money from the MONEY menu and "write a check." We'll first ask you to set up a checking account and then proceed to let you enter the data.

But to get going in an organized way, you may wish to follow these steps. It won't take long, and you'll be building a good foundation for years to come.

STEP #1: SELECT THE OPTIONS YOU WANT

Select Optional Features from the FILE menu, and then Money Options. Press F1 for HELP in making your choices and then the Action Key to accept them. (Remember that none of this will "take" if you quit the program without saving, so it's a good idea to press Ctrl-S from the Menu Bar once you've changed any options.)

HINT: The Action Key is either Enter or F10; the screen will tell you which. You may change the Action Key at any time. To do so, go to the FILE menu, choose Program Setup, then Action Key. Type E for Enter or F for F10.

The simplest thing is to just stick with the settings Managing Your Money comes with and skip to Step #2 now.

But if and when you do want to tinker, here are your choices:

- **Warn if transaction is over- or under-allocated.** With this option activated, we'll warn you if you ever fail to fully allocate a transaction. This is helpful when you're assigning a transaction to multiple budget categories. It will not warn you if you later change the amount of a transaction and fail to reallocate it.

- **Warn if something to send to CheckFree.** This option only appears if you have activated the CheckFree electronic bill-paying service (under CheckFree on the MONEY menu). If you say "Yes" here, any time you have something to send CheckFree and try leaving the program without doing it, we'll warn you. We'll let you leave anyway or transmit first.

  We find out whether you have something to transmit by looking through your MONEY records. If you have a lot of data and find that it takes too long to quit the program, you can say "No" here and we won't warn you. If you do, you'll have to remember to transmit any time you change anything related to CheckFree—create a transaction or merchant, change anything in your CheckFree setup (such as your address or account), or write E-Mail.

- **Five-year Budgeting.** Several years ago this feature inspired a Salt Lake County commissioner to impose five-year budgeting on the County. The practice helped the County build reserves and retain an Aaa bond rating, while keeping taxes level for six years. If you take the time to project your finances into the future, you may wind up with triple-A finances, too. (Meanwhile, I subsequently persuaded that county commissioner, Bart Barker, to leave Utah and come work for me.)

- **Graphs.** Unless your equipment can't handle graphics, you'll a most surely want to say YES.

- **Accounts Payable and Accounts Receivable.** Activating this puts Payables and Receivables on your MONEY menu. We ask you for your last invoice number so we can use it when you print invoices.

- **Where to start the cursor.** On the Spend and Receive Money screens, we fill in the date and, if applicable, the check number, and so normally start the cursor down on the Payee or Payor field. But if you tend to enter your transactions a batch at a time, covering several days, you might prefer to have us start the cursor at the top, in the Date field, so it's easy to change.

- **Reset Date.** When you're entering a stack of Spend or Receive transactions, we'll continue using the last date you entered until you change it, if you say NO to this option. If you say YES, we'll drive you nuts changing the date back to today after each one. (But that's handy if you use Managing Your Money to pay most of your bills, only occasionally entering a transaction, such as a handwritten check, with a prior date.)

- **Display Running Balance on Quick List.** As you go down your Quick List marking transactions to execute, we show how your account balance will be affected. This is very handy, but can slow things down on older machines. If you find speed is a problem, try answering NO to this option.

- **Alert Transaction warning days.** How far in advance, if at all, should we remind you of transactions on your Alert List? Enter 0 if you don't want us to remind you until the day you've scheduled the transaction to be made.

- **Base TAX projections on which year's figures?** Normally, you'd choose THIS YEAR. But we can pass a future year's budgeted figures from MONEY to TAX instead. (It's wise to switch this option back after using it, lest you forget and not notice, weeks from now, that our TAX estimate is based on a future year's budget.)

- **Change your fiscal year (F6).** You almost surely don't want to d this! Most individuals and businesses file income taxes based on a calendar year. But if your business uses a fiscal year that ends in

June, say, reflect that here when you begin using Managing Your Money. For details, press F1 for Help after you press F6.

- **A word about Close Out Past Year.** The first time you start Managing Your Money with a date from next year, we'll add Close Out Past Year (COPY) to your FILE menu. Press F7 to find out more. (Once COPY appears on the FILE menu, F7 will no longer appear here.)

- **Change data set status (F8).** You probably don't need this, either. Your Active data set is the one for the current year; inactive sets are for prior years and don't allow you to enter transactions with this year's date. If you inadvertently answered this question wrong during Installation, just change it here. Changing this back and forth has no effect on your data.

When you're done with Money Options, press the Action Key to save your changes.

STEP #2: SET UP YOUR MONEY ACCOUNTS

By "money accounts" we mean primarily your checking, savings and charge accounts. But you may also want to set up one or more cash accounts (His and Hers?), portfolio-linked CMA accounts, home-equity accounts and perhaps even "noncash" accounts for things like frequent flier miles, depreciation, or your gift of a fur coat to the Salvation Army (see page 374: "Noncash Items").

IMPORTANT! Here's the best way to get into synch with your bank or credit card company:

First, on the Add a Money Account screen, enter the balance from your last statement—usually positive if it's a bank balance, negative if it's a credit card balance—in the field where we ask for "last statement balance." That way, you and they agree on where things stood November 25th (say).

Now, select Spend and Receive Money from the MONEY menu and enter all the transactions the bank doesn't know about yet—the ones made since November 25th, and the ones made prior to November 25th that hadn't yet hit your statement. That's it! It's like handing a baton smoothly from the old way you used to keep track of your checkbook to this new, swifter runner called Managing Your Money.

To start, it's fine to set up just one of your accounts. You can always add the others later.

Setting up accounts is easy, and it's all explained in HELP:

1.   Select Money Accounts from the MONEY menu.

2.   Press F5 to add your new account. Any HELP you need is just a keystroke away: F1.

INCLUDE IN CASH FORECASTING?

At the bottom of the screen we ask whether to include the account in Cash Forecasting. Normally you'd say Yes. If you say No, Managing Your Money's cash-forecaster will know to ignore its balance when it projects your available cash. It will still figure into your Net Worth—you'll still be rich. It just won't show up as ready cash in MONEY's cash projection.

You'd do this for, say, a savings account you've vowed never to touch til the tots turn twenty. In reality, the cash is there; but, to avoid temptation, you'd rather not think of it that way when you select Forecasting from the MONEY menu.

If you set up a **home equity account**, you'd almost surely want to say No. Otherwise, we'd show you deep in the red each month, with the $40,000 you'd borrowed against your house deducted from your available cash. Yet you actually have 30 years to repay that $40,000, so it's not exactly a pressing drain on your wallet.

The same logic holds for **credit card accounts** if you're one who leaves the balance outstanding more or less forever, and only pays the interest. Just say No!

In short: Say No for any account whose balance—positive or negative—you want Cash Forecasting to ignore. This would be any account whose balance doesn't really affect the amount of cash you can lay your hands on: a bank balance you're determined not to draw on; a home equity or credit card account balance you're not planning to repay any time soon.

But you don't have to deal with this now! (Or ever, really.) You can edit a bank or credit card account at any time. If you're just starting with Managing Your Money, press on!

STEP #3: SET UP YOUR BUDGET CATEGORY NAMES

You don't *have* to assign your income and expenses to categories, but being able to is one of the key benefits of using a computer to manage your money. And Managing Your Money makes it very simple. Even if you don't plan to use the program for budgeting, you'll still want to be able to list and total your expenses by category, for tax purposes.

1.   Select Budget Categories from the MONEY menu.

2.   Press F1 and read HELP. I won't take your time repeating it here.

3.   To save you time, we've started you off with a list of common buget categories. Naturally, many won't apply to you. Just arrow down the list and press F3 to delete them. For those that do apply—Clothing, say—but for which you'd prefer a different name—Apparel—just press F2 and change it. Press the Action Key when you're done.

4.   Add categories we haven't thought of—Apparel-His, Appare-Hers, Apparel-Kids. Just press F5. In fact, even if you can't think of any others you need, press F5 anyway to see what that screen looks like, and to read its HELP. It may give you some ideas on how to set up your budget.

When you add a new category, we offer you the option of tagging it with one of our tax categories right away, or postponing that until later. I suggest you postpone it and concentrate on one job at a time. For now, just get your budget categories the way you want them. Later, you can run through all of them and assign tax treatments (i.e., tell us that Church Donations is a "Charity Contribution"). **Postponing this little chore will actually save you time.** That's because any new category you create without assigning a specific tax category is automatically assigned the "Not a Tax Category" tag. And for many of your budget categories, like Apparel, that's exactly right! So you'll only need to change the ones you add that do have tax consequences, like Church Contributions or Royalties or Baby-Sitting Income.

For a list of all the Tax Barrels into which budget buckets may be dumped, see: "Tax Categories."

We give you a Memo field so you can record the assumptions you used to set up your budget ("includes gas and repairs but not insurance").

BUDGETING FOR SAVINGS

At the bottom of the Add Budget Category screen, we ask whether to include this category in Cash Forecasting and whether to include it in Profit & Loss. The first question is the same one we asked on the Add Money Account screen.

- **You don't have to deal with this now (or ever).**

- **But in case you do want to deal with it, you'll see we've already done a lot of the thinking for you, in the budget categories we've started you off with.**

 A budget is a *spending* plan. Money shelled out for rent or groceries is spent. But what of money shelled out for a savings certificate? Or for 100 shares of stock? Or to pay down the balance of your mortgage? It's not really spent, it's just moved from one of your pockets—(your checking account)—to another—(your savings account or brokerage account or the equity in your home).

 Yet some of us, understandably, want to budget for savings as well as for spending. Managing Your Money has a neat trick to accommodate this.

- **Include in Cash Forecasting?** The answer for almost all categories is Yes, because almost all kinds of expenditures, whether for flowers or savings bonds, cut into your available cash. Answer Yes for any expenditure that cuts into your available ready cash.

 Still, you might have a handful of categories you want to tag "No." We'll exclude them from our calculations of available cash in Forecasting (on the MONEY pulldown menu). You might do that if you set up a category called NONCASH CONTRIBUTIONS because you planned to give $500 worth of old clothes to charity each year and wanted TAX to reflect it. Clearly, giving away clothes will not lower your available cash, so it shouldn't be reflected in Cash Forecasting. Likewise, if you planned to stick $50 a month in a cookie jar, and set up a budget category called COOKIE JAR, you might also answer No, because that cash would remain available to you (unless the cookie monster got it). Answer No for any category that does not reduce your available cash.

- Include in Profit & Loss? Answer Yes here for any spending that makes you poorer—CLEANING or MORTGAGE INTEREST or CLUB DUES. But answer No for any "spending" that just shifts money from one pocket to another—SAVINGS or MORTGAGE PRINCIPAL or LOAN PAYMENT. (Paying down a loan reduces the amount of cash in your pocket, but doesn't make you poorer. You have less cash, but you also have less debt.)

  With Income categories, answer Yes to all those that make you richer, like SALARY, DIVIDENDS and GIFTS FROM DAD. But answer No to any that are really just transfers from one pocket to another, like IRA WITHDRAWAL. (When you take money from your IRA, it doesn't make you richer.)

GROUP THE "NO'S" TOGETHER?

While you're at it, you might consider grouping all your savings-oriented budget categories together, by putting the same character at the start of their names.

If you start them all with a Z (Z-RAINY DAY FUND), all your savings-type expenditures will be grouped alphabetically. The expense ones will sit just above the line for *NET PROFIT* (unless you have a category for ZEBRAS). Thus it will be easy to see that, while your budget shows a net profit of only $350, say, that's after putting aside $2,000 for your IRA, $3,000 for a rainy day, $12,000 for mutual fund purchases, and paying down an additional $1,582.38 on your mortgage.

To see what your profit really was, press F6 on the Budget screen and we'll exclude those categories you said not to include in Net Profit. Note, however, that with printed reports, all categories are included in the calculation of net profit, even if you've used F6.

What's the point of all this? We let you exclude categories marked "No" from the Income, Expense, and Net Profit totals. That way, if you're budgeting income of $100,000, spending of $60,000 and savings of $40,000, we won't show you just breaking even, we'll show you making a $40,000 profit. (To see this, select Budget Categories from the MONEY menu. F6 gives you the choice of All categories or only those included in Net Profit—the ones tagged Yes.)

EASIER THAN IT SOUNDS

To summarize:

1.   Leave most budget categories the way they are. Just say "Yes."

2.   For categories that don't make you richer or poorer, answer "No" to "Include in Profit & Loss?" (e.g., "spending" on shares in a mutual fund).

3.   If a category doesn't even change the amount of cash you have available, answer "No" to "Include in Cash Forecasting?"

You can ignore all this if you want. But to make it easy, we've started you off with some "No" categories we thought you might want to use. Feel free to delete them or to add others or to fiddle with them at any time. To see which categories are tagged Yes and No, press F7 until you see the Status screen.

If you follow those steps, you'll be able to use F6 on the Budget Categories screen to exclude from its totals those items that don't really make you richer or poorer.

STEP #4: MAKE BUDGET ESTIMATES

You don't have to do this right away. In fact, if you don't want to make up a budget—or don't need to live within one—you don't have to do it ever!

But most of us benefit from having a plan and being able to track our progress against it. MYM makes this very easy, too. And entering budget estimates means our TAX section can make sensible projections. So, when you're ready:

1.   **Verify the budget categories we start you off with.** Point to the first budget category on your list (the one right after our summary Total Income line) and press F2. Change its name if you like, and check to be sure you're satisfied with the tax treatment we've assigned it (displayed next to "Tax Category"). If not, press F6 to change it. We'll only show you the income-type tax categories for income budget categories and expense-type tax categories for expense budget categories. Select the category you want and press the Action Key to accept it.

     While you're here, you can also add a Memo (press F2 if you need more room) and tell us whether to include this category's totals in Cash Forecasting and Profit and Loss (see Budgeting for Savings, above) in case we've guessed wrong.

     Then press the Action Key to save your changes.

2.   **Delete those that don't apply.** Back on the Budget Categories screen, press F3 to delete any of our sample categories that you don't want.

3.   **Add new ones of your own.** You'll doubtless think of things we forgot. From the main Budget Categories screen, press F5 to add new ones.

> HINT: Page Scrolling Through Your Budget Categories. When viewing the details of a budget category, you can move straight to the next without having to return to your list. Just press the PgDn key. But return to your list as often as you like: you'll see your budgeted *NET PROFIT* at the end of the list grow and shrink as you enter your estimated income and expenses.

4.   **Make budget estimates.** Now point to the first of your budget categories again and press the Action Key to make up its budget— how much do you receive from Alimony each month? (But first see Long-range Budgeting, below.) Press F1—HELP for tips and shortcuts.

     When you're satisfied with this first category, press the Action Key to save your changes, and visit the next category—and the next and the next. (Of course, you're welcome to visit them in any order you want. And you needn't do this all at once.)

You might find it easier to check the tax category for each budget category first (F2 from the Budget Categories screen). Use PgDn to move to each successive category (PgDn saves your changes before moving on). When you're done, go back to the top, press the Action Key and set the budgets, again moving from category to category with PgDn.

NOTE: If you have no idea what you spend, or if you're not keen about taking the time to make up a budget, there's an alternative. Forget it for this year. Just enter your receipts and expenditures as the year unfolds, allocating each transaction to a budget category. Next year, you'll know at a glance what you spend on things. And we'll make up your budget for you, if you like, as part of the Close Out Past Year (COPY) process. Just tell us to use last year's budget or last year's actuals as this year's budget—inflated or deflated by any amount you choose. Or, if you delay COPY through much of next year, you can use this year's "actuals" yourself in setting next year's budgets. We display them right on the screen (press the Action Key from the Budget Categories screen).

Long-Range Budgeting

Before you start entering your budget estimates, you will probably want to **turn on our five-year budgeting option.** (Select Options from the FILE menu, then Money Options.) If you do, our budget shortcuts will automatically fill in most of the numbers for you at the same time as you're doing this year's budget. Your cash forecast will extend a full year or five years into the future; and if you like, TAX will be able to estimate your taxes for that future year.

HINT: Alph*bet!za+^on. There's a way to impose more than just alphabetical order on your budget categories. Say you wanted to group together all the categories pertaining to each of 5 rental properties. You could put an asterisk (or any other non-alphabetic character) in front of all your rental property categories, followed by a 1 for all those categories pertaining to the first property, a 2 for all those pertaining to the second, and so on. Instead of a category called "Maintenance-123 Elm Street," you might use "*1-Maintenance" or "*Elm-Maintenance." Managing Your Money will group all the asterisks together. And within that overall group, each property will have its own little subgroup.

Or you could begin all your household categories—groceries, clothing, family car—with a hyphen ("-") to group them at the beginning of your Expenses list, making it easy to eyeball them all at once for a quick review.

Grouping items together this way may make your data easier to enter and analyze.

To exploit the possibilities here, it may help you to know how a computer "alphabetizes" non-alphabetic characters. Sing this, if you can: ! @ # $ % & * ( ) * + , - . / 0 1 2 3 4 5 6 7 8 9 : ; < = > ? @. Only then do you get to A through Z.

IMPORTANT NOTES:

- You needn't finish the job of setting up your budget before proceeding to Step #5. We're not slave-drivers. You can always add new budget categories or enter your budget estimates later. But unless you're very rich or genetically frugal, do make a budget soon: it's the first step in any successful financial plan.

- Do not enter budget estimates for conventional mortgage or automobile loans. We do that for you as part of entering the loans in Step #5, below.

- Next year, creating your budget will be a snap. We'll do most of the work for you. (See NOTE, on previous page.)

- Read HELP as you encounter each new screen.

STEP #5: SET UP YOUR LOANS

There are basically three kinds of loans: mortgage loans, that follow a standard "amortization schedule" (where the monthly payment stays constant, but is almost entirely interest at first and principal at the end); interest-only loans (where all the principal is repaid in a lump at the end);

and all others, which we call special loans (including nonstandard mortgages, rule-of-78 loans, and crazy loans you make to your brother-
in-law).

- You can enter all three kinds of loans in Managing Your Money.

- As part of the process, you can (and should) set up a Quick List or
  Alert List transaction for each, as I'll explain.

- The loans can be money you owe—or money owed you.

- It's fine to come back to this later, if you're eager to get going.
  There's no need to enter all your loans now. Just remember not to
  make budget estimates for your mortgage payments, because we
  do it for you— precisely—when you set up the loan.

Managing Your Money's ability to handle mortgage-type loans (**which
includes most automobile loans**) is particularly amazing. Once you tell
us the basics, we'll create the proper Quick List or Alert List transaction
for you and enter precise budget estimates. Then, if things change—you
make a principal prepayment, say, or the interest rate on your mortgage
declines—we recalculate everything automatically and even readjust your
budgeted principal and interest payments.

We don't work that magic on special or interest-only loans—but we do
work on them, so be sure to set them up and create their Quick List or
Alert List transactions here. We won't fill out your budget for you; but we
will remember the categories to which you want to allocate the interest
and principal from these loans, make it very easy to record payments (in
whatever amount), and, when you do, update the outstanding balance of
the loan, and hence your net worth, accordingly.

ENTERING A NEW OR EXISTING LOAN

Setting up a loan is easy. Just follow these steps and tell the butler to hold
your calls. When in doubt, read HELP.

1. From the MONEY menu, select Loan Records.

2. Press F5 to add a new one and fill in our blanks—except for the interest rate, if it's a mortgage-type loan. (If it's a special or an interest-only loan, you can fill that in, too.) Where we ask for the
   Payment, enter whatever monthly payment the bank actually de-

mands, less any escrow payment for taxes or insurance, which are entered separately.

The Purpose field is just for your records. It doesn't really matter which purpose you choose. The Type field is important, though, because it determines how we handle the loan. If it's a conventional mortgage— including a typical adjustable-rate mortgage—tag it "Mortgage." Do the same with most car and other standard loans the bank calculates like a mortgage. But if it's a $50,000 mortgage payable in some unconventional way—$10,000 a year, say, for five years, plus 10% interest on the unpaid balance—tag it "Special."

Don't worry too much about the distinction between a "Special" and an "Interest-Only" loan. Basically, they're the same, except that with an interest-only loan we save you a few keystrokes because we know the payment isn't likely to involve principal.

In fact, with special and interest-only loans, don't worry too much about anything. We don't really care how many payments remain or when you took out the loan or what the interest rate is. This is mainly for your record keeping.

But with mortgage-type loans, we do care, because we need to get our "amortization schedule" as closely as possible in synch with your bank's. That way, we can make up precise budget estimates and readjust everything automatically when you pay extra principal or when the interest rate changes.

If it's a new mortgage-type loan, just enter its origination date in the Date of Loan field. But if it's an existing loan, you can do it either of two ways, whichever you find easier:

- If there have been no twists and turns in the interest rate along the way, and no principal prepayments—if, in short, it's been a plain vanilla situation—you can enter the original date of the loan, the original number of payments (360, if it's a 30-year mortgage) and the original amount. Then, after pressing the Action Key twice to record the loan, just point to it and press F2 to edit it. On that screen, enter the actual number of payments you've made to date—presumably, 12 times the number of years you've had the loan. Press F6 and we'll update everything for you and even write a little essay at the bottom of the screen. At the top of the screen we'll tell you the date through which the loan is paid up based on the number of payments you entered. If we show the wrong date, change the number of payments and press F6 again. Or ...

- Enter today's date; the amount of the loan that remains outstanding; and the number of payments that remain to be made. If you don't know any of this, your bank will tell you.

3.   Now press the Action Key. We will freeze the screen and—for mortgage-type loans only—calculate what we believe to be the accurate interest rate for a loan of this size, term and monthly payments. This may vary slightly from your bank's figure, because different banks use slightly different methods of calculation.

4.   If you're not happy with what you've entered, just press F6 and we'll "unfreeze" the screen to let you make changes. Otherwise press the Action Key again to add this loan to your list.

If at that point you decide to make a change, just point to the loan and press F2 to edit it, or F3 to delete it altogether and start again. Read HELP if you're having trouble. And remember: if the interest rate we show varies slightly from the bank's stated rate, it's nothing to worry about; it's just (mathematically speaking) our saying tomay-to when they say tomah-to.

5.   Even if you are happy, as you likely will be, point at your new loan and press F2 to take a look at it. If it's a mortgage-type loan, you can have some fun changing the "payments already made" (and anything else) to see what effect that has on the essay we write at the bottom of the screen. Just press F6 to have us recalculate—and then ESCape when you're through playing around, so you don't accidentally save the bogus scenario you were playing with.

6.   Back on the Loan Records screen, there's one last chore. Press F6 or F7 to link this loan with an Alert List transaction or a Quick List transaction. In order for us to keep track of your loan balances properly, you must record all loan payments with one of these linked transactions.

Which to choose? If it's a mortgage-type loan, I'd choose Alert List: F6. (Should you later wish to switch your mortgage from Alert List to Quick List, just delete the Alert List transaction—Alert List from the MONEY menu—and then come back here and create the Quick List transaction instead.) For interest-only and special loans, choose Quick List: F7. (You have no choice—we'll beep if you press F6.)

When we create your transaction, we'll ask what bank account you ordinarily use to make the payment. An Alert transaction is linked to a specific bank account; a Quick List transaction can be used with any account (tag it "Global").

Optional: Fill in the address and Memo if you like (you'll need an address if you plan to print checks and mail them with window envelopes). Fill in the loan escrows, if any. Press F7 if you're a CheckFree customer and want to make loan payments that way.

Now press the Action Key and we'll ask you to designate the budget categories into which you want us to dump the Interest and Principal from this loan, along with the escrows, if any.

Because home mortgage interest gets special tax treatment, it's important to have a special category for that—"Home Mortgage Interest." For other loans, you might assign them all to a single "Other Loan Interest" category. Or use categories such as "Automobile Interest," "Student Loan Interest" and "Rental Prop Interest"—or separate ones for each of the rental properties you own ("620-Interest" for your property at 620 Hyacinth, but "126-Interest" for the one at 126 Ocean Boulevard). Set this up any way you want.

Likewise, you might want to dump the Principal portion of your various loan payments into categories like "Equity in My Home" and "Automobile" (since by paying off the auto loan, you're essentially paying for the automobile); or generic ones like "Loan Repayment" or even (since paying off loans is a form of saving) "Saving." It's up to you.

If you haven't yet created the budget categories into which you'll want to dump the interest and principal from this loan (and escrow, if any), you can add them on the fly when you get to the screen where we ask you to choose. Just press F5.

Whatever budget buckets you choose for the interest and principal of your various loans, remember: with mortgage-type loans, we fill in the budget amounts for you automatically. Don't do it yourself, or we'll both be doing it. (No great harm, but that would essentially double your budget estimates for these loans, and thus throw them way off.)

When you're happy with the budget allocations you've chosen, press the Action Key to record this transaction, which will now be "linked" to your loan. Whenever in the future you use this Quick or Alert transaction to make a payment, we'll know to update the status of your loan. The loans will be indicated on the Quick List with an M, I or S (for Mortgage-, Interest-only- or Special-type loans) to the right of the Last Use column. (If you make the payment any other way—manually, say, on the Spend Money screen—we won't know about it, and won't update your loan. So always use a loan's Quick or Alert transaction to make its payments.)

DELETING A MORTGAGE

When you delete a mortgage-type loan, any Quick or Alert transaction you created for it will also be deleted, and the amounts we allocated to your budget categories will be pulled back out of those categories so you can start fresh. (But no actual payments you recorded will be deleted or pulled out of your Budget Categories. Delete them, if at all, one by one from the Check Register screen.)

> WARNING! Let US Readjust Your Budget! If you were to lower your budgeted Interest and Principal budget amounts manually (maybe the loan fell through and you're not taking it after all) and then deleted the mortgage, we'd go ahead and "pull the allocations back out of those categories" anyway, not knowing you already did it by hand—and that could leave you with negative budget amounts for those categories.

STEP #7: SET UP YOUR PAYCHECK

The one Quick List transaction that can throw people for a loop is their paycheck. It's confusing, because it's not a simple thing like your $30 cable TV bill. With your paycheck, you are receiving money (your gross pay)—and spending it (the deductions)—all at the same time. So in setting up this transaction, you should allocate your gross pay to an income budget category (Salary) and the deductions to various expense categories.

Let's step through it. To enter a "Quick List transaction" for your paycheck:

1.   Select Quick List from the MONEY menu (or press Alt-Q from the Check Register).

2.   Press F5, then R, (or simply Alt-R) to add a "Receive Money" Quick transaction.

3.   On the screen that appears next, enter the name of your employer.

4.   In the Amount field, enter the actual net amount of your take home pay—the amount of the check. Say you're paid $1,000 a week, but that after deductions the actual check is for $623. Enter $623.

5.   Add a memo if you like.

6.   Now press F9 to allocate the paycheck to budget categories and scroll down to the income category called "Salary" (or whatever you've chosen to call it).

7.   Tab into the Allocation column and enter the gross amount from your pay stub ($1,000 in this example), which is likely to be substantially more than the actual amount of the check.

8.   Scroll down to an expense category, like "Taxes: Federal," and type the amount that was withheld. Notice that our message about how much of your paycheck remains to be allocated changes when you enter a number and move to the next field. You are that much closer to allocating the whole thing.

9.   Now go to the other expense categories that apply—Taxes: FICA, Taxes: State, if that's taken out of your paycheck, Health Insurance, and so forth—entering the proper amounts for each. When you're all done, you'll have allocated your gross pay to "Salary" and all the deductions from it to their proper expense categories. There will be nothing left to allocate. It's easiest to just press F8 on the last category and we'll allocate the rest to it.

10.   Press the Action Key to record what you've done.

11.   Note the name of the account showing at the very top of the Quick List screen. If you deposit your paycheck in this same account each time, that's all there is to it. It's been added to your list of Quick List transactions for this account. If this is the wrong account, or if you sometimes deposit your paycheck in a different account, point to your newly created transaction and press F2. Then press F8 and reassign the account, or make it "global," for use with any account.

From now on, whenever you're working with the Quick List, just place an "X" beside your paycheck and we'll record receipt of the check, add it to your account balance, and dump the proper amounts into your budget categories.

If Your Paycheck Varies From Week to Week

Say you're on commission and no two paychecks are alike. Then what do you do? Well, you can still use this Quick List transaction. At least you won't have to reenter your employer's name. Instead, you'll enter the correct amount of your check and then press Alt-F9 (or F2, F9) to enter the gross pay and deductions. This will still be faster than entering each paycheck manually, because you'll be able to page down the list of categories, immediately spotting those with allocations from the previous paycheck. And because some of them won't change (the $17.37 a week they deduct, no matter what, for health insurance), you'll have a little less to type.

If Your Paycheck Is Automatically Deposited in More Than One Account

We can't record it in a single Quick List transaction. Instead, split it into two Quick List transactions: one you would use to record 90% of your paycheck (say) as a receipt in your checking account; a second to receive the remaining 10% to your savings account. You'd allocate each of the two transactions to your Salary income budget category. As for your deductions—income tax, FICA and all that—you could split them proportionately among the two separate transactions, but it would be much easier and just as good to allocate all the deductions to the larger of the two.

Or set up a Quick List "Receive" for 100% of your paycheck and a Quick List "Transfer" to transfer 10% of it over to the second account.

If You Belong To a Salary Reduction Plan

With a 401K or 403B Salary Reduction retirement plan, you may be paid $1,000 a week, but have $70 of it shielded from income tax by being siphoned off to a retirement plan.

1. In Money Accounts on the MONEY menu, create a new account (called, say, RETIREMENT FUND). Specify IRA/Keogh/401K as the account Type.

2. Create two Quick Receive transactions for your paycheck.

   The first will receive your salary, less the salary reduction amount, into your checking account (or wherever you deposit your paycheck). Set it up as a normal paycheck, but the amount you allocate to your SALARY budget bucket will be your gross pay ($1,000, in this example) minus the salary reduction ($70, so you would allocate $930 to SALARY). All your normal deductions go in this transaction.

   The second Quick transaction will receive the salary reduction into the RETIREMENT Money Account you just created. Press F8 on the Quick List to switch to that account first. Create a Quick Receive transaction for $70 and allocate it to an income category you call 401K INCOME and that you tag "Not a Tax Category" (because no tax is due on this $70). You have thus allocated $1,000 to two income categories.

That takes care of allocating your paycheck. And as your retirement funds pile up, Net Worth will automatically know about it.

(The only problem with this—nonproblem, really—is that Social Security tax is based on your gross salary including the otherwise nontaxable Salary Reduction portion. So if you should visit our Self-Employment Tax screen in TAX, it is likely to burp when you call up your salary numbers from MONEY. You may get a message saying that your Salary numbers don't seem to jibe with the FICA that's been withheld—that too much has been withheld from your $930-a-week. Ah, but what TAX doesn't know is that it was actually being withheld, properly, on the full $1,000-a-week. This burp is harmless. Ignore it.)

If you want to keep track of its investments

If you have a "self-directed" retirement plan (one where you can invest the money in stocks, bonds, mutual funds—however you like), you may want to manage those investments in PORTFOLIO.

In that case, set up an IRA/Keogh/401K-type portfolio in PORTFO-LIO, with a name like "My 401K at Work."

There's no automatic way to deposit money straight from your paycheck in MONEY to a portfolio in PORTFOLIO, so, instead, just do this:

When you enter your paycheck every couple of weeks, enter it in a MONEY IRA/Keogh/401K account as described above. But when you get a new quarterly statement showing your 401K status, "Spend" everything in that MONEY account (payee: "401K Investment," budget category: "Transfer," tax category: none), and manually add that amount to the cash balance of the Portfolio account. Then use it to buy whatever your statement shows you actually did buy that quarter.

Say your plan allows you to split your investment among four separate vehicles, as many do—typically, a government bond fund, an insurance-company fixed income fund, a stock market mutual fund, and stock in your own company. Well, each time you got a statement showing what had been done with your 401K contributions, you could visit PORTFO-LIO and buy the appropriate number of "shares" (if it's company stock or a mutual fund) or "units" (if it's something else) in each one.

Say you were putting this year's contributions into the insurance-company fixed income fund. (Why? But that's another story.) If the latest statement showed that you'd acquired $358 more of it, you could say you bought another 358 units at a price of $1 each in an "other"-type asset, or a "bond" (what a GIC most resembles), called "Aetna-GIC" ("guaranteed income certificate") with the symbol: AETNA-GIC. Periodically, when your statement arrived showing the interest that portion of your 401K had earned, you could go to PORTFOLIO's Record Income screen and enter this interest payment.

But please note that there are other perfectly fine ways of accounting for your 401K, depending on the level of detail you want. Don't feel you have to do it precisely as outlined above.

PART II: NOW THAT YOU'RE ALL SET UP ...

Now that you're all set up, you can start using the program for real.

GETTING STARTED IN MID-YEAR

All well and good, you may be thinking (at least that's what I hope you're thinking), but what about all the transactions that have already occurred this year?

You have three choices:

1. Ignore them. If it's October or November or December, that makes a lot of sense. Begin using Managing Your Money to write your checks, but wait until next year—which is only weeks away—to expect it to organize everything.

2. Go back through all your expenditures for the year and enter them (or perhaps just the deductible ones). If it's January or February or March, that's no big deal. Even if it's later in the year, you may find this kind of fun—and a good way to learn the program.

> HINT: Reallocate. If you change the actual amounts for a category and later want to put things back the way they were, go to the Budgets and Actuals screen (press the Action Key from the Budget Categories screen) and press Alt-A. We'll wipe out any amounts you've entered by hand, find all the transactions allocated to this category, and recompute your actuals for each month. If you have a lot of data, it can take a while because we have to look at each transaction.

3. Don't go back and record your transactions for the months gone by, but, on the Budget Categories screen, press the Action Key to visit each of your categories in turn (use Page Scroll—PgDn—to page through them fast) and enter estimates of your expenditures so far this year in the Actuals column. Start using the program for real from now on. (To unlock the Actuals column, which we safeguard from accidental changes, press F8 first.) If you're switching to Managing Your Money from another program, just use the old program to print a budget report and then enter the budget numbers here.

If you choose door #2, and thus may be undertaking to spend the rest of the afternoon entering hundreds of transactions, remember: save your work every so often—return to the Menu Bar and press Ctrl-S—lest a power failure or some other mishap wipe it out. It's no different from saving your work on a word processor or anything else: it's crazy not to.

STEP #8: SPENDING OR RECEIVING MONEY

1. Select Spend or Receive from the MONEY menu or press Alt-S or Alt-R from your Check Register.

2. Look at the top of the "check" or "receipt"screen. Is this the account you want to work with? We always take you into the account you were working with last. If it's not the one you want, just press F8 to select it. (F8 appears only if you have more than one account.)

    Note that in addition to its name, we display the account's balance, so you know where you stand.

3. In entering a transaction, it's easiest to TAB from field to field:

Number: If you assign a check number, we'll remember it—and assign them incrementally from then on. You can always type over the check number we supply, but ordinarily you won't have to.

   Fine points:

   • If you do type over our guess, we'll start incrementing from that number. But we'll only make it the new "Last Check Number" for this account if it's higher. In other words, if our little counter was up to 1310 and you typed 1343 as the check number, we'd reset the Last Check Number accordingly.

   • But if you made it 1187—to enter a check from your spouse's book of checks, which are lower numbered than yours, we'd only reset the counter temporarily, while you were on that screen. That way, you could keep entering his or her transactions in sequence but then, when next you returned here, be back at 1311. To get back to 1311 even without leaving the screen, just press "F7-Revert to Last Check Number." You'll only see this option when you have, in fact, typed a lower number than the one we're up to. It's our Back-to-the-Future feature.

- To reset an account's Last Check Number—typically, because you accidentally typed in a check number that was too high, and the Last Check Number counter believed you—you need to visit the housekeeping screen for that account. Just select Money Accounts and then point to the one in question and press F2. Now you can just type over the Last Check Number we show. That resets the counter. Press the Action Key to record the change and get back to work.

- To get rid of numbers altogether—in your credit card accounts, for example, which don't use them, just blank out the Last Check Number altogether. From then on, we'll leave that field blank, too. (Monkey see, monkey do.) If you should later enter a check number by mistake, and get us counting again, just return to this housekeeping screen and blank it out again.

- There are no "check numbers" on the Receive screen; only on Spend.

- CheckFree users: When you choose this payment method, the check number field vanishes. You cannot assign CheckFree check numbers.

Date: We supply today's. Type over it, if you like, and we'll keep using the new one you enter until you leave the screen.

Fine points:

- If you'd rather we reverted to today's date after every transaction, tell us in Money Options (select FILE's Optional Features). This might be best if you tend to enter "historical" transactions singly, rather than a batch of them at a time, and don't want to have to bother changing the date back when you do.

HINT: To go back or ahead just a few days, it's fastest to use our Alt- and Alt+ shortcuts. With your cursor in the Date field, just hold down the Alt key and press a few minus or plus signs. (You don't actually have to press the Shift key to tell us you mean "plus" in this instance. We'll know.) Alt+ and Alt- also work on the check-number field—or any other numeric field in Managing Your Money.

- We normally start the cursor on the Payee or Payor field, on the assumption that you'll only occasionally need to arrow up to the Date or Check Number fields to change what we've entered for you. But if you'd like us to start the cursor on the Date field each time instead, perhaps because you are entering a batch of historical data, just tell us in Money Options (select FILE's Optional Features).

- If you are a CheckFree user and specify "CFree" as the payment method, we automatically advance today's date four business days.

  Payee/Payor: Whomever you're paying or, on the Receive Money screen, whoever is paying you.

  Amount: On the Spend screen, enter as little as possible. On Receive, you can go as high as $99 million and change, and we hope you do.

  Category: When you TAB into the Category field, "Not Allocated" will be showing. If you like, TAB right on to the next field—you don't have to allocate income and expenses if you don't want to. But especially for transactions that are taxable or tax-deductible, it's kind of crazy not to. Just use the Up and Down Arrows to scroll through your list of categories or—much faster—Speed Scroll to the one you want. Type G and you're at Groceries (or Gasoline, anyway). Ordinarily, the first letter or two are enough.

NOTE: Once you begin scrolling through categories, to the right of the Category window you'll see either "Income" or "Expense", which is particularly useful if you've got two categories called "Beach House," say—one for the expenses of running it, and another for the income from renting it. If you type "Bea" on a Spend transaction, we'll assume you mean the Expense category and skip the Income one.

If you'd prefer to see your whole list and not just our little one-line window ... or if you want to split the allocation over more than a single category (up to a maximum of 15) ... or if you want to set up some new category you hadn't thought to include ... just press F9 (and then F5 if you need to set up a new category).

By: TAB into this field and, if we're not displaying the proper payment (or receipt) method, just press the first letter of the one you want (or press Spacebar to go into the choice box, scroll down to it and press Enter.) We'll normally guess the most likely method for each type of account—"Check" for a checking account and "Direct" for a credit card account, for example.

Check is the obvious method for a checking account.

CheckFree will be a payment option only if you've activated CheckFree, this is your CheckFree account, and you're entering a Spend transaction. If you select it, we'll add this transaction to the list of items to be transmitted to CheckFree. Because CheckFree transactions require at least four business days to complete, you will have to use a future date. To spare you that trouble, we automatically advance the date four business days (unless you've advanced it even further).

Payable or **Receivable** will be an option only if you've chosen it on the Money Options screen (under Optional Features on the FILE menu). If you select it, the transaction won't show up on your Check Register. Rather, it will be shunted off to your Accounts Payable or Accounts Receivable list, waiting for the day you choose to execute it from there.

Note that if you select Payable, a new field pops up for the "Due Date," which we then display on the Payables screen to help you decide when to make the payment.

Direct would be for items that get taken out of or deposited into your account through some sort of special debit or credit—if, for example, your utility bill is automatically debited to your bank account or your Social Security check is automatically credited through the magic of EFT (Electronic Funds Transfer). This is also the method to use for credit card transactions.

Phone is for those of you whose banks offer bill-payment-by-phone. When you record those payments in Managing Your Money, you can tag them as "phone" payments.

ATM is for transactions done through an Automatic Teller Machine.

Address: I ordinarily bother with these only when I'm going to be printing a check and no reply envelope has been included. (The address will show through my window envelopes.) But you might also want to use it for recording credit card receipts, where one of the things the IRS will want to know is where you had this purported business lunch.

Memo: This could be as simple as your account number or as complex as a detailed accounting of how you arrived at the amount of this payment. Only the first line will print on your check, but pressing F2 opens up room for 31,999 more lines of text, should you have a lot to say. Of course, you can leave Memo blank.

4.   When you're ready, press the Action Key to record the transaction. (Remember to return to the Menu Bar and Ctrl-S from time to time to save your work).

Use Memo Field Codes for "Subcategories"

Don't miss the power of memo search in the Report Generator (on the MONEY menu). It lets you include in your report only transactions that have a certain "character string" (any combination of letters or numbers) someplace in the memo. Thus, if you ever wanted to do reports of money you'd spent on Billy only, and you put a "BBB" someplace in the memo in all those expenditures, the Report Generator could isolate and total only those.

(I chose BBB because it's not likely to pick up other non-Billy items you don't mean to include, like the one with the memo about "Bubble bath for Bobby's birthday." You can use any codes you like, including things like $$ and *Bill* or anything else. You could simply search on "Billy," but that wouldn't pick up any with only the word "Bill." And you could simply search on "Bill," but that would pick up the memo on your purchase at B. Dalton of that Paul Erdman novel, The Billion Dollar Sure Thing.)

For those of us who like to tag our expenditures two or more ways—by rental property, say, and by type of expense and by who actually spent the money (you or your spouse)—memo search is thus a very handy way of having your cake and eating it, too. The budget allocation for this expenditure might be, simply, "Rental Property Expense." But on the memo line, you could have things like "623-Br" to flag it as an expense on the property at 623 Broadway; "Plumb" to let you extract all your plumbing expenditures for a report someday; and "::" to show it was money you spent yourself, versus ";;" for money your spouse spent or ",," for money your daughter spent.

Don't worry about any of this now! I just wanted to alert you to the possibilities.

STEP #9: PAYING DOWN YOUR LOANS

Remember the linked Quick List or Alert List transaction you created as you established each new loan? (If you didn't do it for some of your loans, select Loan Records from the MONEY menu and create them now. Don't worry: we won't let you make duplicates.) You'll find them all on either your Quick List or Alert List, patiently waiting to be used to record payments. (You can tell they were created on the Loan screen by looking at their "Type" in the middle column of the Quick List transactions screen. Where most Quick List transactions are of the "V" type, for Variable, loan transactions are "M," "S," or "I"—Mortgage, Special or Interest-Only.)

To record a loan payment, you should always use its linked transaction. That way, we can keep those loans—and your budget and your tax estimation and your net worth—all up to date automatically.

If it was created as a Quick List transaction, just place an X beside it and change the amount, if it's changed (as it might with a Special Loan where the amount varies from time to time, or with a mortgage loan on which you're prepaying principal). When you're through with the Quick List, press the Action Key.

On Special Loan payments we'll then ask you how much of the payment was for interest and how much for principal. On Interest-Only Loan payments, we'll ask you to confirm that the full amount of the payment was indeed interest. On Mortgage-type loans, we won't have to ask anything.

We already know the principal-interest-escrow breakdown, and we assume any extra you've decided to pay this month is a principal prepayment and adjust all your figures accordingly. It's that simple.

Even so, there are some out-of-the-ordinary events to consider:

Late Penalties

Well, I hope this one is out-of-the-ordinary. From time to time, you may be hit with an extra interest charge for paying your mortgage late. To keep everything in balance, don't simply change the amount of your Quick List transaction from $708.14 (the regular amount), say, to $723.14 (the amount you owe with the late penalty), because we assume any extra payment is a principal prepayment. The check we print will be for the right amount, but your loan amortization will ever after be slightly off.

Instead, record your normal mortgage payment (and print the check if you use Managing Your Money to print checks), and then record a separate spend transaction, allocated to Mortgage Interest (or "Mortgage Penalty Interest" if you're a super purist), for the amount of the extra interest (and print a second check).

Or, if you'd rather not print two checks, first record your normal mortgage payment and then, on the Check Register, point to this new one and press F2 to edit it. Increase the amount to include the late penalty and allocate that extra amount to your Interest allocation. Now print the check.

Late penalties often represent an outrageous rate of interest, even if relatively few dollars. That, coupled with the inconvenience of having to record two transactions instead of one, is yet another reason to try to pay on time!

Principal Prepayments

Okay. You're sending in an extra one-time $5,000 principal payment along with your 67th regular monthly payment. How do you record that in Managing Your Money? Simple:

- *Quick List transactions.* Go to your Quick List and enter the actual amount you're paying—$5,873.13, say, instead of the normal $873.13. When you go back to check the status of that loan after you've executed the transaction, you'll find that we've credited you with the extra principal and recalculated the number of payments remaining. (Paying off principal hastens the pay-off date of the loan.) What's more, we automatically adjust your budgeted principal and interest figures to match the new status of your loan.

• *Alert List transactions.* If you linked this mortgage to an Alert List transaction, select Loan Records from the MONEY menu, point to the loan and press "F8—Prepay Principal on an Alert Loan Transaction." Instead of adding the additional principal to a regular Alert List loan payment, we create a separate transaction. This extra payment goes straight to your Check Register, without passing go and without stopping at the Alert List, and uses the next check number in sequence. You can then write out or print the check. (If the loan payment is being made via CheckFree, this extra payment will still be a regular check.)

HINT: Fancy Loan Amortization. For some fancy footwork on mortgage loans that involve multiple principal prepayments (one-time or periodic) and a series of interest rate changes, select Loan Amortization from the ANALYZE menu. We'll take all these mind-bogglingly complex factors into account and print a customized amortization schedule. We can also show you the difference between a monthly and biweekly mortgage (where you in effect make 13 months— payments a year). We won't carry the results to Loan Records (we'll account for the changes when you really do prepay principal or have a rate adjustment). But ANALYZE's Loan Amortization is a great planning tool.

Interest Rate Changes

When the rate changes on an adjustable rate mortgage loan, select Loan Records from the MONEY menu. Highlight that loan with the cursor, press F2, fill in the new rate, press F6 to recalculate your new monthly payment and the Action Key to save the modified loan. We'll adjust all your budgeted principal and interest amounts to reflect the change. (If the new monthly payment is off slightly, come back and adjust the interest rate a hair until, through trial and error, you get the payment you want. Your bank may be rounding things off slightly differently from the norm. What it calls a 10.5% loan might to us seem like a 10.502% loan.)

Escrow Amount or Loan-Name Changes

If taxes or insurance rates go up and the monthly escrow amounts your bank requires change, delete the linked Alert or Quick transaction (with F3) from the Alert List or the Quick List. Then return to Loan Records, point to this loan, and press F6 or F7 to create a new Alert or Quick transaction. Enter the new escrow amounts as you create the new transaction.

You can change the name of the loan itself just by typing over it on the Loan Records screen. But that won't change the payee name on the linked transaction. To do that, press F2 and F6 as just described. In these days of daily bank mergers, this could come in handy sooner than you think. (If it's set up for payment by CheckFree, you'll find that you can't change the name when you press F6. Instead, delete it on the Alert List or the Quick List and then return to Loan Records to create a new one.)

To Get Back On Track If You've Loused Up Your Loan

If you somehow mis-enter or otherwise louse up the recordkeeping on a mortgage loan, you can delete it (see page 342: "Deleting a Mortgage"). But how do you reenter it—properly this time—in midstream? After all, since you first took it out several years ago as a simple 30-year $75,000 loan, the interest rate has switched four times and you've made three different small partial prepayments.

Rather than try to reconstruct all that, do this. Simply enter the loan for what it is now: a 243-payment (if that's how many the bank tells you you have left) $68,329.88 loan (if that's the outstanding principal as of the last payment) at 10.625% (if that's the current interest rate). Unless your bank is strange, entering the loan this way, odd as it may feel in a world of round numbers, should get you back on track.

> NOTE: We Can't "Un-update" Loans. One of the things we can't do automatically is "un-update" your loan if you should record a Quick List loan payment and later, for some reason, delete it. So if you find you've somehow recorded one payment too many (that is, one more than you've actually made), adjust things by making your next loan payment without using its Quick List transaction (and thus without updating it), to get back in step.

Allocating Loan Proceeds

If you borrow $10,000 in cash from the bank, you record two things: the receipt of $10,000 in your checking account, or wherever you park the money (select Receive Money from the MONEY menu to record the receipt of funds); and the establishment of a new $10,000 loan (select Loan Records from the MONEY menu to record the new loan).

But to what budget category do you allocate the $10,000 proceeds? And what if it's not quite so simple, as in the following example?

From Concord, CA:

"I will be buying a new car soon. Should I consider the loan proceeds as 'income' and the loan payments, 'expense'? And what about the money I'm taking out of my savings account for the down payment? How will all this affect my net worth?"

Let's start with the easy part—your net worth. Enter the car as an asset in NET WORTH (see Chapter 8) and adjust its value each year as it depreciates (unless it's one of those 1923 Stutz Bearcats that appreciate). Enter the loan in MONEY. Its outstanding balance will automatically show up as a liability in NET WORTH and decrease with each monthly payment.

Your net worth will increase by the market value of the car—but decrease by the amount of the loan and the down payment you withdrew from your savings account. Net result: a small decrease, I'm afraid, reflecting the fact that a car generally loses value the minute you take it off the lot.

Now, what about the loan proceeds?

Scenario A: You never even see the money. It goes straight from GMAC (say) to your dealer. All you see is the payment book.

In this case, there's no need to receive any cash. Just set up the loan in Loan Records, along with a Quick List transaction. When you're asked how you want to allocate the principal and interest on the loan, allocate principal to an expense budget category you might call "Auto Equity" (which is also the budget category into which you'd dump the money you withdrew from your savings account for the down payment) and interest to one called "Personal Interest."

Scenario B: You actually get a check for $10,000 which you deposit in your bank account, then write a $10,000 check to your Jaguar dealer.

Allocate the check you receive to "Loan Proceeds" (Not a Tax Category). Allocate the check you write, if it's really a strict auto loan, to the same place: "Loan Proceeds." When you allocate an expenditure to an income bucket, we automatically make it negative—so the money you spend on the car will lower your $10,000 in loan proceeds back down to $0. (If you don't want a new category for just a couple of transactions, use your Miscellaneous category. Or don't allocate these Receive and Spend transactions to categories at all.)

Then set up the loan as described in Scenario A.

(There are other perfectly acceptable ways to record loan proceeds. If you've been doing this differently and you're happy, we're happy, too.)

STEP #10: PRINTING CHECKS

You certainly don't have to, but it makes a lot of sense to print most of your checks with Managing Your Money. Otherwise, you're entering information twice: once, when you write it by hand on the check and then again when you note it on the check stub and/or record it in Managing Your Money. What's more, why should you write out the amount of the check in English and the date? We can do it for you! Why even write out the name of the payee or address an envelope? As described in Step #8 (page 116), if it's someone you've ever paid before in this account, or whom you've added to your Quick List, Payee Search or the Quick List will do all that for you—and print your account number, or anything else you've included, on the memo line.

1. Select Print Checks from the MONEY menu (or Alt-P from the Check Register).

2. Press F8 to select the checking account you want to work with, if we've guessed wrong.

3. If this is the first time you've printed checks with Managing Your Money, press F9 to let us know what kind of checks you'll be using. Just point to the proper style and press the Action Key.

    It may require a little trial and error to get set up properly the first time, or when you change to a new check style or printer (which is why we have F6 on the Print Checks screen to print "line-up" checks). But it shouldn't be hard to get things in synch, even if you're using checks other than the ones we list. Press F6 on the Select Check Format screen to make adjustments or **customize a format** that works for you. HELP behind that screen explains how.

4.   Press F7 and look over the **Check Printing Defaults**. Change any you like and press the Action Key. You shouldn't have to visit this screen often, either.

Unless you're tight for space on your hard disk, you almost surely want to answer NO to the questions about deleting the address and memo after printing. You almost surely DO want to use pre-numbered checks. If you're hand-feeding one check at a time into the printer, you'll want to PAUSE between each one. And if you're using single-sheet laser checks, you'll want to say YES to "formfeed after each check." If you're using continuous-form checks, you'll want to say NO.

5.   Back on the Print Checks screen, tell us whether to print Today's Date on the checks, or to stick with whatever dates you may have used when you entered the transactions. And be sure to tell us the Starting Check Number—the number of the first blank check in your printer. Finally, tell us which checks you want us to print if we haven't guessed right (you can scroll through your transactions on the screen).

Until you get comfortable with printing checks, you may want to print just one check first. For example, if you're printing checks 3347 thru 3355, you might initially instruct us to print only the first check—"3347 thru 3347"—to make sure it lines up properly. Then print the rest.

6.   Print a line-up check if you like (F6). Then print your checks (Action Key).

TIP: Use Blank Paper for line-up checks. Don't waste blank checks on line-ups. They're expensive! Where possible, use blank paper and hold it up to the light with the blank check behind it.

For tips on making sure the check numbers in the program match the ones on your checks, see Step No. 6 on page 361. I'll walk you through the process of printing checks, and tell you how to order checks, next under "How I Pay My Bills."

How I Pay My Bills

It's not practical to print a single check (unless you have a sheet-fed printer or an old printer you use only for checks), so I just write those out of my wallet and make a note to record them next time I'm in the program. (With "duplicate" checks—the kind that make their own copies without carbon paper—you don't even have to record your checks in a check register.)

What is a real time-saver is to use the program to pay lots of bills all at once. I keep a manila folder next to my computer. When bills come, that's where I toss them. Likewise, receipts, brokerage confirmation slips and business cards I want to record. Every couple of weeks, I power up and clean out the folder.

Anytime I write a check (or record one I've had to write out of my wallet), I always set it up as a Quick List transaction. I figure that if I'm paying whomever it is once, I'll probably have to pay him again someday. By now, I have 433 payees on my Quick List and only occasionally have to take half a minute to add a new one. So here's what I do:

1.   I put my bills—and receipts for bills I've already paid by hand—in a stack, face up, like a deck of cards.

2.   I speed scroll to the Quick List transaction for each one in turn, typing an "A" in the "Mark" column, to the right of the first, a "B" to the right of the second, and so on. In most cases, I type in a new amount. (With a few I needn't do even that—it's the same as last time.)

> HINT: Shortcut: Mark from A to Z. If you often pay more than 26 bills, note that there are more than 26 "letters" in a computer's alphabet—see page 336 for a computer's conception of alphabetical order.

Marking them "A, B, C" instead of all X's means they will print out in the same haphazard order I happen to be doing my bills, so the first check will go with the first bill, the second with the second, and so on. Marking them all with X's is fine, too—the checks will print out in alphabetical order. That's nice and tidy, but it means hunting around for which bill goes with which check. Or sorting the bills in alphabetical order.

For those checks I've written out of my wallet, I type the actual dates in the "Last Use" column and enter the actual check numbers at far right.

For those bills I pay by CheckFree, I don't have to do anything special, because the "By" column of the Quick List already remembers this preference (though I can always change it).

3.   I press the Action Key to record my work. At this point the transactions are recorded, as far as Managing Your Money is concerned (provided that I save my work).

4.   I frequently return to the Menu Bar and press Ctrl-S to save what I've done. This isn't required, but prudence is my middle name. (Previn is my middle name, actually, but that's another story.)

5.   I select Print Checks from the MONEY menu.

6.   I tell Managing Your Money which checks I want to print, if it hasn't guessed right, and the actual starting number of the first one in my printer. (I've gotten a lot better at getting them into their little sprockets unmangled.) This is important, because it allows us to match our check numbers to the real ones on your checks. If we've tentatively numbered your checks 400-415, but 400 and 401 go into the trash, we will actually wind up printing those payments on checks numbered 402-417. When you tell Managing Your Money that 402 is the first actual check in your printer, it knows to renumber 400 as 402, 401 as 403, and so on. That way, your check numbers in Managing Your Money will match your check numbers in the real world.

(Should you ever gum this up, you can simply press F2 on the Check Register to visit each of the transactions in turn and renumber them yourself. With Page Scroll, going from one to the next takes just a minute.)

I leave "Use Today's Date?" set to Yes, because the day I print them is a perfectly reasonable date to use. I may have entered the payment in Managing Your Money a week ago and been lazy about printing a batch of checks. But this feature redates the batch to to-day. If you prefer, answer No, and we'll use whatever date, past, present or post, you entered for each check.

7. Under Check Printing Options (F7), I answer "No!" to the questions about deleting memos and addresses after the printing is done. It can be quite helpful to have the memo available for inspection on the screen. And as for addresses, if you should louse up a print-run and have to do it over again, you'll find to your annoyance that, if you've answered "Yes" to deleting them, they're gone. Out print your checks the second time, but with no addresses to show through your window envelopes. So I choose "No."

    If I backed up my budget.dbs file onto 360K floppies, instead of 1.44MB's, and hence risked running out of room one day if I took up too much space for thousands of addresses, I'd choose "Yes" and be more careful with my print runs.

    I answer "Yes" to quality print mode, "Yes" to pre-numbered checks (almost everyone has these), and "Don't Pause" when printing. (See below for notes on sheet-fed printing.)

8. I turn on the printer.

9. I don't bother with line-up checks anymore, because by now I've learned how far in to feed the first check. But if I wanted, I could press F6 to print one. If the printing started too high or low on the check, I'd know to feed the checks in a little farther or less far. (And I'd enter the new "starting check number," now that I were ready to start printing for real.) It helps to make a mark on the printer to line up the check the next time.

10. I press the Action Key and watch my 23 checks come chugging out while I put stamps on the reply envelopes (and on window envelopes for those bills that come without reply envelopes).

11. When the printing's done, I rip them out of the printer—but not the memo half of the last check (I use business-style checks). I could rip out that little tail-end, too, if it were important (it never is), but I leave it as a "leader" to help me feed the checks in next time.

12. I rip the little sprocket runners off the checks all at once, sign them (checking to be sure an extra zero hasn't crept in somewhere), rip

them apart and stuff them in the reply envelopes. I don't bother to rip off the bottom half of the check; I include it just as most businesses do.

Although everything is neatly synchronized, I do try to keep my eyes open, having once dropped an envelope off the edge of my desk and found that I had thus placed the check for American Express in the Book of the Month Club envelope, Book of the Month in Care, Care in Visa—and so on. This led to a lot of swearing, envelope reopening and Scotch taping, which I have since managed to avoid.

13.   I drop them in the mail.

Note that printing checks is little different from printing any other report, except that the paper you use is more valuable. **Printing reports— or checks—in no way affects the data on which they're based.** Whether you print some of them, none of them or nine of them twice, your underlying numbers and records will remain unchanged. (The exception: If we renumber checks for you, as explained above.)

Furthermore, if you did get everything tangled (and it's hard to imagine how you could), you could just choose Revert from the FILE menu and start all over again. I've never had to do this.

Finally, trust me when I tell you there's a learning curve here. What will at first require some time and concentration should quickly become an efficient process. Your first try won't be faster than paying bills by hand. But soon you will be a pro and it should all be quite slick. And having done it this way, all the data's now available for rapid reconciliation, analysis, report generation throughout the year, and tax preparation early next year.

Writing Checks By Hand

If you prefer to pay your bills by hand, you can still save lots of time by recording the transactions on the Quick List transactions screen as you go. Just use Speed Scroll to jump to each payee as you write out the check, or use Payee Search (F6) on the Spend Money screen. It goes very fast and saves your writing out a check stub for your checkbook.

Ordering The Checks You'll Need

MECA Forms, a division of MECA Software, can provide high-quality computer checks, forms and supplies at competitive prices. The checks are custom-designed for Managing Your Money and are guaranteed compatible. You can get continuous-feed checks for a dot-matrix printer or sheet-fed checks for a laser or other page printer.

You don't need permission from your bank. You don't need to send a sample of the checks you're currently using. **All you need do is call MECA Forms toll free at 1-800-992-2951.** Or use the MECA Forms brochure that was included with Managing Your Money. MECA Forms promises to process your order immediately and ship standard items within four to six days.

You can order either personal-size checks or business-size. Managing Your Money works fine with either, but I recommend business-size. You can also order window envelopes. They're a big time-saver: just print and sign your checks, put them into the envelope so the mailing and return addresses show through, and mail.

MECA Forms also offers a complete line of personal and business forms and supplies, such as mailing labels, invoices and Rolodex cards designed to work with Managing Your Money.

To offer you a choice, MECA also endorses Deluxe Corporation as a supplier of compatible Managing Your Money checks. Their service is also excellent. To order from Deluxe, call 1-800-328-0304 and ask for Managing Your Money-compatible checks.

> WARNING: Use higher numbered checks. To avoid confusion when ordering, please specify a beginning check number well above the check numbers of the personal checks you currently use. That way, your computer generated checks will all be big and professional; those you write out of your wallet will be the familiar smaller ones you already have; and you'll be able to tell at a glance from the check number which is which.

> HINT: Printing just a few checks at a time. A great advantage of laser sheet checks is the ease with which you can print them without having to switch back and forth between regular paper and your checks on many printers. With laser, ink jet and most newer dot-matrix printers, you can just feed them in manually while leaving your regular paper loaded.

Printing Checks with a Laser or Other Sheet-fed Printer

If you have a sheet-fed printer, like a Hewlett Packard LaserJet or DeskJet, check-printing is terrific. Just remember to answer "Yes" on the check-printing screen where we ask if you want us to send a formfeed after each check. (A "formfeed" tells your printer there's nothing more to be printed on this page, so go ahead: feed it through and get ready for the next page.)

MECA Forms offers sheet-fed checks. But if you have some continuous-form checks you want to use up.first, just rip off their sprocket strips and separate them before printing instead of afterward. Because of the perforations, you may have to feed them into the printer manually, to avoid jams, rather than stacking them in the paper tray. When you run out of this batch of checks, buy the sprocketless laser kind that come already separated (MECA Forms Style 4922xx business-size or 4923xx personal-size). They work fine in the paper tray.

Printing Checks the First Time

Once you decide which type of checks you want to use—personal or business, with a stub (voucher) or without—you'll need to tell Managing Your Money, so we know where to print everything. From the Print Checks screen, press F9 to select a check format. Highlight your check style on the screen and press the Action Key. You're ready to print your first check!

> NOTE: Edit Check Layout. If we're printing the name of your payee in the wrong place even after you've loaded the correct check style, press F9 on the print-checks screen, point to the type of check you use, press F6 and move things around. Read help for instructions. If you're using personal-size checks, see below.

Printing Checks in "Quality" Mode

We give you the option, when you go to print checks, to print them in "quality" mode. If you choose "Yes" but we don't seem to be rising to the occasion, select Program Setup from the FILE menu and then Printer. Is the right printer selected? Then press F7. Are there strings of numbers entered on the lines for "Near letter quality on" and "off?" If so, are they the right strings? (Check your printer manual.) We will accept on these lines any setup strings you think will make your checks and reports look good, including those your printer requires for bold-faced or emphasized printing.

> NOTE: Laser Printers. You can choose "No," because you're already in quality mode. Or choose "Yes"—it shouldn't make any difference, unless you've chosen to use Quality mode to mean something else.

My checks print funny.

"The numerical amount of my check looks like it's going to fall off the right side of the check. If it were for a larger amount—$10,000.00, say, instead of $9.31—it really would fall off the edge!"

No, it wouldn't. If you've changed the default setting to "right-justified," the larger your number, the further to the left we begin printing it. Just press F9 from the Print Checks screen, point to your check style and press F6. You can change it to "left-justify" this amount instead. Try it that way if you prefer.

I can't get the date to line up

That may be because the date is anywhere from 8 to 10 characters long. A format that looks good when it's 10 characters (12/25/1991) may look less good when it's 8 characters (1/1/1992). But feel free to press F9 and F6 from the Print Checks screen and experiment with the placement of the date.

The printing starts further and further down on each successive check I print.

This can happen if you've instructed us to load the wrong printer setup—e.g., Epson LX instead of Epson LQ.

But a few people have found themselves accidentally adding a phantom line to their checks. We'd then print 18-line checks instead of 17-line checks, and the printing would start one line too low on the second check, two lines too low on the third, and so on.

If this ever happens to you after you've changed the check format (F9, F6 from the Check Printing screen), here's what you're doing wrong. You've got checks that are 60-columns wide and you've told us to place the memo field, say, starting on column 12 (12 spaces from the left margin). That would be fine, only the memo field is 50 spaces wide—whether you use its full width or not. You have it running from column 12 to column 62. Even though that 62nd column is blank most of the time, your printer jumps to the next line to "print" it, anyway. You don't notice it, because the extra character is a blank. The solution is simply to move the memo line, or any other information field you have running past column 60, a few columns to the left, so it won't overflow to the next line.

One user writes: "With your new default, the numerical amount falls off the edge of my personal-size checks. Using your routine to modify the format, I moved the numerical amount 10 spaces to the left but received an error message saying it conflicted with the amount in words. Does this mean the amount in words could overlap the numerical amount?" Yes. "Then I moved both to the left three spaces and it worked."

A little trial and error, in a program such as ours, works wonders. It's the price of flexibility.

STEP #11: A STEP TOO MANY

If you're still with me, you've covered a tremendous amount of ground. And I should think you've had it up to here with steps. Fair enough. No more steps for now. But there are a few more topics you'll probably want to read about in this chapter:

RECONCILING A MONEY ACCOUNT

One of the more tedious money-management chores—so much so that many of us don't do it—is checkbook reconciliation. Yet only if you reconcile your checkbook will you know for sure your records (and the bank's) are accurate. Managing Your Money can make it fast, easy and almost fun (even if, the first time, it requires a little tinkering).

Summary: Enter information from your bank statement at the bottom of the Reconcile Account screen, have us sort your transactions by check number and then mark on the screen those transactions that have cleared the bank. Everything will then reconcile (unless you need to enter something you forgot, or correct something you misentered, or call the bank to point out an error it made). When it does, press the Action Key to complete the process. That's it.

The Full Detail Method (optional!): Select Reconcile Account from the MONEY menu (or press Alt-E from the Check Register). Look at the top of the screen to make sure you're in the right account (you can change it with F8). The "Last Reconciled Balance" should match the beginning balance on your new bank statement. If necessary, go to Money Accounts from the MONEY menu and set it right (highlight the account and press F2 to modify it, then press the Action Key to save your changes). Then come back to the Reconcile Account screen.

At the bottom of the Reconcile screen, enter the ending balance from your current bank statement, and any interest, finance charges and services charges that appear on the statement.

Now go back up to the top of the transaction list (Ctrl-PgUp) and mark the transactions that appear on the bank statement. To make this easy, we display only transactions you haven't reconciled previously; and you can use F9 to sort them as your bank does. (Re-sort at any time if you're hunting for a specific transaction.)

Start at the top of the list, placing an "x" next to each transaction that appears on your bank statement. If you find a transaction that's not in Managing Your Money, press F5 to add it (or Alt-S, Alt-R or Alt-T). If you find an error in a transaction, press F2 to fix it. To check or change only its budget allocation, press Alt-F9.

We track the total of the In and Out transactions as you mark them, and tell you how far out of balance you are. It's fun to watch the numbers change until—yes—you're in balance! (The numbers will be correct only if you've filled in the amount fields at the bottom of the screen first.) Next to "Reconcile on Statement Date," put the statement date.

When you've marked all the transactions on your bank statement, your account should be in balance—and we'll tell you so. When you give the word, we'll put a check mark next to all the cleared transactions on your Check Register. If your balance still doesn't match the bank's, press F1 for Help finding the problem.

HANDLING YOUR CREDIT CARD ACCOUNTS

There are a variety of ways to handle credit card transactions with Managing Your Money. You should choose the one that fits your needs.

The Full Detail Method

You can set up a separate charge account in MONEY for each of your cards. (Select Money Accounts from the MONEY menu, press F5 to add a new one, and type cha in the Type field so we know it's a charge account. Unless the bank owes you money, be sure to enter a negative balance.) Then, as you charge things, bring your receipts home and record the charges in their respective accounts (Visa, MasterCard, etc.) and allocate them to budget categories. You'll have a running balance for each account. When the statement comes each month, reconcile it as you would your checking account.

When you write a check to pay off or pay down one of your cards, you are spending money in your checking account and receiving it into your charge account. You can do it:

* in two steps (record the check in your checking account, then go to your charge account to "receive" the same amount);

* or in one step (select Transfer Money from the MONEY menu or Alt-T from the Check Register);

* or in one even faster step (set up a Quick List Transfer transaction so that, thereafter, you can just mark it off the list as you're running through your other payments).

But however you do it, don't try to allocate the payment to budget categories, because you'd be double counting. Under this "full detail method," you recorded your various charges throughout the month and allocated them to expense categories. Now, you're just transferring some cash from one of your accounts to the other. No additional expense has occurred. There's nothing new to allocate.

A Little Short Cut

Perhaps you're not concerned with the running balance on your cards. You figure that, at worst, every once in a while a waiter will tell you you've bumped up against your limit—whereupon you'll proffer the next card in your deck. If so, rather than setting up 13 different charge accounts and posting transactions to them as incurred, you might prefer to lump all your charge transactions into a single account called "Charge Cards" (or keep American Express separate, say, but lump all your gasoline cards—it's up to you).

Lumping all your charges into one account is less precise—and not for everyone—but easier. When individual credit card statements arrive, glance over them to be sure you weren't hit with somebody else's charges, but don't try to reconcile each one. Just enter the finance charge, if any, as a "Spend" transaction (allocated to Personal Interest Expense)—or don't even bother with that if the amounts are small and you can stand the imprecision. At the end of the year, all 14 of your creditors will dutifully inform you of the cumulative interest you were charged (which doesn't much matter anymore, since it's no longer tax-deductible).

A Little Better Short Cut

Even if that strikes you as appallingly sloppy, this may make sense. It applies whether or not you lump all your charge accounts into one.

Rather than record all your transactions throughout the month more or less as they take place, record them all at once, directly from the monthly statement when it arrives. In fact, just throw your monthly statements into the folder you keep by the computer and tend to this at the same time as you clean out the rest of the folder—pay your bills, print your checks, record brokerage transactions, and so on.

You can enter a separate spend transaction for each item on the statement or—a shorter cut—"spend" the entire amount in one transaction ("Visa Payment") and allocate it over a variety of budget categories. The calculator (Ctrl-N) will make short shrift of adding up the various items that aggregate to each of your budget categories. Or perhaps you'll tot up only deductible expenditures, dumping the remainder into your "Unallocated" category—it's up to you! If you want to explain any of the charges, use the Memo field (pressing F2 to expand it, if necessary).

> NOTE: Charge account balances are ordinarily negative. Bear that in mind when entering your initial balance.

EXPENSE ACCOUNTS

Though it can't fill out your company form, there's a simple way to use the program to help you with your expense accounts.

Set up an Expense budget category called "Reimbursable Expense" (or, if you submit expense accounts to several employers, set up one for each). Then, whenever you record an expenditure you plan to add to your expense account, dump it into that budget category.

When you're ready to prepare your expense report, select Report Generator from the MONEY menu; press F7 twice; mark just the budget category called "Reimbursable Expense" and press the Action Key to save your selections and back up. Now choose the dates your report should cover, select Budget & Tax Category Reports and press the Action Key. When you see the transactions you want, press F4.

I would suggest you print two reports:

Use the Allocation Report Format screen to specify that the first report's transactions be arranged by Budget Category (even though they're all from the same category, this causes us to print a grand total), followed by Date and then Payee. (Include, also, the Amount and Memo.) Put a Y on the first two lines in the right column so we include both a grand total and a day-by-day subtotal.

Now print a second report just like the first, only put Payee on the second line of the Report Format screen and Date on the third. Switch 'em. Now we'll subtotal by payee. (We could do that in the first report, too, if you put a Y beside the third line, too, but chances are you wouldn't like the resulting clutter of mostly meaningless one-item subtotals.)

If you get into the habit of entering your expenses in a format that matches your employer's needs, you can take this a step further. Say you precede all hotel charges with an "H-"—"H-Airport Marriott," "H-Universal Sheraton,"

"H-Cambridge Hyatt." And all airline charges with an "A-" and all meals with an "M-." When we print our report (the second one), you'll get neat groupings of your hotel, air and meal expenses.

There are a variety of ways to play with this depending on your needs, but this should give you an idea of the possibilities. (Note that you can save the customized report formats you come up with. There's no need to reinvent them each month. Press F6, enter a name at the bottom and press F5.)

However you choose to format the report, out will come all your Reimbursable Expenses for the months you specify. If you print them "to disk," ordered by date (see page 298: "Printing to Disk"), you'll quickly be able to add any needed detail that wasn't already in the memo. Just use our word processor (Ctrl-W) to call up the report you save.

If your company accounting department is at all flexible, it should welcome your neatly printed report, allowing you to staple it to the standard form with the simple notation: "See attached."

Naturally, this all makes most sense for people who have already chosen the Full Detail Method for charge cards described on page 369—I'm not one of them—and for whom, therefore, most of the entries they'll need for the expense report will already have been recorded in Managing Your Money.

And When You're Reimbursed …

If you do adopt a system like this, what you could do when you received an expense check would be to receive it into your checking or savings account (wherever you actually deposit it) but allocate it not to an income category, like "Expense Reimbursement," but to your "Reimbursable Expense" expense category. Whenever you allocate income to an expense category, we automatically make it negative. So by doing it this way, the figure for this budget category would rise when you were owed money and fall back to zero when you'd been reimbursed.

(You'd probably want to set your monthly budget for this category at zero, as you expect no net out-of-pocket expense, and have it dump to the "Not a Tax Category" tax barrel—although if your employer ever failed to reimburse you, you could presumably claim the shortfall as an unreimbursed employee business expense.)

More detail? If your expenses aren't fully reimbursed and you need to file a Form 2106 with your taxes, you'll need to account for meals and entertainment separately from your other exenses. In this case, create an Income category, "Expense Reimbursements," and two Expense ones, "Reimb. Expense-Meals" and "Reimb. Expense-Other." Tie them to the three Form 2106 Tax Categories we provide.

You can be as elaborate as you want. One user we know, who takes about a dozen trips a year, has one income and two expense categories for every trip. He places a period at the beginning of each category, so they all sort to the top of the list, and he abbreviates the name of the city he visits. If he visits the same city more than once, he numbers them. His second visit to Washington, D.C., last year produced the Income category ".DC2 Reimbursements" and the Expense categories ".DC2 Meals, Entertai" and ".DC2 Other Expenses."

In short, many people will be best served doing their expense reports the same way they always did. But for some, Managing Your Money may help to organize the process.

MEDICAL EXPENSES AND REIMBURSEMENTS

You can handle medical expenses and reimbursements in much the same way. Set up a budget bucket for medical expenses, dumping, naturally, to one of the Schedule A medical tax barrels, and allocate all your medical expenditures there. Allocate your reimbursement there, also.

Whenever income is allocated to an expense category, we automatically take it to be negative. Say you spend $100 on a medical bill and then got a $90 reimbursement. By allocating that income to the same expense category, the total we'd show, and pass through to Schedule A in TAX, would be $10—the amount of your unreimbursed medical expenses.*

---

*The "Annual Total"—we show on the budget summary screen may not reflect this negative amount until the following month. Say it's July and that in May you spent $500 on reimbursable medical expenses but received $200 of reimbursements. Our annual total would show $300, just as you'd expect—the $500 expense less the $200 "negative expense." So far so good. But now, still in July, you receive the remaining $300 reimbursement you were waiting for. You'd expect, once you entered that negative expense, to see an annual total of zero. Yet until August rolled around, we would still show it as $300. Why? Because for the current month "July" our Annual Total figure is always based on the greater of your budgeted amount (probably zero, in this case) or your actual amount (LESS than zero, in this peculiar case). Once the month is over, we use the actual amount (negative $300) in figuring the Annual Total, so from then on it would look exactly right.

If you'd like a way to keep track of your reimbursements, to be sure they're really coming as they should, and if you've activated our Accounts Receivable option (select Optional Features from the FILE menu, and then Money Options), do this:

When you pay a medical bill, go also to the Receive Money screen and enter there the name of the reimbursor and the amount for which you expect to be reimbursed. In the "By:" field, select "Receivable." This tells us you haven't actually gotten the cash, but that we should add this item to your Accounts Receivable list.

You may wish, also, to note the number of the check and/or some other features of the bill, including the invoice number, for identification purposes. In other words, instead of calling the payee, "Blue Cross," you might call it, "Blue Cross re:#2405" and put the invoice number and "2/14 Appendectomy" in the memo.

Then, when the reimbursement arrives, select Receivables from the MONEY menu and record it on that screen.

NONCASH ITEMS: CHARITABLE CONTRIBUTIONS, DEPRECIATION, PARTNERSHIP LOSSES

In MONEY you can set up a thing we call a "noncash" account. This allows you to enter transactions that affect your taxes but involve no cash—and to do so without lousing up your Cash Flow projections in MONEY or affecting your net worth in NET WORTH.

Just select Money Accounts to set up a noncash account (or several, if you'd like one for depreciation and another for donations of old clothes and a third for partnership income and expense). Ignore the "cash balance" displayed for this account on the Money Accounts screen. We know it's not really cash. If it bothers you, you could always spend or receive the exact opposite amount to set the balance to zero; but you may find it helpful always to be able to see at a glance, for example, the total of your noncash tax deductions—for that's presumably what this figure will represent.

Charitable Contributions

If you give $2,300 in stock to the Red Cross, "write a check" for that amount in a noncash account, allocating it to your "Charitable Contributions" budget bucket. Even though it's in a noncash account, you might want to make the payee, "Red Cross—STOCK!," so that in print-outs you're reminded this was not a contribution of real money and to include the backup you'll need to satisfy the IRS. The memo line in this case might read, "100 shares, Wrather Corp. common, vsp 3/4/1978." (VSP is short for "versus purchase," so you and your broker and the IRS know which Wrather shares these were.)

(If you do give shares, then go into PORTFOLIO, locate this tax lot on the Display Assets screen, and press F2 to edit it. Simply lower the number of shares you originally purchased by the number you've given away—you softie—and, on the comment line, note something like, "Excludes 100 shares given to Red Cross 12/25/1991.")

Depreciation

For depreciation, simply visit your noncash account and write a "check" for each depreciation charge you want to record, dumping, presumably, into depreciation budget buckets that dump, in turn, into the appropriate Schedule C, E or F tax barrels.

We don't automatically calculate depreciation schedules for your equipment, nor update them as you start each new year; but once you've devised your depreciation schedule for a particular item, you might set it up as a Quick List transaction. Make the first four letters of the payee DEPR, say, so all your depreciation items will be grouped together—DEPR-Mack Truck, DEPR-Answering Machine, and so on. If you like, you could append the year of acquisition, too—"DEPR-Mack Truck —88." In the memo area, note whatever else you need to know, including the depreciation method (straight-line, etc.) and the actual numbers for the years to come. That way, next year you can just mark all the DEPR's on your Quick List, updating those where the amount has changed (the correct amount will be sitting a keystroke away on the memo line). I actually have an annual reminder in The Reminder Pad that reminds me to do this in January of each new year.

Note: Depreciation Is for Business Only

If you don't know anything about depreciation, you're lucky. It applies only to people who run their own businesses. And since the first $10,000 worth of business equipment you buy each year—fax machines and the like—may ordinarily be "written off" all at once (consult your accountant, TaxCut, or a tax guide about "Section 179 Property")—you may not have to know anything about it even if you do run a small business.

So the fact that the central air conditioning unit in your home is depreciating each year is of no consequence to Managing Your Money.

Otherwise—if you own rental properties, for example—you will want to create budget categories for depreciation. Say you just bought a $275,000 building which you may depreciate over 27.5 years. That means you get to deduct $10,000 of depreciation each year against the rental income from the building. (I'm simplifying. Check with your accountant about how much depreciation you get to take the first year, how to depreciate some of the things that came with the building, and how much of the purchase price you cannot depreciate because it represents the value of the land.) To be sure TAX knows about this each year, you'd want to "Spend" that $10,000 each year ... but not with real cash, because it's just a bookkeeping entry. That's why you spend it in a noncash account.

Rental property depreciation will ordinarily be assigned to a Schedule E tax category. Farm depreciation, to Schedule F. Any other depreciation, like the depreciation on the mainframe you just bought for your consulting practice, to Schedule C.

Partnership Gains and Losses

To record $5,300 in partnership income that's being reported to the IRS, even though the sons-of-guns never sent you a nickel, let alone $5,300, just "receive" the income in your noncash account. It will show up in your budgets and (assuming you've set up a category called Partnership Income dumping into the Schedule E tax barrel) on Schedule E in TAX.

Early each year you can "spend" your estimated tax losses or gains from each partnership, writing a noncash "check" to, or recording a noncash "receipt" from, each. Then, as estimates of your losses shrink or grow (mine generally grow), you just go back into this noncash account and edit the transactions. Your TAX estimates will always be up-to-date.

You can also do a variation on the Quick List transactions scheme described above for DEPR, only this time, enter on the memo line of the Quick List transaction the year-by-year profit and loss estimates from the offering brochure.

Note that to account for partnerships properly, you'll also need "Not a Tax Category" budget buckets for "Partnership Cash In" and "Partnership Cash Out," because sometimes you actually do get cash from a partnership, even though that's not what the IRS goes by in taxing you; and often you have to send cash to keep the partnership afloat, even though that's not what you get to deduct. (These real cash transactions are naturally recorded in your real checking account.)

FROM CHAPTER 4: TAX

A TAX ESTIMATOR

This section of Managing Your Money estimates your tax liability based on 1991 or 1992 tax brackets and rules (your choice). It doesn't give any significant tax advice. But many users find it valuable for figuring their estimated quarterly tax liabilities (if any) and for making decisions that have tax consequences.

To see how it works, just press F1 for HELP behind the Form 1040 screen—and as you encounter each screen thereafter.

HOW SHOULD I PROCEED?

1.   Select Form 1040 from the TAX menu. Form 1040 is the main TAX screen, and will automatically reflect changes you make in the others.

2.   Press F7 to update the entire TAX section with the proper numbers from elsewhere in the program. Bang. In a single keystroke, if you've entered your budget **in MONEY, you'll have a pretty decent estimate of your Federal income tax.** Or press F8 if you'd rather update only those starred (*) on this screen.

3.   Press F1 for an explanation of exactly what the numbers we pull in represent: your actual transactions so far this year, plus your budgeted income and expenses for the remainder of the year.

4.   ESCape to the Menu Bar and select Tax Tables and Parameters to see whether we've loaded the right ones for your filing status (single, joint) and tax year (1991 or 1992), and to see how to change them (Merry Widow, unMarried with Children, Divorce Court). Please also read the next section: "What If the Tax Laws Change?"

> SHORTCUT: From the Form 1040 screen, you can reach any schedule, A-F, simply by pressing its letter. And you can move among these six schedules the same way.

5.   Visit each schedule in turn and read its HELP for a further explanation of what we've done. Change anything you like. Visit the Form 1040 Worksheet, Self-Employment Tax form and the Alternative Minimum Tax screen as well. These schedules and other screens also have an update key that pulls information from MONEY. Many of them have places to fill in some information manually, too.

WHAT IF THE TAX LAWS CHANGE?

In most respects, you should be able to change right along with them. Just select Tax Tables and Parameters from the TAX file menu.

Plus Plan members will be apprised, where possible, of changes they should make to reflect changes in the tax code. It is also our intention to include updated tax data with each annual update to the program.

> HINT: Managing Your Money comes to you with the save area empty. If you load User-defined tables before you press F8 to save some, we'll dutifully replace all the real TAX numbers with blanks. No harm. Just use F7 to reload 1991 or 1992.

What-if: If you want to play some games—to enter the Brazilian tax brackets, say, in case that minor bank fraud you masterminded seems about to unravel—go right ahead. Then, if you can get a couple of Senators to ravel it back up again for you, just go to the last field on the screen (Ctrl-L), press the Spacebar, choose 1991 or 1992 (the numbers TAX never forgets), and press F7 to reload those tax tables.

The Save Area: Note, in fact, that because TAX never forgets these numbers, you can always recover them-but that changes you do want to make to the 1992 numbers, should Congress make changes, will be wiped out if you should ever reload 1992.

That's why we provide a "save area" for your changes. Just press F8 to save your "user-defined" tax parameters. Should you ever lose them, whether they're only slightly different from the numbers we provide or wildly different (because they're Brazilian), Ctrl-L to the last field, choose User-defined, and press F7 to load them back again. Your numbers will stay there until you overwrite them by using F8 to stick some different set of tax parameters into the save area.

Important!

- There's more on the Tax Tables & Parameters screen than meets the eye (or that will fit on one screen, anyway). To change things like the threshold for medical deductions, the Social Security tax rates, and so on, press PgDn to see the next screen and PgDn again to see the third.

- If you do switch from 1991 to 1992, or vice versa, or if you do make changes to the Tax Parameters, be sure to visit each of the TAX screens that may have been affected by your change-such as the Self-Employment Tax screen-so that the change can take hold. You needn't do anything on those screens; just visit them for an instant and return to Form 1040.

ESTIMATING A FUTURE YEAR'S TAX

Form 1040 will ordinarily pull in your current year's numbers, but FILE's Money Options screens lets you pull in your budget estimates for next year instead—or even for any of the following three years if you've activated our five-year budgeting option.

Naturally, the answers we give will be iffy at best, in part because no one knows what crazy things Congress may do, and few of us can budget accurately five months into the future, let alone five years. Still, you may have occasion to play with this, for next year's taxes if not 1996's. And you're free to change the tax laws temporarily, as described above, to craft what you consider the most likely scenario.

After you've changed the year in Money Options, be sure to change it back before you try to estimate this year's taxes.

FROM CHAPTER 7: PORTFOLIO

PORTFOLIO AT A GLANCE

This is a full-fledged portfolio management system. Most of it is self-explanatory. But here, as a reference and overview, are some of the features, and how to reach them, that may not be obvious from glancing at the Menu Bar:

Buy Assets

>Buy Multiple Lots of an Asset: Alt-F5
>Cover a Short Sale: F7

Sell Assets

>Regular and Partial Sales, First/Last-Acquired Sales
>Sell Short: F7

Update Prices

>Update Prices, Yields or Special Codes
>Update the Index You Compare Yourself to
>See or Change the Meanings of Special Codes: F8
>Change an Asset's Symbol: F7
>See All Tax Lots of a Given Symbol: F2
>Sort by Name or Symbol: F9

Record Income

>Dividends, Interest, Return-of-Capital Distributions, Automatic Reinvestments

Split Stocks

>Stock Splits and Stock Dividends (but not dividend reinvestments—see HELP)

Portfolios

>Set Up a New Portfolio: F5
>Revise or Delete a Portfolio: F2 or F3
>Analyze Your Brokerage Commissions: F7
>Quick-Edit Commissions: F7, Action Key
>Transfer Assets Between Portfolios: F6
>Disaggregate All Aggregated Assets (careful!): F8

Display Assets
  View or Change the Particulars of an Asset: F2
  Delete an Asset: F3
  Print Unsold, Sold or Short Assets (as sorted): F4
  Rotate to Show Current Value, Name or Original Cost: F7
  Sort by Symbol, Value, Purchase Date, Gain, Maturity,
  Appreciation: F9
  Work with Unsold Assets, Short Assets, Sold Positions or Good-
    Til-Canceleds: Action Key
  Aggregate Multiple Lots of a Single Asset: F6
  Disaggregate Asset: F2

Analyze Assets
  Capital Gains Analysis: F6
  Capital Gains Advice and Sale Candidates: F6, Action Key
  Select Specific Symbols for Analysis: Action Key, F7, ActionKey
  Appreciation Display: Action Key, Action Key, select
    Appreciation, Action Key
  Yield Display: Action Key, Action Key, Select Yield, Action Key
  Yield Summary Analysis: Action Key twice, select Yield, Action
    Key, F7
  Special Codes (by Percent) Display: Action key twice, select
    Special Codes %, Action Key
  Performance vs. Index Display: Action Key twice, select
    Performance vs. Index, Action Key
Graph by Risk, Recommendor, etc.: Action Key twice, select criteria, F9
  Aggregate Display: Action Key twice, select Aggregation, F9

View Income
  View Your Dividend and Interest Receipts for the Year

Financial Reminders
  View Automatically-Generated Reminders

Bullishness Index
  A Good Day to Buy? To Sell?

Managing the Market (if activated)
  Updates Prices Over Your Phone Line

Report Generator
  Customized Reports in Addition to the F4 Reports Everywhere
  Else

Schedule D: Select in place of Matching Assets, then Action Key
Delete Old Sold Assets: Alt-F3

Alt-key Shortcuts

To make navigation more convenient for experienced users, we've provided some shortcuts:

- Display Assets is PORTFOLIO's Grand Central Station, just as the Check Register is in MONEY. From here you can press Alt-B to Buy Assets, Alt-S to Sell the Asset you're pointing to, Alt-R to Record Income, and Alt-U to Update Prices. And when you press ESCape, you'll be back looking at the portfolio you were working with (press F8 at any time to switch to another).

- From Buy Assets, Alt-S will take you to Sell Assets, and from Sell, Alt-B will take you to Buy. This is handy if you're entering a batch of buy and sell transactions all at once.

WHAT EXACTLY IS A PORTFOLIO?

A portfolio is any collection of assets you care to lump together. Typically, each separate brokerage account will be set up as a separate portfolio. If you keep track of a stamp collection, you could say it's part of your Merrill Lynch IRA portfolio—but presumably it would make more sense to set up a portfolio all its own, called, perhaps, "My Stamps." You might group all assets in your 401K into one portfolio. Mutual funds can be grouped together in a portfolio called "My Mutual Funds," or each given its own private portfolio, or grouped by fund "family"—Fidelity, Vanguard—you're the boss.

We'd like to record all your assets here, or at least most of them—stocks, bonds, rental properties, certificates of deposit—you name it. Portfolios are simply "file folders," if you will, to help you organize these assets into logical groupings. You may designate four different kinds of portfolios: Taxable, IRA/Keogh/401K, Hypothetical or CMA.

HINT: Set up CMA's even if you don't have any. You can use CMA as the "type" for a taxable portfolio even if it doesn't officially have check-writing privileges. The advantage is that you'll then get a record in MONEY of all the dollar Ins and Outs of your portfolio—the dividends you've recorded, the proceeds of sales, and so on. And you'll be able to record the transfer of funds from your checking account to this portfolio in one fell swoop in MONEY. You'll have a Check Register record of all the inflows and outflows. It's a neat trick. (You wouldn't want to do this for Hypothetical or IRA/Keogh/401K accounts, however, because then we'd treat them like real, taxable CMAs.)

- Most portfolios are taxable. A regular brokerage account, for example (or your stamp collection), you'd tag taxable. This would be true even if it contained some tax-free bonds, because while the interest on those bonds may not be taxed, the gains and losses realized when you sell them are taxable.

- If it were one of those brokerage accounts that allow you to write personal checks against it—a so-called cash management account (CMA)—you'd tag it CMA. We'd treat it just like a taxable account, only we'd know to link it to your corresponding CMA account in MONEY. Managing Your Money can keep track of up to 9 such linked accounts.

- If it were an account under the shelter of some sort of retirement account, you'd tag it IRA/Keogh/401K. We'd be sure to include it in our calculation of your net worth (and also in the Retirement Planning section of ANALYZE). But we wouldn't tell TAX about any of your gains or losses or dividends, because they are not taxable.

- If it were a play-money account, or one that for any other reason you didn't want us to count in figuring your taxes or net worth, you'd tag it hypothetical. (PORTFOLIO's Report Generator will print a Schedule D for a hypothetical portfolio, in case it's a real one you're tending for someone else. Or you may exclude it (with F6 on the Report Generator screen). Your choice.

Once you've created a portfolio, you can't go back and change its type—from taxable to CMA, say, if you've begun writing checks on your brokerage account.

THREE STEPS TO GET STARTED

To get going with PORTFOLIO, there's a three-step process: first you set up at least one portfolio; then you fill it with the assets it already contains; then you adjust its cash balance.

STEP #1: SETTING UP YOUR PORTFOLIO

In order to list your stocks and bonds (and whatever else) in PORTFO-LIO, you must first "Add a Portfolio" for us to put them in.

1.   Press Alt-P from the Menu Bar, select Portfolios from the PORT-FOLIOS menu and press F5.

2.   Read HELP and set up a portfolio. Don't bother with the "Initial Cash Balance"—for now, leave it blank. We'll adjust it in Step #3.

Cash Management Accounts

Many of you have the kind of checking accounts that are tied to broker-age accounts. So do I. They're funny animals because they are part check-ing account—MONEY—and part portfolio—PORTFOLIO.

Managing Your Money allows you to set up as many as nine of these spe-cial, linked accounts—CMA1—CMA9. Tag an account "CMA1" in MONEY and we automatically create its counterpart in Portfolio (on the PORTFOLIO menu).

> NOTE: It doesn't matter which you set up first, the Money Ac-count or the Portfolio. But it's a little easier to set it up first as a Money Account, because then there's nothing else to do. The CMA is added in PORTFOLIO automatically. If you set it up first as a Portfolio, we burp and take you to fill out the Add Money Ac-count screen before proceeding.

Once your CMA account is set up, buying a stock or bond automatically reduces your cash balance in PORTFOLIO—and in MONEY. Selling a stock or receiving a dividend raises both balances. Meanwhile, paying the rent in MONEY automatically decreases your balance there—and in PORTFOLIO. The balances will match perfectly in MONEY and PORTFOLIO, but not be double-counted in NET WORTH.

Suggestion: Money Market Mutual Funds—CMAs

Your CMA probably "invests" cash balances in a money market mutual fund. As a practical matter, rather than recording these as mutual fund shares, and having to buy and sell shares (always at $1 per share) every time the slightest thing happens, your life will be much simpler just counting those "shares" as cash, which they essentially are. Once a month, when your statement arrives, just select Receive Money from the MONEY menu and allocate the receipt to your Interest Income budget category.) Because it's a CMA, the receipt in MONEY will automatically be reflected in your PORTFOLIO balance as well.

Suggestion: Money Market Mutual Funds—non-CMA accounts

For a regular brokerage account that sweeps cash into a money market fund, you could do this: First, "buy" 1 share of an asset called "MONEY FUND" or some such for a penny. The idea is simply to get something with that name in your portfolio. Thereafter, whenever you want to record money market interest income, select Record Income, point to MONEY FUND and record receipt of this interest. Your cash balance and budget allocations will fall right into place.

STEP #2: ADDING A NEW ASSET

Now that you've added a portfolio, back up to the Menu Bar and select Buy Assets—or just point to the portfolio and press the Action Key and F5.

Here's where you build a profile of the asset. One nice feature is that you won't have to do it over each time you buy the same asset. (Some things will be new—the price, commission, date and number of shares, as well as any comment you care to make—but the other characteristics you've assigned will appear automatically.) Fill in as many of the blanks as you can. You can always add or change something later. Here's how:

Symbol: Wherever possible, use the actual stock, bond, mutual fund or option symbol of your purchase. (Consult your broker, Standard & Poor's Stock Guide or the Dow Jones News/Retrieval Service.) If you're compiling a portfolio of rare stamps, or including them in some other portfolio, assign any symbols you'll find easy to remember. Just be sure not to use a stock symbol. "GI-1945" is fine for your GI Joe 1945 commemorative, but "GI" alone is Giant Industries.

> HINT: For easier updating. If you get your price quotes from the newspaper, you may wish to lead off all New York Stock Exchange names with an asterisk (say), all American Stock Exchange names with a hyphen, all NASDAQ names with a period—and so on. Then, when you select Update Prices, press F9 to sort them by name. Using these little prefixes, your assets will be grouped and listed in the same order as you find them in the paper, which makes for easier updating. (See page 336 for "alphabetical order.") On the other hand, if you do follow enough different securities to make this scheme helpful, we hope you'll consider automating the process with Managing the Market instead.

Name: Use any abbreviations you want, though the ones you find in the stock pages of the newspaper may be easiest. We pay no attention, other than to include the name when we print your Schedule D.

Number of Units: If you're buying a *stock* or *mutual fund*, just enter the number of shares.

You may enter *fractional shares*. When you do, the "4.237" you type will seem to be rounded to "4" on most of our displays—but we'll know! The correct number of shares is in memory; there's just not room to display it. To check us (or find out just how many shares you do have), select Display Assets and press F7 once or twice.

Stand-alone *money market mutual funds*, used essentially as checking or savings accounts, should be set up as Checking or Savings accounts in MONEY. But if they're tied to your brokerage account and you don't write checks against them, handle them as described in the "Suggestions" on pages 383–384. Or, if you do write checks against them, handle them as the cash component of a CMA account as described there, too.

If you're buying *bonds*, multiply the number of bonds—and divide their purchase price—by 10. This conforms to the manner in which bond prices and yields are quoted by your broker and in the paper: as a percentage of their $1000 face value. Instead of saying you bought 1 bond for $1000, enter 10 at $100.

Say you bought "100,000 face of Connecticut-13's-of-2001 at 112," as a broker might put it. In English, that means you bought 100 State of

Connecticut bonds, each with a face value (like all bonds) of $1,000. But that you paid 112 cents on the dollar for each—$1120 per bond, $112,000 in all. And that, because they're "13s," they pay 13% interest on their face value—$130 a year (though paid semi-annually)—until they are redeemed for $1000 each in the year 2001, unless called earlier.

You'd enter 1000 as the number of units, 112 as the price, and 13 as the yield.

If you're buying *options* (a put or call on 100 shares of stock), enter each one as "100" to conform to the way prices are quoted. Instead of saying you bought one Nike call for $350, which you did, say you bought 100 at three-and-a-half (3.5). (See: "Puts and Calls.")

If you're buying *futures* contracts, also called *commodities*, the same reasoning applies. Don't say you bought one contract on 5000 bushels of beans, say you bought 5000 units at $7.56 each—the price per bushel. That way, you'll conform to the way prices are quoted. (And it will also bring home the enormity of the risk you've undertaken.)

If you're buying *precious metals*, enter them by the ounce, because that's how prices are quoted.

If you're buying *stamps* or *coins* or *art*, enter each separate item as "1" unit unless the price is so high ($80 million) that you have to pretend it was actually "100 Van Gogh" at $800,000 each.

If you choose to enter *Real estate* here, and you're buying a $2,500,000 house, enter 1000 units at $2500. (Or simply list it as an asset directly in NET WORTH.) You can't enter 1 unit at $2,500,000 because there's not enough room on the screen to allow prices of more than six places (plus three decimal places) and still display all the information we want.

Mortgages you own, and any other *loans due you*, could be recorded as bonds, of a sort, in a portfolio here (call it "Loans I Own"), but most users will find it more sensible and effective to enter them in the Loan Records section of MONEY.

If you're buying a $10,000 *certificate of deposit* here, enter it as a bond, which is essentially what it is. But because you won't be looking up its price in the paper, you needn't bother with dividing it into 10 units to conform to the way bond prices are quoted; just enter 1 unit at $10,000. This could be in a separate portfolio you set up called "My CD" or as part of a larger one called "All My CD's"—whatever way suits you best. Every month or quarter, just up its price to its new, higher value.

If you're keeping track of *frequent flier miles*, enter them—in a "hypothetical" portfolio—as 2490 units (nautical miles) for a trip to California, symbol TWAFF (TWA Frequent Flier, as distinguished from TWA the stock), price $0.02, if you agree with me that each mile is worth about 2 cents. You'll see an aggregate number of miles for each of your airlines in the aggregate format of our portfolio analysis, and even a rough estimate of what all those miles are worth. (Their value is more than hypothetical, but might not impress your banker if included on your balance sheet.)

If you're buying ***anything else***, use whatever system makes sense to you. I mention the frequent flier miles not because I see much point to keeping track of them this way (it might be easier to use a noncash account in MONEY) or much point to keeping track of them at all (what's wrong with the monthly statements the airlines all send?), but to suggest that there's more you can organize here than stocks and bonds.

Purchase Date: Use the "trade date" (the day you made the transaction) not the "settlement date" (the day your payment is due). Remember, if it's June 5, 1992 and you want to record a trade you made yesterday, you need type just the number 4. When you leave the field, we make it: 6/4/1992.

Price Per Unit: Enter the price per unit (share, ounce, bushel, etc.) as described under "Number of Units" above.

> NOTE: Remember! With bonds, you didn't buy 1 bond for $995 (even though you did), you bought "10 for $99.50". With options, you didn't buy 1 GM 40 call for $360 (even though you did), you bought "100 for $3.60".

Commission: If you don't know it exactly, take a guess or leave it blank until the confirmation slip arrives. (Note our shortcut for that: F7, Action Key on the Portfolio screen.) If no commission is involved, just leave this blank.

Yield: Tell us how much cash your asset pays per unit each year. If it pays no dividend or interest (or rent), enter zero or just leave this blank.

For a *stock* that paid a 30-cent-a-share quarterly dividend, you'd enter "1.20" (because 30 cents a share per quarter works out to $1.20 a share per year).

For a 12.5% *bond*, you'd enter "12.5" (because you'll be getting $125 in interest per bond each year, but we entered each bond as 10 to conform to the way bond prices are quoted).

For the $600 monthly rent from an $80,000 *rental property* you had recorded as "1000 units at $80 each," you'd enter "7.20," because that is the yield per unit per year ($600 x 12 months = $7,200 a year for the whole property, or $7.20 a year for each of the 1,000 units into which you've divided it). If you entered that property as 1 unit at $80,000, then the annual yield per unit would be "$7,200."

For *mutual fund shares*, your yield estimate—of necessity less precise than for a stock or bond—would include just the dividends and interest, if any, you expect the fund to pay out, per share, during the year.

Tax Status: Tell us whether income from the asset is fully Taxable (as is most often the case); Free of Any Tax (tax-free municipal bonds issued by an entity within your state); subject to Federal Tax Only (U.S. Treasury securities, like Treasury bonds and Savings Bonds, are not subject to local income tax); or subject to State Tax Only (tax-free municipal bonds issued by a state other than your own will be subject to your local income tax).

You can leave this field blank if you're not sure, or if the asset is owned in a hypothetical or IRA/Keogh/401K portfolio where the tax status doesn't matter anyway. But it only takes a second to tag GM dividends as "Taxable"—which you should do even if this particular lot of GM shares is in a hypothetical or IRA/Keogh/401K type portfolio. After all, the next 50 shares of GM you buy might be in your regular brokerage account. You may as well get GM set up in Managing Your Money properly from the start.

Type: Choose one. (Use the Spacebar to jump into the choice box; then arrow up and down to see them all. Use Enter to choose.) For a kind of asset we haven't thought of, use "Other" or "Special Coded" (I'll explain below). For a deferred annuity, use our catchall "Savings Bond/SPDA" (Single Premium Deferred Annuity).

Accrued Interest: You won't see this field unless and until you tell us that this asset is a bond. But if it is, the confirm your broker sends may well include a charge for accrued interest. If so, just enter it here.

CUSIP: Every publicly traded security has a CUSIP number (Committee on Uniform Securities Identification Procedures)—even those without a regular symbol. No need to enter this if you don't want to, but especially for some of your more obscure holdings it might come in handy one day. Look for the CUSIP number on your broker's confirmation slip.

Maturity Date: Leave this blank for a stock; but if it's a bond or a certificate of deposit, it "comes due" as of some date. (For a bond that can be called early, you may prefer to use the call date.) Option expiration dates can be entered here, but you needn't bother: our Financial Reminder screen determines the expiration date from the symbol.

We use the maturity date two places: Financial Reminders, to remind you the asset is maturing, and Display Assets, where F9 offers to sort in order of maturity date. If you accept this offer, all the assets with no date specified (like stocks) will come first, but never fear: at the end of the list will be your bonds and CD's, in order of their maturity dates.

Price Objective: If you enter one, we'll remind you when you reach it.

Mental Stop Loss: If you enter one, we'll remind you when you reach it. Of course, you can also enter real stop loss orders with your broker. As you know, these assure that even if you're off in Africa and not paying attention, you will be "stopped out" of your stock, now $44 a share, if, say, it should ever drop to $39.75. That way you know that the most you can lose is $4.25 a share, even if you should come back to find the stock down to $11.

The two problems with this are, first, that if the stock should encounter some major bad news, closing at $40.25 a share one night but opening the next day at $23, your broker will dutifully sell your shares at $23. He's obligated simply to sell as soon as they dip to or below the stop-loss price you specified. So you're not entirely protected. Second, what often happens is that you do indeed get stopped out at $39.50—only to see the stock bounce back to $44 and beyond. This is called getting whipsawed. The floor of the exchange is ankle high in whipsawdust.

Risk: Short term Treasury obligations entail virtually no risk. But 30-year Treasury bonds do entail risk, because if interest rates should rocket, the price of long-term bonds (even safe ones) will plunge. All stocks entail some risk, but some entail a lot. You may certainly leave this blank, but by categorizing your assets by risk, you allow us to show you the risk distribution of your portfolio(s).

Beta: This is a measure of a stock's or portfolio's volatility relative to the market as a whole. A stock that moves with the market has a beta of 1. A ponderous blue chip that goes up or down only half as fast has a beta of one half—.5. A stock that zooms and plunges at every turn may have a beta of 3 or 4. If you care about betas—I don't—find a place to look them up and fill them in. Otherwise, settle for your own risk classification (above), which amounts to much the same thing.

Or use this box to enter **Value Line rankings**, if you're a Value Line fan. The heading will still say "Beta," but you and I will know. Value Line ranks stocks from 1 to 5 for timeliness. If you enter those rankings here, you will be able easily to determine, for example, the proportion of your assets ranked 1 or 2 for timeliness.

HINT: F9 to back up. If you're like me, you will use special codes a lot, both in PORTFOLIO and in the Card File. For convenience, you'll find that F9 not only takes you into your list of special codes, but back out as well. The screen shows ESCape as the key to back up, as always; but it's even easier to tap in and out with F9.

Liquidity: Fully liquid assets are those that are readily converted to cash. Illiquid assets (a better term might be frozen) include non-marketable partnership interests, stock in a family business, "letter stock"—that sort of thing. Semi-liquid assets are those you can sell, but not right away or all at once, like 75,000 shares of some stock that normally trades just 200 shares a day, a CD that doesn't mature for another six months, a Renoir, or a parcel of land that could take a year to unload. Again, you may leave this blank; but by taking a moment to fill it in, you can then always see your assets broken out by liquidity.

Industry Group: Choose one. If you don't find anything that fits, choose "Other" or assign a Special Code (see below).

Recommendor: Likewise.

Special Codes: Here's one of the things that makes Managing Your Money so flexible. We've provided 52 tags for you to assign any way you like—26 upper-case letters and 26 lower-case. Press F9 here to assign meanings to these letters—and then to refresh your memory whenever you forget. F6 toggles between the upper- and lower-case codes.

For example, you could code stock tips from three newsletters A, B, and C, so you can quickly separate and compare the performance of each. If you've set up a portfolio for your stamp collection, you could have special codes for "Commemoratives," "Plate Blocks," and "First Day Covers." You are only limited by your imagination.

> HINT: An extra 40 codes. Only lower- and upper-case letter codes are included in the special codes display. But for retrieval purposes—to pull out just those assets you've tagged with a question mark, say—you can add 40 more codes by using all the numbers and symbols on the keyboard. See how we've assigned 1, 2, 3 and the question mark? Wherever we give you a chance to add, change or display special codes, we also let you see the crib sheet that will remind you what they mean. While looking at the crib sheet, you may add new codes or change the meaning of existing ones.

> HINT: Multiple Lots. You've entered your first purchase of AT&T, and now you want to enter the next eight lots you've purchased. Enter the Symbol, Name and Type of Asset on the Buy Assets screen, then press Alt-F5. You can enter a whole list of purchases of that asset in short order.

To see how your assets break down according to these various criteria, select Analyze Assets, mark the portfolio(s) you want to analyze, and press the Action Key twice, the letter "S" for the special codes display, and the Action Key again.

The easiest way to keep your special codes up-to-date is the Update Prices screen. The right-hand column on the Price Update screen shows all the codes you've assigned. Scroll down through your various assets, adding, changing and blanking out codes as you go.

Index: Enter here the current level of the Dow Jones or the Standard & Poor's 500 or any other index you care to compare yourself against. (Just be sure to be consistent and use the same index for all your assets.)

If you leave this box blank, we'll assume your asset performed no better or worse than the index. Otherwise, we'll be able to give you an analysis that says, in effect, "Since you bought these 50 shares they've climbed 23.1%—versus just 17% for the Dow." And another that compares the performance of your entire portfolio against the Dow (Analyze Assets, mark the portfolio(s), Action Key twice, "P," Action Key again).

Lot Comment: What you enter here will apply to the current tax lot only (that is, not all your GM shares, just these 50). Often, you won't have anything to enter here when you first buy shares. (If I place a "market order," I enter the purchase right away and use this space to record the time I placed the order and the oral confirmation number the broker gives me, just in case for some reason the order somehow were not executed. Then, when the written confirm comes, I come back and enter the commission, edit the actual price at which the trade was done, and delete this little comment). Where the Lot Comment may be more helpful is in the months and years to come. For example, if the shares rise in value and you decide to give some of them to charity (be sure to wait at least a year and a day), you might enter a comment like this: "Owned 100 shares in this tax lot; gave 30 to Red Cross on 12/4/1992." You needn't enter any comment— but can go on at monumental length with F2 (from anywhere on the screen) if you do.

Symbol Comment: Record anything that applies to all your lots of this asset—all your GM. Perhaps you'd like to keep a running record of stock splits or your broker's excuses. You might put the latest earnings estimate, or your rationale for buying it in the first place, or the name it used to go by before it merged, or the number of shares into which it's convertible (if it's a convertible bond). Visit this field and press F2 to expand it.

When you've filled in everything you'd like to keep track of, press the Action Key to add this asset to your portfolio.

STEP #3: ADJUST YOUR CASH BALANCE

When you're all finished filling a portfolio with the assets it contains, reselect Portfolio. The cash balance we show will be negative to the tune of the cost of all the things you just "bought." (If you actually had just bought them, this is how much you'd have had to dug into your pocket to pay for them; but you already owned them, so the number we show will be wrong.) Just press F2, Tab down to "Cash Balance," and type the correct current net cash balance (or margin debt) over the one we show so that our records agree with your broker's. While you're there, note that you have an expandable (F2) Memo field for comments about this portfolio.

And what is the correct cash balance? If your broker starts to confuse you with "the credit in type 1 and the debit in type 2 and the phantom short balance," interrupt politely and ask, "Cut to the chase, Herb. If I closed my account today and transferred all the securities and short positions elsewhere, how much cash would I get—or have to send you to pay off my margin debt?" That's the number that matters. Chances are, if your account is at all complicated by short sales or not-yet-settled transactions, let alone futures contracts, your broker won't know. For all his or her fancy computer screens, he'll have to call someone in the back office who can actually make heads or tails of this. But it should be possible to figure out who owes whom without actually having to close out your account and transfer the securities to see.

From now on, whenever you buy things, we'll automatically lower your cash balance by the amount of the purchase; whenever you sell, we'll automatically dump the net proceeds into your cash balance.

• When your cash balance is positive, it's just that: a cash balance. When it's negative, because you owe the broker money, that's called a margin balance. Buying stock "on margin" is like buying a TV "on time" (well, sort of). You're putting up only part of the money now and borrowing the rest.

If you actually do send your broker a check one day, or every time you make a purchase, add this cash influx to your cash balance on the Portfolios screen (point to the portfolio, press F2 and type over the balance). Likewise, subtract an amount equal to any cash withdrawals you make.

- Adding to and subtracting from your cash balance is easy if it's all round numbers. Anyone knows that $5,000 plus $2,500 equals $7,500. But for real world situations, you'll find Ctrl-N handy. Just position the cursor on the portfolio cash balance in question; press Ctrl-N to summon the calculator and then F6 to pull the current cash balance down into it. Now just add or subtract the amount of your deposit or withdrawal, press Enter twice, and you're done. Try it!

- If you'd like an "audit trail" of these additions and subtractions—a written record of when you added or withdrew cash and where that cash came from or went—use F2. That is, while still on the Portfolios screen, with this portfolio highlighted, press F2 and jot down your entry in the memo area—"March 3, 1992: withdrew $5,000." Pressing F2 again will expand that little area into a huge blank page, on which you can set up a little table and watch it grow over the years as you add notations.

  (Of course, if you set this up as a CMA-type portfolio, its checking account side in MONEY will reflect all the inflows and outflows automatically. The only thing is that, because CMA's are all considered by Managing Your Money to be real and taxable, you wouldn't want to use one for a hypothetical or tax-deferred portfolio.)

  The Portfolio memo area is also a good place to keep running notes on dealings with your broker generally. What instructions have you given him or her? What assurances has he or she given you? Who's the branch manager?

- If this is your butterfly collection and not your Paine Webber account, it presumably has no cash balance, positive or negative. Just blank out the number we show and—unless you keep cash in your lepidoptery kit or have burdened your collection with a butterfly-now-pay-later loan—just reset it to zero whenever you make a purchase or sale.

Management Fees

If your monthly brokerage statement shows some fees apart from those tied to a specific purchase or sale—an IRA "management fee," for example—do two things. First, subtract this charge from your cash balance, just as your broker did. But then select Spend Money and, in any account, "spend" zero dollars, but press F9 and allocate the amount of the management fee to a budget category like, "Investment Fees," which gets dumped in the Schedule A "Investment Man. Fees" tax barrel. The payee for this odd transaction should be whomever you paid the management fee.

- If you have told us to warn you if a transaction is over or under allocated (Money Options under Optional Features on the FILE menu), we'll warn you when you enter this transaction. Just tell us that yes, you really did intend the allocation to exceed the transaction amount.

  Because you spend zero dollars, we don't lower your bank balance. But because you allocate the amount of the fee to the proper budget category, it will show up on Schedule A of TAX and in MONEY Report Generator reports of your deductible expenses. (Unfortunately, investment management fees are counted as "miscellaneous deductions," which currently are deductible only to the extent they exceed 2% of your adjusted gross income.)

YOUR FINANCIAL REMINDERS

Select Financial Reminders and we remind you:

- when an asset has met or exceeded the price objective (if any) you set when you recorded its purchase;

- when an asset has fallen to or beneath the mental stop loss level you set;

- when your holding is about to go long-term (not that it much matters as of this writing, because the tax code no longer gives much benefit to long-term capital gains);

- when options are nearing expiration;

- when bonds or CD's set up as bonds are nearing maturity.

HINT: Be sure to select Optional Features on the FILE menu, and then Portfolio Options, to match our work habits to your requirements! Don't miss "F6 - Alter Financial Reminder Criteria" on that screen. (And don't forget to record your changes with the Action

> Key, and then to save your work before you leave the program—preferably as soon as you get back to the Menu Bar, with Ctrl-S.)

RECORDING DIVIDENDS AND INTEREST

To record a distribution from an asset:

1.   Select Record Income from the PORTFOLIO menu.

2.   Point to the asset that's thrown off the income. If you have this asset in more than one portfolio, be sure to choose the right one. But within a single portfolio, it doesn't matter which one you point to! Any tax lot will do.

3.   Press the Action Key.

4.   On the window that pops up, tell us the date you received this income (it must be this year, the amount, and then the "Status."

   - **I received cash** means GM sent a check that you want us to put in one of your MONEY accounts.

   - **Broker held for me** means the check went to your broker, and we should add to your portfolio cash balance accordingly. This option will not appear if you're recording a dividend in a CMA portfolio. That's because dividends your broker receives for you in a CMA are just like getting cash and having it instantly direct-deposited to the checking account side of the CMA—so that's just what we do. Choose "I received cash" as the status for all CMA income you receive.

   - **Automatic Reinvestment** means there was never any check at all Instead, your dividend was used to buy new shares.

5.   When you've filled in these three fields, press the action key. We need to ask more questions.

6.   On the Record Dividends and Interest screen that appears next, you can record receipt of:

   - **Dividends**

   - **Return of Capital** distributions (also known as liquidating dividends—see HELP)

- **Mutual fund capital gains distributions**
- **Regular Interest**
- **Tax-free interest** (from municipal bonds)
- **AMT interest** (subject to the alternative minimum tax calculation but not regular income tax)
- **Reinvested dividends** and distributions

Usually this is all quite straightforward, but there are some fine points.

Ordinarily, stocks will simply throw off ordinary dividends, bonds will throw off interest, and mutual funds will throw off some combination of things you'll be advised of by the mutual fund. Change anything we may have guessed wrong.

7. After filling in the appropriate fields, press the Action Key. If this is a hypothetical or IRA/Keogh/401K portfolio, that's all there is to it. You're done, ready to record another dividend or interest payment or else to go on about your business.

   But if it's income in a real, taxable portfolio (which includes all CMA portfolios), there's one more step. When you press the Action Key, you will get yet one more window. Just what you can tell us on this window depends on the kind of portfolio the asset is in (regular or CMA) and the kind of dividend this is (cash, broker-held-for-me or reinvested).

   - At the top of the screen, you'll see which MONEY account is currently active and also the current balance in that account.

     Below that, you'll see the kind of distribution you're getting ready to execute—tax-free, "Schedule B" (meaning that some or all the income should be reported on Schedule B of your tax return) or "Schedule D" (meaning that the capital gains portion will show up on Schedule D).

     Don't be concerned if the Amount shown on this screen is $0.00. If this is income "Broker Held for Me," or that was "Automatically Reinvested," then there's zero cash to be deposited in one of your MONEY accounts—which explains the zero amount. But we bring you here anyway so you can allocate the income to budget categories, for tax purposes. (There's no cash to deposit, but there may be income to keep track of and report to the IRS.)

But maybe you did receive cash. If you received it in a non-CMA account, F8 will appear. Press it to select the MONEY account into which you deposited the dividend check. (If it's a CMA portfolio, F8 won't appear; we'll assume the cash went straight to the MONEY side of the CMA, as in fact it did.)

- We also allow you to select the proper budget allocation for this income. Just speed scroll to the proper Income category—DIVIDENDS, most likely, or BOND INTEREST or CAPITAL GAINS DISTRIBUTION.

  If you haven't set up the one you want, press F9 and then F5 to add one. (Note that the tax treatment of your dividend and taxable-interest categories will be pretty obvious. They both should be linked with "Schedule B" tax categories. But if you set up a budget category for capital gains distributions, you won't find a corresponding Schedule D tax category with which to link them. That's OK; just leave it unlinked as "Not a Tax Catgeory," because PORTFOLIO and TAX automatically know how to treat them. The budget category(ies) you set up for interest that's free of federal tax should be tagged—naturally—"Not a Tax Category.")

HINT: Partially Taxed Interest. Interest from U.S. Treasury securities is subject to Federal but not local income tax, and income from tax-free municipals may be subject to local income tax if they're issued outside the state you live in. While we do not make this distinction on the Record Dividend screen directly, you may set up as many different Income budget categories as you like, dumping each kind of interest into its appropriate category, and thus keep track of each separate type of taxable income.

If the distribution you're recording combined two or more types of income—part ordinary dividend and part capital gains distribution, say—press F9 to split the amount.

When you're all set, press the Action Key. Now your part of the job is done. Here's what we do:

- If cash was involved, we deposit it in the proper MONEY account. There, you can see (and edit) it as you would any other transaction. (Changes you make in MONEY will not affect PORTFOLIO's View Income screen, however.)

- Your budget allocations will be dumped into the categories you selected.

- A record of the dividend will be added to View Income (on PORTFOLIO's pulldown menu).

- With automatic reinvestments, we create a new lot for your new shares, which we offer to aggregate with the old ones. If you accept (yes! say yes!), you can later disaggregate and reaggregate them as often as you like.

- Amounts you specify as capital gains distributions will figure into PORTFOLIO's capital gains analysis (select Analyze Assets) and also be reflected on Schedule D in TAX.

- Amounts you specify as return of capital distributions will lower the purchase price of your shares. In other words, if you had 100 shares of a stock for which you paid $20 a share, and now record a $500 return of capital distribution, we will do what the IRS requires. Namely, we won't report that $500 as taxable income, but we will adjust the "basis" of your shares from the $2,000 you paid in all to the $1,500 they cost you after getting $500 of your capital back. Thus the purchase price shown in Managing Your Money would now be $15 a share.

VIEWING YOUR DIVIDENDS AND INTEREST

Select View Income from the PORTFOLIO menu and you'll see each distribution you've recorded—and be able to sort them nine different ways (Ctrl-L, F9). Press F4 to order up a report.

This screen breaks out the portion of each distribution, if any, you tagged "capital gains distribution" and lumps into the "Schedule B amount" column the portions you tagged ordinary dividends and taxable interest (we call this the Schedule B column, because Schedule B is where you report dividends and interest to the IRS.)

- Note that income is listed on this screen for all portfolios, including hypothetical and IRA/Keogh/401K. But don't worry: only income attributable to Taxable and CMA portfolios will have their tax data passed through to TAX.

- If you paid accrued interest when you bought a bond, you'll find that amount listed here, as negative income, and an ACC to its right (for ACCrued interest). And if you received accrued interest when you sold a bond, you'd see that income here with an ACC to its right.

- Where cash was involved, you'll also be able to see a record of your receipt in the Money Account into which you deposited it.

FROM CHAPTER 8: NET WORTH
YOUR NET WORTH

This section of Managing Your Money summons everything we know about you from other sections (if you press F6 on the first screen), gives you a chance to add as many other items as you like-such as a room-by-room household inventory-and then tallies your net worth.

It draws pie charts of your assets and liabilities (F9 at every level of detail, if you're equipped for graphics). It prints three different kinds of balance sheets, in varying levels of detail, depending on the style and format that will most please your banker (F4 from the first screen).

It shows you the capital gains tax liability, if any, implied in the value of your appreciated securities. And it maintains and graphs a monthly record of your monthly progress—or regress (Net Worth History).

Finally, it includes Asset Allocation to help you decide how best to deploy your assets among various classes — stocks, bonds, real estate and gold, for example — to achieve your investment objectives with the least possible risk.

HELP explains all.

ADDING A NEW ITEM

Your Net Worth includes three types of assets and liabilities:

- Extract items, which we draw from elsewhere in the program, like the savings accounts you own and the loans you've told us you owe. You can change the names of any of these extract items just by typing over them—but read the warning at the end of this chapter before you do.

- Aggregate items—like "My Art Collection"—which are headings you create to house a bunch of individual items.

- Individual items—"Van Gogh's Irises."

To add a new aggregate or individual item:

1.   Select Your Net Worth.

2.   Highlight either Assets or Liabilities, depending on which this item will be. (Anything you own is an asset. Anything you owe is a liability.)

3.   Press the Action Key and then F5.

4.   Describe the new asset or liability. Enter, for example:

      Bicycle $300.00   Individual

5.   Press the Action Key to save what you've done.

Or designate it an Aggregate item—Bicycle Collection—and then, pointing to it, press the Action Key to descend a level and add the individual (or aggregate) items that comprise it. Racing Bikes and Mountain Bikes could be aggregates you set up under the main aggregate, and each of those could have dozens of individual bikes listed one by one, with their individual values. When you move back up a level, the sum of those individual values will appear as the total value of the Aggregate.

DEBT/EQUITY RATIO

Note the debt/equity ratio we provide for you on the first Net Worth screen. Having a net worth of $1 million is one thing when you own $1.2 million in assets and have $200,000 in debt (a debt/equity ratio of 20%) and quite another when you own $10 million in assets but owe $9 million (a debt/equity ratio of 900%). I know a lot of people would prefer the second situation (controlling $10 million in assets is a lot more exciting than a measly $1 million), but not me. In my experience, assets evaporate a lot more frequently than debts.

(Why does $1.2 million in assets and $200,000 in liabilities work out to a debt equity ratio of "0.2"—20%? Because we're not dividing your liabilities by your assets, which in this case would round off to 0.17. Rather, we're dividing your liabilities by your net worth, also known as your "equity," which in this case would be an even $1 million.)

UPDATING YOUR NET WORTH

There are three ways to update your Net Worth:

- Automatically. Visit Net Worth Options on FILE's Optional Features menu and tell us to do it for you automatically every time you visit Your Net Worth. I don't do this myself, as I'll explain in a minute.

- Semi-automatically. Do it yourself whenever you want to by pressing F6 on the first Your Net Worth screen. That will update all the extract items below.

- Line-by-line. Go down a level to your list of assets and press F6 on each line, to see how each extractible item has shrunk or grown since the last time you came here. Then do the same for liabilities.

I use a combination of the latter two. Because I track more than one portfolio, it's a fast way to see how the day's price changes have affected the value of all the portfolios taken together (but separated by certain types of securities, and breaking out the gain and loss from short sales separately). Then I jump back to the top level and press F6 to update everything else.

> NOTE:It takes a minute. One reason not to have us update your net worth automatically every time you visit is that, depending on the amount of data you have and the speed of your set-up, it can take a little while. In fact, if you update it line by line, you'll notice that the first item you update that's extracted from the MONEY section will take a while, as Managing Your Money computes everything from that section. Any other lines extracted from MONEY will then update the instant you press F6. Likewise, the first PORTFOLIO item you choose to extract individually will take a while. Any others will then be instant.

WHAT WE EXTRACT

Here's what each extract item extracts:

ASSETS	From MONEY:
Checking Accounts and Cash	Your combined balances
Savings & Money Mkt Accts	Your combined balances
Accounts Receivable	Your total accounts receivable
Loans I Own	Principal owed you on loans lent

From INSURE:

Insurance Cash Value	Cash value from whole life policies in insurance policy organizer (not reduced by policy loans, which we expect you to set up as loans in MONEY)

From ANALYZE:

Pension/Profit-Sharing Plans	As entered on retirement planning screen

From PORTFOLIO:

Portfolio Cash	The combined positive cash balances of your taxable and CMA portfolios
Marketable Securities	Total value of common stock, preferred stock, mutual funds, options, futures contracts, other and special coded assets in your taxable and CMA portfolios
Unrealized Gains on Shorts	Unrealized gains from short positions in your taxable and CMA portfolios
Bonds	As entered in your taxable and CMA portfolios
Savings Bonds/SPDAs	As entered in your taxable and CMA portfolios
Metals & Collectibles	As entered in your taxable and CMA portfolios
Real Estate	As entered in your taxable and CMA portfolios
Tax Shelters	As entered in your taxable and CMA portfolios

	From MONEY and PORTFOLIO:
IRA/Keogh Portfolios	The sum of your assets plus the cash balances in all your IRA/Keogh portfolios and MONEY accounts

LIABILITIES

	From MONEY:
Balance on Mortgages	Principal remaining on mortgage loans
Balance on Auto Loans	Principal remaining on auto loans
Balance on Credit Cards	Total of your credit card account balances
Balance on Home Equity Loans	Total of your home equity loan accounts
Balance on Education Loans	Principal remaining on education loans
Balance on Personal Loans	Principal remaining on personal loans
Balance on Other Loans	Principal remaining on other loans
Accounts Payable	Total you've entered
Negative Bank Balances	Any asset-type Money accounts with negative balances

	From PORTFOLIO:
Margin Debt	Total negative cash balances in your taxable and CMA portfolios
Unrealized Losses on Shorts	Unrealized losses from shorts in your taxable and CMA portfolios

TRACKING YOUR NET WORTH OVER TIME

Select Net Worth History at least once a month and press F5 and then the Action Key to add that month's net worth number to a monthly table we'll build over the years. If you've selected the automatic update option (Net Worth Options on the FILE menu), we'll automatically update your Net Worth History when you visit Your Net Worth.

Adding past years' data. To get a running start and make our graph look interesting, press F5 and enter figures going back as far as 1980, if you have any idea what your net worth was then.

Graphing limitations. Note, however, that our bar and line graphs here—F9— will only handle as many as 20 consecutive entries, and that the time line is not proportional. Each of the up-to-20 entries you have us graph appears to be an equal time period even if the first one covers 1980-1990 and the rest are the 19 months since. We'll use the last 20 months unless you give us a different date range.

One entry per month. We only accept one net worth number per month—new ones for that month overwrite old ones—but surely yours doesn't fluctuate that much from week to week to make this a problem. If you add this month's Net Worth on the 15th of the month, feel free to come back on the 31st and add it again; the new number will replace the old one.

Appreciation rates-F6. Point to any date and press F6. We'll calculate how much your net worth has appreciated (or depreciated) since the date you pointed to and how fast it's been growing each year. Enter a date and press the Action Key; we'll project what you'll be worth then if you continue getting richer (or poorer) at the current rate.

INDEX